UNSEEN DANGER

Local and state officials watch in awe on April 16, 1983, as a subsidence along Route 61 south of Centralia gushes steam. Both the hole and the steam were caused by the Centralia mine fire. (Photo: David DeKok, News-Item)

A Tragedy
of People,
Government,
and the
Centralia
Mine Fire

BY

David DeKok

UNSEEN DANGER

University of Pennsylvania Press · Philadelphia · 1986 upp

Copyright © 1986 by David DeKok
All rights reserved

Library of Congress Cataloging-in-Publication Data

DeKok, David.
  Unseen danger.
  Includes index.
  1. Mine fires. 2. Mine gases. 3. Coal mines and
mining—Pennsylvania—Centralia. 4. Centralia (Pa.)—
History. I. Title.
TN315.D45 1986   363.3'79   85-31454
ISBN 0-8122-8022-9
ISBN 0-8122-1226-6 (paper)

Printed in the United States of America

Designed by ADRIANNE ONDERDONK DUDDEN

Contents

List of Figures

Centralians celebrating on the steps of the U.S. Capitol on November 18, 1983, after Congress appropriated funds for relocation   279

MAPS

List of Acronyms

AML Fund   *Abandoned Mine Lands Fund* (federal)

ARC   *Appalachian Regional Commission* (federal)

ARDA   *Appalachian Regional Development Act* (federal)

CCHD   *Centralia Committee for Human Development* (local citizen group)

CHA   *Centralia Homeowners Association* (local citizen group)

CHD   *Campaign for Human Development* (Catholic Church)

DCA   *Department of Community Affairs* (state)

DER   *Department of Environmental Resources* (state)

DMMI   *Department of Mines and Mineral Industries* (state)

EPA   *Environmental Protection Agency* (federal)

FEMA   *Federal Emergency Management Agency* (federal)

OSHA   *Occupational Safety and Health Administration* (federal)

OSM   *U.S. Office of Surface Mining* (federal; Department of the Interior)

PEMA   *Pennsylvania Emergency Management Agency* (state)

PennDOT   *Pennsylvania Department of Transportation* (state)

USBM   *U.S. Bureau of Mines*

Acknowledgments

I began this book in November 1980, when it appeared to me that the Centralia mine fire problem was close to solution. Less than three months later, I was sitting with friends in the Hardshell Bar in Shamokin when a Centralia man whose name I do not remember asked if I knew that a boy, that day, had fallen into a steaming hole opened by the mine fire.

My reporting of the Centralia story between 1976 and 1980 had, in fact, been only an introduction to the events that followed. Centralia and its mine fire were to make world headlines that year, and I would write 383 stories about the mine fire for *The News-Item,* my employer, between February 14, 1981, and December 1, 1983, the day it was announced that President Reagan had approved funding for a mass relocation of the Centralia community. My colleague, Jake Betz, wrote a number of other stories.

John H. Reid, who was then publisher of *The News-Item,* deserves special praise for devoting the resources of a small newspaper to this one, important story. His support was in the best tradition of American journalism.

Many persons contributed their thoughts and remembrances about the Centralia mine fire for this book, and I would like to thank them all. Secretary of the Interior James Watt, Governor Dick Thornburgh, and U.S. Senator Arlen Specter declined to be interviewed, although Specter did offer a collection of his press releases on Centralia. It was refused. Interviewing former Congressman Daniel Flood was not possible due to the poor state of his health.

Two persons in particular helped me enormously in bringing this project to fruition. One is Dr. Walter Brasch of Bloomsburg University, who provided invaluable advice at every stage of the work, and the other is Michael Steinberg, my literary agent, whose tireless efforts on behalf of this book will never be forgotten.

I would also like to thank Teresa Carpenter of *The Village Voice* for her early advice and assistance; Arthur Evans, Robert Gable, and the rest of the staff at the University of Pennsylvania Press; Kathy Robinson, the Press's former executive editor; Catherine Gjerdingen, whose sensitive copy editing helped me greatly; Elizabeth Warner, T. J. Tristan, Amy Fabian, and Marian Maurer, for help in production; John Taylor of *The Pittsburgh Press;* David Morris of the Harrisburg *Patriot;* Dr. Jack Holmes of the political science department of Hope College, for background information on Secretary Watt; Fred Prouser, Stephen Perloff, David C. Haupt; and Ron Ungvarsky, for photographs; Thomas Koch, for his excellent maps; Louis Pagnotti III; the Freedom of Information staffs at the Interior Department, U.S. Bureau of Mines, U.S. Office of Surface Mining, and Appalachian Regional Commission; the staffs of the Mount Carmel Public Library, Shamokin-Coal Township Public Library, the State Library and State Archives in Harrisburg, and Pennsylvania State University Library in State College; and Nancy McBride, Charlene Rubendall, Bob Sandri, John Gruneberg, and Kate Bradley, for their interest and encouragement.

And last, I would like to pay tribute to the many other newspaper, wire service, magazine, television and radio reporters who did stories on the mine fire. Centralia is a shining example of the power of the press to help correct grave social and environmental ills through factual, fair reporting. May it not be the last.

Shamokin, Pennsylvania   DAVID DeKOK
December 29, 1985

1
A Bad Day

Former Centralia mayor John Coddington in his store on March 19, 1981, the day he was overcome by gases from the mine fire. By coincidence, he was interviewed and photographed for a newspaper story about eight hours before he collapsed. (Photo: David DeKok, News-Item)

SOMETHING was wrong at the Coddington apartment. An ambulance had raced up Locust Avenue and pulled in at John Coddington's former gas station, where he and his family still had a small store and upstairs apartment. The neighbors who saw this feared the worst, knowing the Coddington home had more poison gas from the mine fire than most in Centralia.

Men and women hurried outside and gathered in the cold near the ambulance. They could smell the sulfurous fumes venting from the tall pipe off to one side of the station. Had the carbon monoxide that found its way into their homes from the fire in the old coal mines of Centralia finally claimed a life? It was an article of faith in this Pennsylvania village that neither the U.S. Department of the Interior, now headed by Secretary James G. Watt, nor their own Governor Dick Thornburgh would do anything to stop the fire until it claimed a life. Such cynicism was born of too many years of watching the local, state, and federal government vacillate over how to deal with the fire; now it had become a raging monster that threatened to destroy their community.

The ambulance attendants emerged from the building carrying a stretcher. On it was John Coddington, the sixty-two-year-old former mayor who had become something of a spokesman for those residents of Centralia who lived day-to-day with the very real dangers of the mine fire. Not every family in Centralia was affected by the fire, but it was a nightmare for those who were.

Coddington had been overcome by gases but was still alive, albeit delirious. The attendants lifted the stretcher into the ambulance, closed the door, and drove away. It was March 19, 1981.

■ ■ ■

Centralia had just under one thousand residents in 1981, the year the mine fire came to national and international attention. It was an isolated village,* straddling a high, narrow valley in the Appalachian Mountains of east central Pennsylvania, at the southern tip of Columbia County. It was also part of what is called the Anthracite Region, after the hard, shiny, high-BTU coal that is mined in that region and nowhere else in the United States. Philadelphia was 125 miles to the

---

*Under Pennsylvania law, Centralia is a borough, a term that applies to communities of a certain small size that have their own governing council. The term, which is English, is little known in much of the United States. Village conveys better the kind of small, intimate place Centralia is—or was.

CENTRALIA

PITTSBURGH

NEW YORK

HARRISBURG

PHILADELPHIA

WASHINGTON D.C.

Location of Centralia in relation to major eastern cities.
(Map credit: Thomas Koch)

southeast of Centralia, New York City 190 miles to the east, and Pittsburgh 230 miles to the southwest. Beneath the village was a labyrinth of abandoned tunnels where miners had dug coal for over one hundred years to fuel the boilers of industry and heat the homes of the eastern United States. Surrounding Centralia was a land ravaged by strip mine pits.

Once life in Centralia had been wonderful, a legacy of the close social ties that result when people share a common hardship and danger like coal mining. The mine fire, which ignited in 1962, had gradually wrecked that pleasant life. Like the victims of the toxic waste tragedies at Love Canal, New York, and Times Beach, Missouri, the people of Centralia had to cope as best they could with illness and the threat of death. They faced the possible loss of home and community, of all they had worked and saved for. As a final blow, they faced official indifference and even political hostility to their plight. When the people of Centralia finally rebelled, it was too late to save their village. They had no desire to leave Centralia, but by 1981 it was increasingly clear that many of them, if not all, would have to go. The events of March 19 showed how far the situation had deteriorated after so many years of government bungling and neglect.

■ ■ ■

John Coddington, his wife Isabelle, and his son Joe had lived in the apartment above the gas station for much of their lives. Coddington was born in Centralia and went to work in the mines the evening he graduated from high school. He didn't work there very long, but it was long enough to give him a moderate amount of anthrasilicosis in his respiratory system. The disease is better known as black lung, the plague of coal miners everywhere. It would make Coddington much more susceptible to ill effects from the mine fire gases forty years later.

His first gas station was located a quarter-mile south of where it would be in 1981. In the late 1950s, when the state changed the course of Route 61, the main highway through Centralia, Coddington moved his station to South Locust Avenue. It was a fateful act; beneath the new site was a mine gangway that would lead directly to the heart of the mine fire.* The gangway would allow carbon monoxide, carbon dioxide, and oxygen-deficient atmosphere produced by the mine fire easy access to Coddington's home and those of his neighbors through cracks in the rock and the foundations of their houses.

---

*A mine gangway is a relatively level tunnel that connects mine breasts, tunnels that slant upward to follow the vein of coal.

By 1981, daily life for the Coddingtons and the other mine fire families had assumed a horrible routine of visits by the state gas inspectors, clanging gas alarms that only seemed to sound in the middle of the night, extraordinary drowsiness, nausea and headaches caused by the gases, and worry. Yet they tried to maintain their lives in as ordinary a fashion as possible. To a visitor, the only sign that something was wrong might be the electronic carbon monoxide monitor, ticking softly and rhythmically, printing out a continuous paper tape, often sitting in the living room next to the television set or piano.

State gas inspectors Edward Narcavage, Wayne Readly, and Jeff Stanchek had the task of making certain that none of the mine fire impact zone residents died from the gases.* That morning they arrived at the Coddingtons' home around 9:00. It was the first stop on their rounds, which included fifteen houses or apartments and St. Ignatius Elementary School. In some homes they checked the air at one location, but at the Coddingtons' home and others they did several tests. Although the Coddington readings were not at the danger level that morning—they would have been considered extraordinary in any normal community—the inspectors and families knew that safe gas levels could become fatal five minutes later. The gases were that unpredictable.

Narcavage, the chief inspector, was especially worried that day about the backfilling of a subsidence hole across the street from the Coddingtons. He feared gases that had vented from the hole would now enter nearby homes.** The subsidence had been backfilled on March 16, just three days earlier, and on March 17 the Coddingtons had a serious gas alarm. The monitor showed 100 parts per million— the highest possible reading on the dial—and the tape showed the gas lingered for 42 minutes. It was an unusually long incident, particularly since the Coddingtons opened all the windows in the house as soon as the alarm sounded.

■ ■ ■

That day in Harrisburg, the state capital, the technical operations subcommittee of the Centralia Mine Fire Advisory Group was reporting its conclusion that the only way to attack the Centralia mine fire and be

---

*The inspectors were employees of the Pennsylvania Department of Environmental Resources, but the U.S. Office of Surface Mining paid all costs of the gas monitoring, including their salaries. OSM is a division of the U.S. Department of the Interior.

**A subsidence occurs when the earth and rock above a mine chamber suddenly collapses. It can create a deep hole at the surface or barely ripple the ground, depending on subsurface conditions. A mine fire can cause a subsidence by causing a mine roof to expand, then contract and crack.

certain of success was to totally excavate it. In laymen's terms, that meant digging more than 140 acres of burning coal out of the ground.

Subcommittee chairman David Simpson, chief of the U.S. Bureau of Mines field office in Wilkes-Barre, acknowledged there were severe drawbacks to the plan. It would cost an estimated $87 million, result in demolition of about 109 homes and other structures in a community that had only about five hundred, force relocation of Route 61 and a major natural gas pipeline, and greatly worsen the quality of life in what was left of Centralia. Eight to ten years of blasting, dust, truck traffic, and noxious gas odors would not be pleasant. The southern half of Centralia would become a gaping pit as deep as 400 feet, at least for several years. But no one could think of a project that was cheaper, less damaging, and still had a reasonable chance of solving the mine fire problem once and for all.

■ ■ ■

When Narcavage returned home to Mount Carmel that evening, the weatherman was calling for a very cold night with high relative humidity—85 percent. Narcavage wondered aloud to his wife if that would mean a lot of gas alarms. High humidity held the gases closer to the ground and increased their concentration in the houses.

When a gas alarm sounded after 4 P.M., quitting time for the three inspectors, the families were supposed to call one of the regular DER mine inspectors. But they often called Narcavage, and he never failed to respond. His supervisor had complained that he was running up too much overtime and had ordered Narcavage a few days before not to respond to any more night gas alarms. He was to tell anyone who called to contact one of the approved inspectors on the list. The problem was that the other inspectors were often hard to reach.

■ ■ ■

Kathy and Bob Gadinski had purchased their large house on South Locust Avenue in the summer of 1978. It was on an opposite corner from the Coddingtons, and directly across the street from Tony Andrade's house. They knew about the mine fire when they purchased the house, but no one had a mine fire gas problem at that time. A Bureau of Mines official assured them the mine fire would never reach their house "in ninety-nine years." Now the Gadinskis had a mine fire gas problem, although they didn't believe it was as bad as that of the Coddingtons or Andrades. Bob Gadinski, a high school earth science teacher, called their home "a live-in earth science laboratory."

On March 19, as they were watching the 6:00 news, Mrs. Gadinski felt unusually tired and sleepy. She asked her husband when they were going to get their gas monitor back. The Gadinskis had given theirs to the Andrades, whose monitor had kept breaking down. They considered the mine fire gas problem at the Andrade house to be much worse than their own and felt it wasn't right to hold onto their good monitor while the Andrades fretted over their defective one. They had now been without a monitor for seventeen days.

Bob Gadinski was feeling quite tired, too. Their conversation slowed and dropped off to nothing. Before many minutes had passed they fell into a heavy, dreamless sleep that meant carbon monoxide had entered the home and was affecting them.

■ ■ ■

The Coddingtons dined out that evening, returning home shortly before 7 P.M. All three noticed a heaviness in the air when they stepped into the apartment. A faint odor of sulfur was present. After forty-five minutes of watching television, Mrs. Coddington noticed her husband had dozed off. This was not unusual anymore. Coddington had told a group of state legislators who had visited Centralia the previous week that the mine fire was the best cure for insomnia ever invented. Dr. Joseph Weber, an Ashland internal medicine specialist,* would later tell Coddington extraordinary drowsiness is an early symptom of oxygen deprivation. It was common in many of the homes affected by the mine fire.

Coddington struggled to stay awake. At 9 P.M., Joe told him he should go to bed, that it made little sense to sleep sitting up on the couch. His father agreed and walked off slowly to the master bedroom. Mrs. Coddington and her son were becoming drowsy, too, and she finally got up and opened several windows, shutting off the furnace to conserve oil. It was bitterly cold outside, about 15 degrees, but there was no wind. They were used to this by now, but the cold was nonetheless unpleasant.

The high humidity that night prevented the mine fire gases from dispersing, and a pocket of oxygen-deficient air formed in the bedroom where Coddington slept. When he shut the door, there was even less chance of proper ventilation. A healthier person might have coped, but Coddington's diseased lungs made him more vulnerable to the low oxygen, Dr. Weber said later. With his reduced lung capacity he could not extract enough oxygen for his body from the bad air in the room.

*Dr. Joseph Weber agreed to be interviewed for this book at the request of the Coddingtons but insisted that John Coddington be present during the interview. Dr. Weber does not discuss his patients' cases in most instances, but he was extremely helpful and informative after his conditions were met.

At about 9:45 P.M. Coddington awoke, confused and gasping for breath. He sat up and tried to get out of bed but lost consciousness and hit the floor with a sickening thud. Horrified, Mrs. Coddington and her son ran to the bedroom, where they tried unsuccessfully to rouse Coddington. Mrs. Coddington, afraid her husband had suffered a heart attack, told Joe to call Centralia Ambulance. It did not immediately occur to her that the mine fire gases might be the cause of his collapse.

Joe first called Kathy Gadinski, a physical therapist, believing she might have some idea of what to do if his father indeed was having a heart attack. The call woke the Gadinskis from their gaseous slumber, and they came over. Joe then called Peter Wysochansky, one of the ambulance drivers, told him what happened, and asked him to bring the ambulance up to the house.

Wysochansky, who arrived with Roy Kroh and Raymond Reilley, assumed Coddington had become the first serious casualty, perhaps even the first fatality, of the mine fire gases. He asked Mrs. Coddington if they had had a gas alarm. "No, no, we didn't," she said. "Well, I'm not sure." She was still very confused by the entire affair.

Gadinski decided to check the oxygen meter in the living room. He pushed the button on the gauge and it showed the oxygen level in the room was 18 percent. He wondered why the alarm had not sounded. It was supposed to sound if the oxygen level dropped below 19.5 percent.

Coddington opened his eyes as the men lifted him onto the stretcher but he was not really seeing any of them. Suddenly he sat up on the stretcher, waving his arms. Unable to quiet him, they finally strapped him down.

Before leaving the apartment, Mrs. Coddington called Narcavage, as she or her husband always did when the alarm sounded. She would not feel safe returning to the apartment until he had checked the gas levels and assured her everything was all right. Narcavage was stunned. His first impulse was to rush over to the Coddington home, but he had explicit instructions from his supervisor not to do this. He told her she would have to call one of the approved night inspectors. Mrs. Coddington thanked him and hung up. It was time to go to the hospital and she didn't have time to call anyone else.

About that moment, the oxygen monitor began to buzz in Terry Burge's house trailer, located about 150 feet behind Coddington's station. He got up, shut it off, and opened the windows, a routine procedure by now for this taciturn, unflappable state employee. He saw the flashing red light of the ambulance at Coddingtons and hurried over to investigate.

Reilley and Kroh climbed in the ambulance with Coddington; Wysochansky closed the door behind them. As he drove onto Route 61, he radioed the hospital that he was bringing in a male patient from the mine fire impact zone in Centralia, a possible victim of low oxygen and carbon monoxide. Kroh and Reilley gave Coddington three liters of oxygen during the ten-minute ride to the hospital. It was not an easy task; he fought the mask and tried to squirm out from under it.

At the hospital, the emergency room team hooked Coddington to oxygen and a heart monitor, which indicated he hadn't suffered a heart attack. Gadinski, meanwhile, had gone to call another inspector after being informed by Mrs. Coddington that Narcavage could not come. The other inspector was not home, so he left a message. Gadinski decided to give Narcavage another call and later was glad he did. After Mrs. Coddington's call, Narcavage's wife and daughter pleaded with him to go help the Coddingtons. When Gadinski called from the hospital, it was all he needed to make up his mind. He dressed, gathered his equipment, and arrived at the Coddington home at 10:30 P.M.

Oxygen and time were having a salutary effect on Coddington. About thirty minutes after he was wheeled inside the hospital, he opened his eyes—this time with life and perception in them—and blurted out, "Pete? What are you doing here?" Wysochansky told him it appeared he had been overcome by mine fire gases in his home.

Dr. Joseph Weber was familiar with the mine fire from newspaper accounts and from conversations with Isabelle Coddington, his patient. He knew Coddington's symptoms were similar to those of a person suffering a stroke, but he also knew oxygen deprivation could produce such symptoms. Coddington did not exhibit any of the specific signs of a stroke, such as partial paralysis, but persons sometimes exhibit total confusion and thrash about when a stroke is beginning. Paralysis came later. The problem was that confusion, convulsions, and unconsciousness were just as likely to be symptoms of oxygen deprivation.

The more Weber thought about it, the less likely it seemed Coddington had suffered a stroke. He was no longer confused, he was not developing paralysis, and he certainly did live in an environment of oxygen deprivation. The diagnosis was bolstered by the results of a blood gas test, which showed a moderate decrease in the amount of oxygen in Coddington's blood, even after Coddington had received several liters of oxygen in the ambulance and at the hospital. After sending Coddington to intensive care, Weber cautioned Mrs. Coddington and her son not to stay at the apartment that night. She wholeheartedly agreed; they would stay at her daughter's home near Ashland, two miles away.

Narcavage was on his way upstairs to the Coddington apartment when Terry Burge caught up with him. Burge's carbon monoxide alarm had sounded at 11 P.M., and under the circumstances it bothered the Burges greatly. Narcavage could hear the oxygen alarm buzzing upstairs in the Coddington apartment, but the Burge alarm took first priority. The carbon monoxide had dissipated by the time he reached the trailer, but the monitor showed there had been 40 parts per million at the time of the alarm.

Narcavage waited at the Andrade house across the street until the Coddingtons returned around 12:30 A.M. to pick up some clothes. Before they entered the apartment he ran the gas tests. There was no carbon monoxide, but carbon dioxide was at 0.5 percent and oxygen at 19.5 percent—a full percentage point less than when they checked it that morning. And this was after the windows had been open for three hours. "You're lucky John fell off the bed," he told them. "If he hadn't, and you'd just gone to bed, I don't think any of you would have woken up again."

2
Men and Resources

Centralia, Pennsylvania, in spring 1981, before the demolition of homes began. (Photo: David DeKok, News-Item)

FIRES do not spread very quickly or very far underground unless man has created passageways the fire can follow. The mine fire that felled John Coddington would not have existed but for the vast network of abandoned mine tunnels under Centralia. Much digging can be accomplished in a century; on mine maps, the subterranean world beneath Centralia resembles a huge beehive or a house of cards.

Once Centralia was a wilderness, of course, but it is difficult to find many traces of that wilderness today. There are still patches of forest, true, but scratch the surface or look around and you will find evidence that miners were here long before you.

The first Centralia miners were Welsh, English, and German. Not long after came a mass of desperate emigrants from Ireland, strangers all to the terrors of mining, but needed in the mines nonetheless. They had fled the potato famine and wanted only food, at first. Later, joined by Polish, Russian, and Ukrainian emigrants, they demanded more than simple existence in return for the wealth they created for Centralia coal companies and the nation at large.

The Centralia valley was part of the vast wilderness of northeastern Pennsylvania, much of which native tribes sold to Pennsylvania colonial agents in 1749 for 500 pounds. Colonial settlers explored at least part of the Centralia valley in 1770 while surveying and building the Reading Road, which linked Reading, 54 miles south of the valley, with Fort Augusta, a frontier outpost 31 miles to the northwest along the Susquehanna River at the site of present day Sunbury. Much of the trail later became Route 61. It is likely the road builders saw evidence of the valley's anthracite coal riches as they hacked their way over Locust Mountain to what would become Centralia, 84 years later.

The eastern third of the Centralia valley was joined to Robert Morris's wilderness empire in 1793. Morris, a Revolutionary War hero and signer of the Declaration of Independence, acquired most of western New York, large tracts of Pennsylvania, and the future site of Washington, D.C., before going bankrupt in 1798. His Centralia lands passed to the Bank of the United States while he suffered in the squalor of Philadelphia debtors' prison for three and a half years. Morris earned nothing from the Centralia valley. He would be one of the few owners who did not.

Stephen Girard, a former French sea captain turned Philadelphia banker, purchased Morris's Centralia lands and sixty-eight tracts further east at an auction in Philadelphia in 1830. Girard had heard rumors of a fortune in anthracite coal buried in the mountains of central Pennsylvania, and he spent $30,000 to acquire the lands on the chance it was true. His surveyors found the coal fortune that rumor foretold. One of them wrote home:

> I have run lines where no human being ever trod, over mountains as steep—nay, steeper than the roof of any house . . . embodied in which must be immense quantities of coal. At one place in the vicinity of the first encampment, Mr. Allen had a vein opened to ascertain the quality as well as the extent. The coal turned out to be of an excellent quality, the vein uncommonly extensive, running directly into a high mountain, apparently inexhaustible.

The anthracite coal rush was on. Despite its apparent riches, however, the Centralia valley was ignored by the coal companies until 1854, when the arrival of the Mine Run Railroad at the village of Big Mine Run about one mile southwest of present day Centralia made it possible to transport coal out of the valley. Centralia's own coal rush then began in earnest. Mining camps were hacked out of the forest, and mining companies moved quickly to exploit the black riches of the valley.

The master architect of Centralia's coal rush was Alexander Rea, a mining engineer for the Locust Mountain Coal and Iron Company, which had owned a large portion of the valley since 1842. Rea went to Centralia, built a house, summoned his family, and drew up plans for a village. The locale had been called Bull's Head, after a tavern erected in 1832, and later Centreville. There was another Centreville in Schuylkill County, however, and the Post Office would not allow a second one, so Rea named his village Centralia. It would be, he hoped, a center of commerce.

Two mines opened in Centralia in 1856, the Locust Run and the Coal Ridge. The Hazeldell Colliery followed in 1860, the Centralia in 1862, and the Continental, located on Girard Estate land, in 1863. The Lehigh and Mahanoy Railroad, a branch of the Lehigh Valley Railroad, reached Centralia in 1865, allowing Centralia coal easy access to eastern markets.

Rea did not live to see all the success that might have been his. He was ambushed and murdered in October 1868 while driving his buggy along the road between Centralia and Mount Carmel. He was perhaps the most celebrated victim of the Mollie Maguires, an Irish-American terrorist organization that committed murder and arson in the name of protecting Irish miners.

The Irish in Centralia escaped the potato famine but little else. In many ways, they were still subject to the hated English. English and Welsh miners saw the Irish as a threat to their hold on the better-paying jobs in the mines. They remembered how the mine owners in Northumberland and Durham counties in England had used unskilled Irish to break a strike. Mine superintendents and foremen were almost without exception English or Welsh. Some despised the Irish for their Roman Catholicism and unabstemious way of life.

The oppression was real, both economically and socially, but disinterested historians have judged the Mollie Maguires less protectors of the Irish than criminals out to serve their own ends. Mollie Maguirism lasted from 1862 to 1877, when many of the alleged leaders were hanged. Their crimes, real and legendary, gave them a permanent place in the Anthracite Region's folklore. Descendants of the Mollies were said to still live in Centralia in the early 1980s.

One local legend says Father Daniel Ignatius McDermott, the first Roman Catholic priest in Centralia, placed a curse on the community for its support of the group after three Mollies gave him a beating in 1869 in retaliation for his denunciations of the organization. The priest prophesied, so the legend goes, that a day would come when only St. Ignatius Roman Catholic Church would remain standing in Centralia. This tale was the subject of much discussion in the village in 1981, when the mine fire situation began to look particularly hopeless.

Centralia miners did not achieve any real measure of economic or social justice until the great United Mine Workers strike of 1902. John Mitchell, the able and charismatic young leader of the union, first led his 150,000 miners out on strike in 1900. The union won a modest wage increase that year, largely because Republican National Committee chairman Mark Hannah intervened to prevent the strike from damaging President William McKinley's re-election bid. In 1902, neither side was in a mood for compromise. The miners wanted more pay, better hours, and formal recognition of the union. The owners wanted the union smashed. George Baer, president of the Philadelphia and Reading Coal and Iron Company, which owned the Bast Colliery in Conyngham Township near Centralia, expressed the owners' attitude best: "The rights and interests of the laboring man will be protected and cared for, not by labor agitators, but by the Christian men to whom God in his infinite wisdom has given control of the property interests of the country, and upon the successful management of which much depends."

The strike began May 12, 1902. The tightly disciplined miners, aided by tactical and financial support from other unions, cut off most of the nation's anthracite coal. The East Coast was particularly hard hit, and when the strike continued into October, civil authorities began to worry that people would freeze to death. Public sentiment remained firmly with the strikers, however.

Nowhere was the strike more popular than among the Centralia miners. According to the *Ashland Advocate* of October 3, 1902, 122 striking Centralia miners surrounded a train carrying strikebreakers when it arrived at the Lehigh Valley Station in Centralia on October 1. The men on the train had been recruited by the Lehigh Valley Coal Company, which now owned all mines in Centralia and most in Conyngham Township. The strikers ordered the men to "cease work under penalty of being harshly dealt with." The strikebreakers left and the miners submitted to arrest quite peacefully.

The mine operators capitulated to pressure from New York banker J. P. Morgan and agreed to submit the strike issues to arbitration. The miners went back to work on October 23. President Theodore Roosevelt, who had been unable to end the strike, appointed a blue-ribbon commission to hear the arguments of both sides. It met through the winter of 1902–3, heard witnesses, including four miners from Centralia, and ruled in favor of the union on March 23, 1903. The UMWA received a 10 percent wage hike and a nine-hour day at ten hours' pay.

Centralia and Ashland area miners celebrated the victory April 1, 1903 with a parade down Centre Street in Ashland. "It Was A Gala Day For Labor" trumpeted the *Advocate,* and indeed it was. The weather was beautiful and flags fluttered above the crowd. Mounted horsemen passed, then carriages bearing local dignitaries, the American Band of Centralia miners, then more bands and more units of miners. Breaker boys wore their John Mitchell buttons, while their elders carried "suggestive banners." They believed they had won the greatest battle ever between labor and management.

Anthracite production reached its all-time peak in 1917, 100 million tons, but declined with the entry of the United States into World War I. Scores of young men from Centralia volunteered, causing a mine labor shortage in the village. After the war there were strikes and more strikes in the industry, and the public, so supportive of the union in 1902, began to weary of the constant disruption of supply. By 1925, the year of the last great strike, fuel oil was cutting into the home heating and industrial boiler market. Anthracite production dropped from a postwar peak of 77.6 million tons in 1923 to 64.2 million tons in 1929.

The stock market crash that year forced Lehigh Valley Coal Company to close all five of its Centralia area mines, throwing thousands of men out of work. The mines did not reopen for six years. Philadelphia and Reading's Bast Colliery stayed open until 1933, when an explosion of mine gas ignited an uncontrollable fire. After flooding the mine to extinguish the blaze, the company decided the sad state of the economy did not justify reopening it. Hundreds more lost their jobs.

To help feed their families, some Centralia miners turned to bootleg mining in idle mines owned by the major companies. A limited market for coal still existed during the Great Depression, and bootleg miners could undercut prices charged by the established companies because their overhead was minimal. Those who owned the mines considered it thievery, and company detectives were known to shoot without asking questions if they found miners working an area illegally.

One of the mining techniques used by the bootleg miners was called pillar robbing. Centralia mining companies, like most in the Anthracite Region, engaged in room-and-pillar mining. Rooms would be carved out of the coal veins, and a certain number of pillars—solid sections of coal—would be left to help support the roof. A substantial amount of coal was left behind in pillars, and bootleg miners would sometimes work a mine from back to front, taking out the pillars—"robbing back"—as they went. Mine roofs often collapsed after the pillars were removed, partially filling the rooms with broken rock and timbers. This practice was used extensively in the Centralia area and would greatly complicate efforts to contain the mine fire.

Some miners returned to work in 1935, when Robert Birtley purchased the Centralia Colliery from Lehigh Valley. One of his subcontractors, Edward Whitney, strip-mined part of the old L. A. Riley Colliery, leaving a pit that came almost to the Odd Fellows Cemetery. The cemetery, operated by the Independent Order of Odd Fellows, a fraternal organization, lay about 350 yards east of Centralia.

World War II restored additional mine jobs, but only temporarily. Fuel oil all but destroyed the anthracite market after the war. Centralia, with no means of support other than coal mining, and no new industry in sight, might well have become a ghost town. After enduring so much hardship and sorrow, however, the people of Centralia struggled to retain what was left and prepared for a post-coal future. Centralia Council acquired the rights to all coal beneath the village in 1950, the only community in Pennsylvania to take advantage of a 1949 state law allowing such purchases. Subsidence was a growing problem in the Anthracite Region, and mining engineers said further mining beneath Centralia, particularly pillar robbing, risked a catastrophe.

The 1950s were a peaceful, happy time in Centralia, perhaps the first the citizens had ever known. The village was in decline, true, and population had dropped by almost two-thirds since the boom years of the nineteenth century. The wreckage of one hundred years of mining was everywhere. Centralians lived out the decade, however, without the major calamities of previous years. They owned the coal beneath them and were no longer under the heavy hand of the Lehigh Valley Coal Company. The village finally controlled its own destiny.

It was the kind of small town where people really did look after each other, where everyone was related to everyone else. Life revolved around family and the church, especially the Roman Catholic church. People found jobs far away, often in Harrisburg, but preferred to commute rather than uproot themselves from Centralia. Ben Marsh, an assistant professor of geography at Bucknell University, believes the hard and dangerous work in the mines forged social ties in Centralia and other Anthracite Region communities that were much stronger than those found in many places. Men needed each other to survive in the mines, and that carried over to the world outside. "You're talking about people literally right off the boat," he said. "A tiny universe of experience. They have a highly impoverished view of the rest of the world, so they are highly dependent on who they know. It's a life built on a sense of social ties. You take that away and there's nothing."

The past was behind the people of Centralia. The worst seemed over, but it was not. The last and most terrible battle was about to begin.

3
Council's Fire

Centralia's municipal landfill pit extended almost to this corner of the Odd Fellows Cemetery in 1962. St. Ignatius School is the one-story building at upper left, while the steeple of St. Ignatius Church can be seen just to the right of the school. (Photo: David DeKok, News-Item)

THE fire began, one can argue, at the May 7, 1962 meeting of the Centralia Council. The actions agreed to that night seemed so innocent, but tragedies often begin with the best of intentions.

The councilmen might have realized later the outcry they would face if the truth became known. Memories were allowed to fade, or were altered over the years to provide a less damaging account of how the mine fire began. Some of the clues were always there in the council minutes written by John Koschoff, Sr., the secretary. Until recently, the key to interpret the clues was missing.

The minutes for May 7 state that Councilman John May reminded the others—Joseph Tighe, Robert Burge, Joseph Hannah, Patrick Shearn, Michael Jurgill, and Mayor George Winnick—that Memorial Day was approaching and suggested council tidy up the new Centralia landfill. No one needed to be reminded where the landfill was. One end of the long pit—the strip mine excavated by Edward Whitney in 1935—brushed the northeast corner of the Odd Fellows Cemetery.

Council had made the pit a landfill in early 1962. New state regulations had required closing the old dump west of St. Ignatius Cemetery, Burge says, and council wanted a landfill to deter people from dumping in the eight unofficial dumps scattered around the Centralia area. Councilman Joseph Tighe, who handled landfill matters, had begun looking for a new site. An obvious choice was the abandoned strip mine pit near the cemetery. There was a good access road, and the pit was 300 feet long, 75 feet wide, and 50 feet deep. Properly tended, it could serve Centralia for years. Tighe negotiated a lease with Lehigh Valley Coal Company, which owned the pit, and obtained the blessing of the cemetery trustees. The trustees disliked having a landfill so close to their burial ground, but people had dumped there illegally for years, and the trustees hoped regulated dumping in the pit would end the odor and rat problem and eventually fill in the pit itself.

George Segaritus, the regional landfill inspector for the state Department of Mines and Mineral Industries (DMMI), liked the site but was concerned about several holes in the walls and floor of the pit. Pennsylvania strip mines often sliced through old deep mines, and this one was no exception. He told Tighe the holes would have to be filled with incombustible material. That way if there was a fire, it would not spread to nearby mines. Tighe arranged to have the holes filled; at the

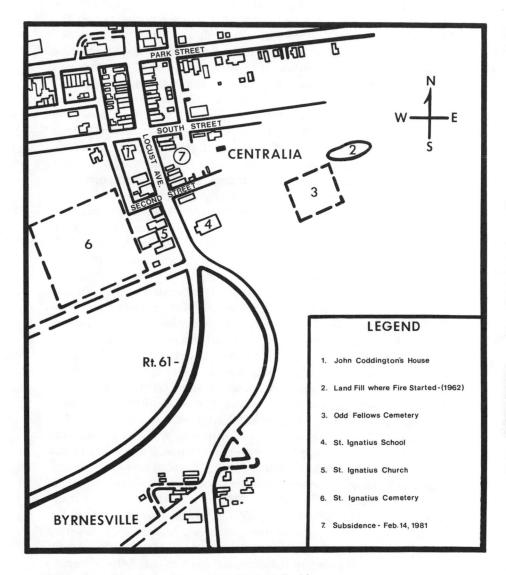

Mine fire impact zone. (Map credit: Thomas Koch)

March 5 council meeting he reported that "five more holes" had been sealed. Segaritus must have found the work acceptable, because he arranged for a state permit for the landfill. Council received permit No. WD–443–R on June 20 along with a cancellation notice for permit No. WD–309–R3, which had authorized the old dump behind St. Ignatius Cemetery. The new landfill was open Wednesdays and Saturdays, and council had a worker there to make sure people did things properly.

The May 7 council minutes show no objections from any of the councilmen to May's proposal to clean up the landfill for Memorial Day. Who could object to that? Memorial Day was an important holiday in Centralia, for many of its men had fought in the nation's wars, from the Civil War on. Every year, members of the American Legion in Centralia would form a color guard and march behind it from cemetery to cemetery, firing volleys to honor the dead. Families went to the cemeteries to tend the graves of their departed loved ones and to socialize with other families. It was important for the cemeteries to look good. This might seem irrelevant, small town history except for one thing: Centralia Council's method of cleaning a dump was *to set it on fire*.

It does not say this in Secretary Koschoff's minutes, probably because state law prohibited deliberately setting dump fires. Francis Goncalves, in 1962 a member of Centralia Fire Company and president of Centralia Planning Commission, and later a member of and president of Centralia Council, said it was common practice back then for the volunteer fire company, at the behest of council, to set fire to the various dumps every spring. Firemen would stand by to extinguish the blaze after it served its purpose, which was to rid the dump of foul odors, rats, and excess papers, Goncalves said. "Every year, Holy Wednesday we used to call it, before Easter, we used to go and burn the dumps. We had nine of them in town. And we used to put them out the same night. Rinse them with the firetruck. Two or three loads on every one. We used to disturb the stuff [refuse] and all," he said. This was the key to interpreting the council minutes.

From the minutes of June 4, 1962, it is possible to reconstruct what happened on Sunday, May 27, the day chosen for cleaning the landfill. Council arranged to borrow a front-end loader for the day from a local strip mine operator. As the minutes state, "May 27, 1962, loader from Bill Farley cleaned up the dumpsite prior to the 30th." Five firemen had been informally hired by council to put out the fire after the cleanup was completed. The minutes show that James Cleary, Jr., the fire chief, Thomas Krupinski, assistant fire chief, Charles Michael,

Donald Leiby, and Mike Krolick each submitted a bill to council for six dollars "for fighting the fire in the landfill on May 27, 1962."

It was clearly a planned fire. Why else would members of a volunteer fire company be paid for fighting a fire? Far more firemen would have been at a regular fire—particularly on a Sunday, when few were working—and none would have been paid. The plan was probably to use Farley's loader to scoop up trash and deposit it in a central pile before setting the pile on fire. If the landfill had been burning before the work crew arrived, it would have been pointless to bring a loader, which has rubber tires. A bulldozer, which has metal tread instead of tires, would have been needed.

Someone struck a match. As fire consumed the papers, black smoke rose. When most of the paper on the surface of the landfill was gone, the firemen poured on water until they could no longer see flames. They left, believing the fire was out. Unfortunately, the fire had burned deeper into the many layers of garbage than anyone suspected. George Segaritus says dump fires have an uncanny knack for surviving the best attempts by firefighters to extinguish them. The fire smoulders at the lower depths, he says, then flares up when the paper above is sufficiently dry.

Smoke and flames were visible again the evening of Tuesday, May 29, when George Jones, president of the cemetery trustees, walked out to the cemetery to make sure the water tanks were filled for Memorial Day. Jones was dismayed to see smoke rising beyond the eastern fence of the graveyard. He opened the iron gate, walked to the edge of the pit, saw the fire, and returned to town to inform Tighe. The June 4 minutes say that after receiving Jones's complaint about the fire, Tighe and May "acted promptly to have the fire put out at the borough landfill."

Charles Michael remembers that he, Cleary, and Krupinski went to the landfill around 9 P.M. "the night before the 30th," hooked up several hoses to a hydrant on Locust Avenue, and ran water on the dump fire until almost 2 A.M. Michael denies being at the dump on Sunday, May 27. He insists he did not return home from his job at U.S. Steel in Bristol, near Philadelphia, until May 29. The bill paid by council would seem to indicate otherwise.

Cleary insists fires at the landfill and the other dumps were routine and frequent, although no other such fires are mentioned in the minutes for meetings that year. "Every Saturday there was a dump fire," he said. "We didn't think much of it." He implies the landfill was already on fire when members of the fire company—Cleary says he was away working that day—went to the pit. "Council asked us, on account of the 30th of May coming up, if we could put some water on it," he said. Would council have left the fire burning—assuming there was a fire—if a holiday was not approaching?*

Tighe told council at the June 4 meeting, according to the minutes, that *two* fires had occurred at the landfill since the May 7 meeting. Yet the firemen submitted bills for only one. It is another clue that what happened that Sunday was out of the ordinary.

Tighe denied it was the practice of council to have the dumps set afire, and denied specifically that the May 27 fire was set. He believed that what is today called the Centralia mine fire is actually a much older fire that once burned a few hundred feet west of the landfill, and which he said was partially excavated years ago. He did not recall when this was, but held an almost desperate belief that this old mine fire set the landfill on fire on May 27, 1962.

He was not the only one to hold this theory, or a variation of it. Some, like Cleary and Robert Burge, believe the old Bast Colliery fire of 1932, which legend says was never fully extinguished, reached the landfill area in 1962. They believe the dump fire was unrelated to the Centralia mine fire.

One who disagrees with that theory is Frank Jurgill, Sr., who says he operated a bootleg mine with his brother in the vicinity of the landfill between 1960 and 1962. They walked through many of the tunnels that later caught fire, Jurgill says. "If it would have started down at the Bast Colliery or somewhere else, when we had a coal hole [mine] there, we would have had to be in it," he said. The gases would have killed them. Tighe said Jurgill told him the same story. It did not shake his belief that the old mine fire ignited the garbage in the pit.

It remained for Joseph Scovack, another member of Centralia Fire Company in 1962, to confirm that the fire company did set fire to the landfill that spring. Scovack, who is the brother-in-law of Donald Leiby, one of the five firemen of May 27, says he just can't believe it was that fire which spread to the mines, judging by how deep in the garbage it was little more than a week later. "Now, maybe it traveled that fast, but it just doesn't seem possible." Scovack said.

---

*Of the other firemen listed in the June 4 minutes, Leiby does not recall if he was at the landfill on May 27, 1962, although he says it was possible, and Krupinski remembers putting water on a fire at the landfill, but little else. Krolick has since died. Leiby agrees with Francis Goncalves that it was the practice then to clean the dumps by temporarily setting them on fire.

Perhaps there is no way to prove that the fire of May 27, 1962 became the Centralia mine fire, but the weight of the evidence supports that conclusion. None of this has been told before, and given the awful consequences of that day, it is not hard to imagine why.

■ ■ ■

The fire in the landfill proved maddeningly stubborn. It flared up the week after the June 4 meeting, and once again Centralia Fire Company hooked up the hoses. About a week later, council rented a bulldozer for the fire company to use in trying to put out the burning garbage. Charles Kasenych, one of the bulldozer operators, found the pit work highly unpleasant.* The stench was horrible and the fumes made his head spin. Kasenych stirred up the garbage so the firemen, among them Joseph Scovack, could douse lower layers with water. Sometimes, he recalls, he would push aside some garbage and the flames would leap up.

After a few days, the firemen made an astonishing discovery. There was a hole almost fifteen feet long and several feet high at the base of the north wall of the pit near the cemetery. It had been concealed beneath the garbage and dirt and was not filled with incombustible material. The hole led into the labyrinth of old mines and is more than likely the avenue by which the landfill fire spread into the coal mines. Council had failed to find and close the one hole that the fire needed.

Tighe said he had no idea the hole was there, and suggests it might have been created by the old mine fire burning up from below. Segaritus, on the other hand, hints he knew it was there. "There were holes," he said, "but you couldn't see how far the coal came up. . . . You couldn't see the coal."

Elmer Wills, a Centralia resident, wrote a letter to state Secretary of Mines Lewis E. Evans in late June, informing him of the landfill fire. Evans sent a letter to Segaritus on June 28 directing him to investigate. Segaritus, however, had gone on vacation. His superior, Deputy Secretary of Mines James J. Shober, Sr., opened the letter and wrote back to Evans on July 6, telling him that a telephone caller had already brought the fire to his attention. "After receiving the telephone call, I contacted the field investigator," Shober wrote. "He informed me that he was aware of the condition and had contacted the authorities of Centralia. The council hired a bulldozer to push the refuse around, and

---

*The other operator was Leon Jurgill, Sr., who much later became one of the more strident critics of families who supported relocation to escape the mine fire.

wet it down [the refuse] with a fire hose. Before Mr. Segaritus went on vacation, he notified me the fire was extinguished."

It was not, unfortunately. The garbage began to smolder once again, and foul odors drifted into St. Ignatius Church, prompting a complaint to council from Monsignor William J. Burke that was reported at the July 2 meeting. Councilmen Patrick Shearn and Michael Jurgill resigned at the meeting. Shearn quit for health reasons, but no reason was cited for Jurgill, who was the councilman in charge of fire department matters.

One member of council telephoned Clarence Kashner in nearby Shamokin, a city in Northumberland County. Kashner was president of the Independent Miners, Breakermen, and Truckers, an organization of men who ran small mines or coal-hauling businesses. He was often called by the Northumberland County Commissioners to organize emergency mine fire projects, which the county paid for.

Kashner looked at the smoldering garbage and the large hole and saw a mine fire in the making. He telephoned Gordon Smith, an engineer at Shober's DMMI office in Pottsville, described what he saw at Centralia, and told Smith he could dig out the burning material with a steam shovel for about $175.

Smith told him such a project would have to go through channels. Kashner, knowing that quick action against such fires is essential, was furious and told Smith he would have a mine fire on his hands if the proposal was delayed in that way. Smith said he was sorry, but there was nothing he could do.

In mid-July, probably about the nineteenth, Segaritus made his monthly inspection of the Centralia landfill. Despite the fire, Centralia Council had continued to allow dumping in the pit. Segaritus was horrified by what he saw. Not only was the garbage again on fire but thin wisps of steam curled out of fissures in the north wall of the pit. Segaritus telephoned Art Joyce, a state mine inspector from Mount Carmel, and asked him to bring his gas detection equipment to the pit. Joyce tested the gases emitting from the large hole and the small cracks and concluded from the amount of carbon monoxide present that the old mines were indeed on fire.

Joyce and Segaritus reported their findings immediately to Shober in Pottsville and Tighe in Centralia. Council president Burge called a special meeting for July 25. It can be inferred from the minutes that DMMI asked Centralia Council to prepare two letters. One was to Lehigh Valley Coal Company, formally notifying it of the fire and describing what council had done to try to extinguish it. The other was an appeal to Secretary Evans for state aid in putting out the fire, a type of communication that would become depressingly familiar to Centralia Council in years to come. A copy of the letter survives in the State Archives in Harrisburg, and it makes curious reading:

> The Borough of Centralia has been operating a waste disposal area under permit No. 443R, issued by the Department of Mines and Mineral Industries.
>
> In spite of all precautions to operate the waste disposal area within the provisions of the applicable law, a fire of unknown origin started on or about June 25, 1962, during a period of unusually hot weather.

After describing efforts to extinguish the fire, the letter concluded:

> It now appears that the coal seams may have ignited, resulting in a mine fire, the control of which is beyond the capacity of the Borough. It is, therefore, respectfully requested that consideration be given by the Department of Mines and Mineral Industries to extinguish the mine fire as a project within its operations.

The letter was signed by Mayor George Winnick, Burge, and John Koschoff, Sr., the secretary. Council clearly had decided to conceal the true origin of the fire, perhaps out of fear that Centralia would receive no help if the truth was known, or that some members of the fire department might face legal action. Charles Michael, one of the five firemen of May 27, was at the July 25 meeting. The letter also indicated that council members, at least in 1962, did not believe in the "old mine fire" theory.

The letter's reference to hot weather may be the germ of the spontaneous combustion theory of how the landfill fire started, accepted to this day by most state and federal officials who have worked on the Centralia matter. Why council picked June 25 is unknown. There had been no press coverage of the early days of the fire by the Mount Carmel *Item* or the Ashland *Daily News,* so there was no ready source of contradictory information. Centralia residents were unlikely to contradict council; few knew the truth anyway.

Inexperienced as they were in dealing with the state bureaucracy, the councilmen perhaps never thought the fire would go unextinguished and that they would be called to account. Segaritus, despite his age and ill health, was eager to be interviewed and seemed desperate to prove he had done his duty as a dump inspector. Perhaps he did the best he could, given that his territory included seven counties.

None of them were bad or evil men, and the horror of what they unintentionally set in motion must haunt them. Many persons who had nothing to do with the fire of May 27 would suffer.

4
Natural Forces

Christine Kogut and Charles Gasperetti, Jr. stop to talk near one of the large vent pipes installed by the U.S. Office of Surface Mining in fall 1980 to vent deadly gases created by the Centralia mine fire. The fire also created huge volumes of hot steam (upper right) by vaporizing ground water. (Photo: David DeKok, Weekly Reader)

WHILE the men of Centralia Council waited to find out if state government would rescue them from their dilemma, the uncontrolled mine fire moved farther and deeper into the labyrinth of mines beneath Conyngham Township. The fire created a deadly world of intense heat and poisonous gases. The blackness of the old mines changed to bright, glowing orange and flickering blue, occasionally punctuated by a brief, brilliant burst of yellow when a mine timber erupted in flames. This was a world where no human could live, hotter than the planet Mercury, its atmosphere as poisonous as Saturn's. At the heart of the fire, temperatures easily exceeded 1,000 degrees. Lethal clouds of carbon monoxide and other gases swirled through the rock chambers.

The fire drew its oxygen from elsewhere in the mines, pulling it in ever greater volumes through the many passageways to the surface left open when the mines closed or created later by bootleg miners. The Centralia mine drainage tunnel, which emptied into Big Mine Run about a mile east of Centralia, could alone provide enough air to keep the fire burning for a long time. Even in the unlikely case that all the openings could be found and sealed, the fire could actually draw air through the earth itself.

Centralia lies at the midpoint of the Western Middle Field, one of four subregions in central and northeastern Pennsylvania that together constitute the Anthracite Region. The others are the Eastern Middle Field, of which the principal city is Hazleton, the Southern Field, which gave rise to Pottsville (the Gibbsville of John O'Hara's writings), and the Northern Field, which encompasses Wilkes-Barre and Scranton. Together they have an area of only 484 square miles, but their relatively small size belies the tremendous amount of energy and potential for human and environmental misery they contained.

The four principal coal veins under Centralia—Buck, Seven Foot, Skidmore, and Mammoth—appear to be a set of bowls, one inside the other, when viewed in cross section. At the bottom is the Buck, above that the Seven Foot, and so on, each vein separated from the next by 30 to 150 feet of non-coal rock. Together, the veins form the Centralia basin, or syncline. The rim of each bowl is the vein's outcrop, the place where it reaches or comes near the surface. At the south end of Centralia, just beyond the Buck outcrop, is the Locust Mountain anticline. Here the coal ends for several dozen feet before beginning again on the other side of the mountain, where the much smaller village of Byrnesville lies. At the north end of Centralia, again just beyond the Buck outcrop, is the Centralia anticline. The four veins under Centralia dip steeply from south to north, then rise just as sharply to the opposite anticline. They are elongated from east to west.

The Centralia fire was in the Buck vein, not far from the outcrop at the south end of town. Three hundred fifty yards to the west was St. Ignatius Elementary School, which was operated by the Roman Catholic Diocese of Harrisburg, and the first row of homes of Centralia. To the east lay a wilderness of abandoned mine lands.

It is a tenet of popular wisdom that fires cannot burn downhill, but for mine fires that is not true. George McElroy, a scientist with the U.S. Bureau of Mines, wrote in his 1938 study of anthracite mine fires that an ample source of air will allow a mine fire to burn rapidly both up and down a coal vein. Downhill about 900 feet to the north were the homes on East Park Street.

Most of the time a mine fire gains ground like any fire, by consuming the fuel in front of it. McElroy wrote that a mine fire can also propagate by means of hydrogen explosions, sometimes far from the mother mine fire. Very hot mine fires liberate hydrogen from anthracite coal, and hydrogen is explosive in the presence of oxygen. All that is needed is a spark.

A mine fire makes it easier for itself to spread by conditioning the coal around it. Heat as low as 200 degrees traveling ahead of the main fire is believed to drive water out of the coal, making it much easier to ignite than normal anthracite, which is notoriously difficult to light.

As a mine fire moves through old workings, it damages their stability. Timbers burn away, support pillars are dangerously weakened, and hot steam destabilizes fill material placed in old mine openings. The result can be a subsidence, or cave-in. Sometimes a subsidence goes all the way to the surface, creating a sudden opening that, if caused by a mine fire, spews steam and poison gases. Other times only a slight depression appears, usually when the initial point of collapse is far beneath the surface. The first type of subsidence is by far the more dangerous. A tragic subsidence in 1928 in Homestead in western Pennsylvania claimed the life of 17-year-old Edward Schaff who dropped into a mine fire when the earth opened suddenly. Homestead was far from Centralia in time and distance, but its warning remained valid.

Fighting a mine fire is considerably more difficult in the Anthracite Region than in the Bituminous Region in the western part of the state, where the coal veins are mostly flat and often relatively close to the surface. With deeply plunging veins there is the possibility of deep mine fires, and, according to McElroy, the steep anthracite veins promote circulation of heat generated by a mine fire.

There were three places Centralia Council could turn for help in fighting the mine fire. One was the Columbia County Board of Commissioners in Bloomsburg. The three-member board was the chief governing body of the county. Commissioners in some coal counties, like neighboring Northumberland, would fund projects to fight small mine fires, which Centralia's still was. The Columbia County Commissioners, unfortunately, had little understanding of the problems of a coal community. Centralia and Conyngham Township were the only coal areas in the county, which was largely agricultural. Centralia was largely Roman Catholic, Irish, and Slavic; the other four-fifths of the county was mostly Protestant, German, English, or Scottish.

There were two government agencies in 1962 that could help Centralia, the Pennsylvania Department of Mines and Mineral Industries (DMMI) and the U.S. Bureau of Mines, which is part of the Interior Department. The two agencies had engineers with long experience in fighting mine fires, but only limited funding for such work. People at the field level in each agency knew how to fight a mine fire, but key elected officials in Harrisburg and Washington had little appreciation in 1962 of the extent and seriousness of abandoned mine land problems in the Anthracite Region.

Both agencies were founded to protect the miner. The General Assembly created the forerunner of the Department of Mines and Mineral Industries in 1870 after the Avondale mine disaster. Congress created the Bureau of Mines in 1910 in response to several other mine disasters. Inspectors from the state agency policed active mines to enforce state safety regulations. The Bureau began as a research agency, studying and reporting on mining methods and mine safety, although it later acquired its own corps of inspectors.

On occasion, mines caught fire from gas explosions, unattended lanterns, or any number of other reasons. The state mine inspector's job was to make sure the mine owner extinguished the fire and repaired all damage before allowing mining to resume. In one extreme case, Lehigh Navigation Coal Company fought a fire in one of its mines near Summit Hill for over eighty years, from 1859 into the 1940s, at a cost of some $2 million.

Some companies ran out of money fighting fires in their mines, and from the late 1920s fires in abandoned mines or mines owned by bankrupt companies became a major problem. In such cases, or when a company could not extinguish a fire, it became the responsibility of the municipality or county to pay for putting it out.

In the case of *McCabe* v. *Watt* in 1909, the Pennsylvania Supreme Court emphasized municipal responsibility and extended it to state government as well. The Finn Coal Company had spent a sum equal to its entire capital stock in attempting to extinguish a fire in Carbondale before abandoning the effort. McCabe and the City of Carbondale obtained a court injunction ordering Watt and the company to continue the effort. The Supreme Court ruled otherwise, concluding its opinion:

> If the lives and property of the citizens of Carbondale are menaced by the burning coal mine and the efforts of the owner are unavailing to extinguish the fire, the municipality should take hold of the situation with a strong hand and abate the so-called nuisance just as it would stop the flames of a surface conflagration.
>
> This fire has reached the public enemy stage, and it should be so regarded and treated by the public authorities. To hold that a state or county or other municipal division, each or all of them, cannot provide protection to the lives and property of citizens threatened with destruction by fire, would be to place the seal of impotency on governmental functions and to deny that protection the law should afford an enlightened people.

The Department of Mines, until 1929, was not authorized by the General Assembly to do anything about mine fires except give advice, despite the court opinion. State mine inspectors, in a practice that continued into the 1970s, would ask neighboring coal companies to extinguish abandoned mine fires, and often the companies did so. No law, however, *required* anyone to take action.

Pennsylvania's elected leaders had failed to provide new programs and funding in response to the steep decline and eventual demise of the anthracite industry after World War II and the damaged lands left behind. DMMI did have a budget line item in 1962 for "Abandoned Coal Mine Services," which ran the gamut from extinguishing mine fires, pumping water out of abandoned mines, and antisubsidence projects, to stopping acidic mine water from leaking into the state's renowned trout streams. In the fiscal year beginning July 1, 1962, DMMI was given $1,447,710 to pay for all this work, a pittance, given the scope of the problem. State officials estimated in 1985 that $15 billion worth of abandoned mine cleanup projects remained to be done. Even allowing for inflation, the amount of work that faced the state in 1962 was staggering.

At the federal level, the situation was little better. Fighting mine fires in both active and abandoned mines was an early and continuing concern of the Bureau, but only from the standpoint of research and advice. Not until 1948 did Congress give the Bureau any money to carry out its own mine fire projects. Public Law 738 of 1954 formalized the appropriation, but limited it to no more than $500,000 a year. To qualify for Bureau funding, a mine fire had to be in an inactive mine and threaten a sufficient quantity of coal reserves. That it might threaten a community was not enough. The Bureau was allowed to pay no more than 50 percent of the cost of a project; someone, usually the state, had to pay the other half.

Congress did not always appropriate the full $500,000, according to Charles Kuebler, a Bureau engineer who would play a major role in fighting the Centralia mine fire. Even when it did, no more than $100,000 was usually allocated for the Anthracite Region, he said. Projects were designed for the amount of money available, not for what the situation required. Many mine fire projects went forward with no assurance money would be available the following year to finish the work. Congress, too, had ignored the wreckage left behind by the anthracite era.

What little state and federal mine fire funding was available in Pennsylvania in 1962 went first to fight big mine fires like the one called Cedar Avenue, which had the potential to spread under twenty-five percent of Scranton and Carbondale. Much of the remaining money went to fight smaller mine fires in the Scranton and Wilkes-Barre areas, a reflection of the political savvy and clout of their legislators and the greater visibility of mine fire problems in this densely populated corridor.

A letter dated April 9, 1962, from Secretary of Mines Lewis E. Evans to Scranton City Clerk Frank DeSarro illustrates the situation. "As you know," Evans wrote, "this department has done considerable work in the Scranton area. In fact, a large portion of the money made available to us has been spent in this area."

All these factors would hamper an effective attack against the Centralia mine fire.

5
Missed Opportunities

A small part of the Centralia mine fire as it appeared after being exposed during an excavation in 1969. (Photo: U.S. Bureau of Mines)

CENTRALIA Council should have admitted its mistake and then pressed its elected representatives to make certain that either the state or federal government extinguished the mine fire. Council did send the letter to Evans, but it then ran from the mine fire and let state government do as it pleased. This would be a fatal error.

Deputy Secretary of Mines James Shober, Sr., had one overriding concern: to protect the small number of miners who worked underground in the Centralia area from the poison gases he knew the mine fire would generate. In 1962 there were between twenty-three and thirty working mines and between one hundred and two hundred men employed in them, depending on whose figures one accepts. Time was of the essence if these mines were to be saved. The danger the mine fire would eventually pose to Centralia seems to have been a distinctly secondary concern.

Shober conferred with Charles Kuebler, research director at the U.S. Bureau of Mines Anthracite Research Center in Schuylkill Haven, on July 25 and arranged for a meeting to be held at the mine fire site on August 6. Representatives of Lehigh Valley Coal Company and Susquehanna Coal Company were invited to the meeting. Members of Centralia Council were not, although Hannah and Tighe attended anyway. The Bureau and DMMI disliked involving local officials in the decision-making process about mine fire work. This was a matter among miners.

Lehigh Valley owned the strip-mining and deep-mining rights to the pit area but was in no position to extinguish the mine fire. The company had been out of the mining business for several years and was now chiefly a landlord, leasing out mining rights wherever possible. Much of its Centralia area coal was leased to Pagnotti Coal Company of West Pittston, near Wilkes-Barre, in 1959, although not at the site where the mine fire burned. Strip-mining rights in the pit area had been leased to Jeddo-Highland Coal Company, and deep-mining rights to Susquehanna, which in turn sublet them to a number of small mining concerns.

Shober expected that the coal company officials would tell him they could not afford to mount a project to stop the mine fire, and Kuebler had told him it would take at least three months to mount a federal project. He therefore announced at the August 6 meeting that he expected Evans to approve his recommendation that the state bear the entire cost of digging out the fire, about $30,000.

In later years, Centralia residents would remember the August 6 meeting as the one at which Alonzo Sanchez's offer to take on the mine fire was rejected by the government and the coal companies. Sanchez, a Centralia strip mine operator, had told members of Centralia Council he was willing to dig out the mine fire at minimal or no charge, so long as he could keep any coal he recovered without paying royalties on it to Lehigh Valley. He would drill boreholes to find the perimeter of the fire and to ascertain how much coal was there. If there was enough to make it worth his while (it is safe to assume there was), then he would dig out the fire.

When Sanchez spoke to Shober and the others at the August 6 meeting he was told the state was going to do the project and it had to go out on bids. Probably Shober rejected the offer because there was no need to accept it. Although it would have saved the state money and assured that the fire was extinguished, the project would have been delayed by the exploratory drilling and perhaps by legal tangles over the mining rights, thereby increasing the risk to the miners.

Later, people in Centralia would recall incidents like this and wonder if there had been a conspiracy among government officials and private interests to let the fire get so bad it would drive the people out, enabling someone to grab the village's coal and make a huge profit. There was no conspiracy, of course, but it became a popular explanation for the bungling that occurred.

State mine inspectors were in the Centralia mines every day now, checking for the carbon monoxide they feared would one day be there. A mine fire's most lethal byproduct is carbon monoxide. Odorless and tasteless, it can overcome a person gradually, almost imperceptibly. On August 9 they found what they were looking for, and all Centralia area mines were ordered closed the following day.

A hue and cry went up from the miners. They demanded quick state action to stop the fire so they could return to work. Local 8707 of the United Mine Workers of America met in Centralia on August 12 and passed a motion calling on Secretary Evans to do all he could to extinguish the mine fire. On another front, Clarence Kashner of the Independent Miners, Breakermen, and Truckers was arguing with Evans for a quick project to end the fire threat. He probably told Evans how his offer to dig out the fire had been refused by DMMI mining engineer Gordon Smith in July. Many of the miners idled by the fire belonged to Kashner's group.

Evans already had Shober's recommendation for a quick project at Centralia. A former miner and United Mine Workers official himself, Evans doubtless was sympathetic to the plight of the miners. It was also an election year. Governor David Lawrence could not run again, and Richardson Dillworth, the Democratic nominee, would need the miners' Democratic votes if he was to defeat Congressman William Scranton, the Republican nominee. Evans wrote back to the United Mine Workers on August 15, telling the union men he had authorized a project to extinguish the mine fire. Bids would be opened August 17. Evans telephoned Kashner on August 15 and told him the same, adding that because of the urgency of the matter the state Attorney General's office had given permission to skip the usual requirement of advertising for bids. Bids would be collected by hand from interested contractors in the Centralia area. Two days later the contract was awarded to Bridy, Incorporated, of Atlas, near Mount Carmel, and on August 22 work began. Edward Bridy's bid was in the neighborhood of $20,000, but the exact figure is lost.*

■ ■ ■

Where was the Centralia mine fire? Was it one hundred feet from the dump, or two hundred feet? How fast was it moving, and in which directions? Bridy did not have answers to these questions, and DMMI had informed him he could not do any exploratory drilling in order to find out. He was simply to follow the plans drawn up by engineers Bill Taby and Gordon Smith. They did not believe the fire was very big or very active, and exploratory drilling would delay for weeks the reopening of the mines. Digging out a mine fire without first doing exploratory drilling was a radical departure from procedure. DMMI's engineers could hazard a guess where the fire was, based on where steam was issuing from the rock, but that often gave an inaccurate picture. Bridy was told to begin digging on the north rim of the dump pit and move outward about two hundred feet, simply expanding the pit perimeter. The problem was that as soon as Bridy's shovel tore into the mine chambers, a huge volume of air would rush in and fan the fire.

Steve Kisela, a bulldozer operator on the first Centralia mine fire project and now a strip mine contractor himself, recalled that his boss wanted to encircle the fire with a trench—dug from the outside in—and prevent it from spreading any closer to Centralia. At that time the fire was still far enough from the first line of Centralia homes that a trench could have been excavated without any structure demolition.

Bridy was unable to overtake the fire for various reasons. Kisela

*With only a few exceptions, DMMI documents on the Centralia mine fire from the years 1962 to 1970 have been lost by the Department of Environmental Resources, its successor agency.

said by the time a section was drilled, blasted, and excavated, the fire had moved ahead of the excavation. Bridy was using a 2.5-cubic-yard capacity shovel, small for this type of work. Since the coal vein sloped downward at a steep angle, as the fire moved northward it also moved deeper, exponentially increasing the cost of digging it out. Bridy was only allowed to work a single, eight-hour shift per day, five days a week, and was given the usual holidays off. One legend about the mine fire says the war to extinguish it was lost on Labor Day weekend in 1962, when work ceased for five days.

DMMI originally believed Bridy would need to excavate 24,000 cubic yards of earth to extinguish the mine fire. By the time the project ran out of money and was terminated on October 29, Bridy had excavated 58,580 cubic yards of earth and still the fire was out of control.*

In an assessment of the state's Centralia mine fire work written in the spring of 1963, Gordon Smith was quite candid about the poor design of the Bridy project. "The plan of attack was ineffective, since it was learned the fire penetrated the coal pillar and the underground workings faster than could be excavated." Roger Howells, another former DMMI engineer, agreed and particularly criticized the failure to do exploratory drilling.

In 1961, DMMI and the Bureau each spent over $50,000 for exploratory drilling to find the limits of the Cedar Avenue mine fire in Scranton, and they agreed to spend $15,000 apiece on an exploratory drilling project in April 1962 at the Coal Run mine fire near Shamokin. Why wasn't exploratory drilling ordered at Centralia? Howells suggests cost was the reason, and he is probably partially correct. But the real reason could well be the urgency to extinguish the mine fire so the mines at Centralia could reopen. In their rush to assist the miners, Evans and Shober lost a crucial opportunity to extinguish the Centralia mine fire when it was still of a manageable size.

There does not appear to have been much concern among Centralia residents about the fire at this time, although John Maloney, a miner who lived at the corner of South and Wood Streets in one of the houses closest to the mine fire, came home angry on August 6 after hearing that Sanchez's offer to dig out the mine fire had been refused. He had no idea a state project was in the works. One of the state mine inspectors told Maloney to always keep a window open to vent any mine fire gases that might enter the house. Mrs. Anne Maloney says

---

*Final cost of the project was $27,658. At some point during the work, Secretary Evans authorized an additional $7,644 beyond the original bid price.

they followed the advice faithfully, though at that time they had no idea how long that window would remain open.

Centralia Council lost interest in the mine fire after the first state project began, as Tighe conceded. "In the first place, it was not in the borough," he said. "We had no jurisdiction. Once the state takes over, you have no say." The mine fire is not mentioned in council's official minutes between October 1962 and September 1964. Council considered the mine fire to be the concern of the Conyngham Township Board of Supervisors, a very shortsighted attitude. True, the fire burned in the township, but Centralia lay directly in its path. This apathy would persist in varying degrees for years. There is no evidence the township supervisors took any interest in the fire at this time.

Even before the excavation project was terminated on October 29, Shober was planning a new project he hoped would succeed where the trench failed. He telephoned Evans on October 23 and proposed a flushing project to stop the Centralia mine fire. Evans approved the work the following day.

The goal of any mine fire flushing project is to smother the fire by denying it the air it needs. It is also intended to prevent the fire from moving farther into a mine. Crushed rock would be mixed with water and pumped down into the mines ahead of the fire, or even into the fire itself. There were piles of culm nearby that could be ground up into flushing material.* Water would be a problem. There simply wasn't very much available from the municipal water system. Shober's engineers estimated the flushing work would cost $40,000. When bids were opened on November 1, the low bid of $28,400 came from K&H Excavating, Mount Carmel, owned by Robert Kerris and Edward Helfrick.

This would turn out to be a particularly star-crossed project. The first bad omen was the unseasonably heavy snowfall Centralia experienced in October. The second came on the first day of work, when the drill used to sink boreholes to the fire area became stuck and melted.

The drilling and flushing were conducted along a semicircle at the edge of the dump pit, the holes spaced twenty feet apart. George Segaritus, the DMMI dump inspector, observed the work on several occasions and vividly described what happened when the water-rock slurry was pumped down a borehole into the heart of the underground

---

*Culm is a byproduct of raw coal after it is processed through a breaker. It is a mixture of coal, rock, and dirt. Huge piles of culm dot the Anthracite Region and occasionally catch fire.

fire: "When you dumped water in it, it created like a volcano. And oh boy, when that busted, did that shake things and make a noise. It was red hot mad!"

There seems to have been a deviation from the original flushing plan. Gordon Smith wrote several months later that the flushing holes were to have been drilled "a safe distance and pitch from the fire." A Bureau of Mines report dated December 12, 1962, states, "Most of the holes drilled have been in the immediate fire area, and at the rate the money is being expended it is doubtful that this contract, when completed, will arrest the fire."

The bitter winter of 1962 greatly hampered K&H. Water lines froze, reducing the already inadequate supply to a trickle, and the machine used to grind the culm into flushing material froze solid one windy night during a blizzard.

One thing above all ensured the failure of this project. Helfrick says the DMMI inspectors, worried that the ten thousand cubic yards of flushing material allocated for the project would not be enough, refused to let him fill the boreholes completely. "If it looked like one hole was taking too much material, they would tell us to stop and go on to the next one," he said. This meant that if the flushing material did not extinguish the mine fire, the fire could eventually leapfrog the barrier. Even when the seal was tight to the roof of the mine, the fire could jump the barrier through cracks in the roof rock.

The money was running out. Shober told the Bureau of Mines in December he might ask the agency to take over the Centralia project. He appealed to Evans for more money. Evans approved an additional $14,000 for Centralia in the waning days of the Lawrence administration. The secretary had done what he could for Centralia. It would be up to the new governor, William Scranton, and his secretary of mines, Dr. H. Beecher Charmbury, to keep the work at Centralia going.

6
Scranton's Grand Plan

William Scranton, governor of Pennsylvania from 1963 to 1967. (Photo: National Archives)

Dr. H. Beecher Charmbury, Pennsylvania Secretary of Mines and Mineral Industries from 1963 to 1970. (Photo: Pennsylvania State University)

GOVERNOR William Scranton would become one of the more distinguished and revered political figures in Pennsylvania history, serving as congressman and governor, running for president in 1964, and much later serving as U.S. Ambassador to the United Nations. His commitment to using state and federal tax dollars to clean up the environment in the coal regions of Pennsylvania is less well known than his other achievements, and it is particularly unfortunate that his administration's handling of the Centralia mine fire will remain a black mark on his record. Scranton's Secretary of Mines, Dr. H. Beecher Charmbury, threw away the last chance the state had to extinguish the Centralia fire at a reasonable cost. Charmbury's mishandling of Centralia set in motion a chain of events that would end, twenty years later, with the destruction of the village.

During the campaign in the fall of 1962, Scranton made no secret of his desire to greatly increase state funding to clean up Pennsylvania's abandoned mine land problems. He wanted tough new laws to force strip mine operators to reclaim the land they disturbed with their pits and would insist on more funding from the General Assembly for backfilling abandoned strip mine pits. He saw a need for new state funding to extinguish the many burning culm banks in the coal regions and more money to stop the leakage of acidic mine water into rivers and streams. Lastly, he wanted more money to fight mine fires.

Scranton was the great-grandson of coal baron Joseph Hand Scranton, who helped found the Lackawanna Iron and Coal Company in 1853. Although the governor grew up on an estate outside the city, he was very familiar with the region's environmental problems. They were hard to avoid. There were seven burning culm banks in the Scranton area alone.

It was an experience with one of these burning banks during the summer of his 1960 campaign for Congress, Scranton says, that convinced him of the need for strong governmental action. He was campaigning door-to-door in the village of Throop, north of Scranton, on a day when fumes from the nearby Marvine culm bank fire descended on the community. "The effect of that wind blowing that smelly culm bank fire all over the place almost made me have to give up the walk," Scranton said. "And that said to me this was no condition for people to be living under."

Scranton's choice of H. B. Charmbury as Secretary of Mines was a logical one, given his priorities at the beginning of 1963. Charmbury, who was chairman of Pennsylvania State University's Department of Mineral Preparation, had conducted extensive research into burning culm banks and acid mine drainage. These two problems, along with abandoned strip mines, ranked highest with the new Republican governor. Mine fires placed a poor fourth.

Charmbury could not have been more different than Lewis Evans, his predecessor. Charmbury was a respected academic, and his interest in abandoned mine land problems was academic, too, not shaped by a life in the mines as Evans's was. Evans considered Scranton's plan to clean up the coal regions an unfair reward to the coal companies that caused them—and said so publicly during the Scranton-Dillworth election fight in the fall of 1962. While this can be dismissed as political rhetoric, it reflected an attitude common to many state legislators in Harrisburg. Scranton says he faced it repeatedly during his four years as governor. Ironically, it might have been better for Centralia, if not for the rest of the coal regions, if Richardson Dillworth had been elected governor in 1962. He probably would have kept Evans as Secretary of Mines, and Evans was clearly committed to helping his fellow miners at Centralia.

■ ■ ■

Plagued by bad weather and lack of sufficient water to the very end, the K&H flushing project at Centralia ran out of money on March 15 and the work was terminated. The total cost was $42,420. Edward Helfrick, who much later became a state representative, then a state senator, believes his firm could have defeated the mine fire in 1963 if only it had been given another $10,000 to $12,000—a paltry amount given later expenditures at Centralia. He admits it would have been necessary to go back to some of the boreholes they flushed and inject more crushed rock to ensure a tight seal.

Gordon Smith, who replaced James Shober as Deputy Secretary of Mines on February 26—Smith was a Republican—considered the mine fire neither abated nor controlled, as is made clear in a proposal for additional Centralia work he would write in April, although later in the document, he equivocates, saying the K&H flushing project appeared to have deterred the fire's spread to the north and west, though not to the east, away from Centralia.

DMMI was capable of initiating an emergency mine fire project quite quickly. It had opened bids on the second Centralia project only seven days after Shober proposed it to Evans. Clearly, either Smith or Charmbury, and probably the latter, decided around this time that DMMI could not afford to spend more money at Centralia that spring.

It was not that there was no money, for Charmbury had committed $369,000 to other DMMI projects that began in March. There was the Blitz Program to backfill abandoned strip mines, for example, budgeted at $240,000 and a public relations showpiece for the Scranton administration.

Gordon Smith, to his credit, did not give up on the Centralia mine fire. Smith was born in Centralia and spent the first twelve years of his life there. His father was inside superintendent for the Lehigh Valley Coal Company. Smith visited Centralia on April 11, 1963, and observed surface evidence that the eastern boundary of the mine fire was seven hundred feet from its point of origin in the dump. Holes in the earth spewed steam, which indicated to Smith the fire was becoming more intense. He returned to his office in Pottsville and ordered a complete engineering study of the mine fire. With the results, he drew up a three-option proposal to save Centralia that could begin on July 1 with the new fiscal year.

Plan A, favored by Smith, involved digging a trench around the fire, then backfilling it with incombustible material to create a fire wall. The projected cost was $277,490. Plan B offered a smaller trench, one that would not completely encircle the fire. The circle would be completed, however, with a flush barrier. The price tag for this plan was $151,714. Plan C was a "total and concerted flushing project" that would be better funded and bigger than the K&H flushing project. The cost was projected at $82,300.

In his formal proposal to Charmbury, submitted in May, Smith described the urgency of halting the Centralia mine fire: "The most serious threat is the possible communication of the fire to that part of the seam [coal vein] underlying the town. This can happen if prompt remedial action is not taken." Despite Smith's warning, Charmbury rejected all three options. He does not recall ever seeing them. Clearly, stopping the mine fire was not a high priority for Scranton's secretary of mines, as it had been for Lewis Evans. Perhaps Charmbury's decision was influenced by Scranton's order, handed down shortly after he was sworn into office, that DMMI spending for the upcoming 1964 fiscal year was to be reduced by 25 percent. This is the budget that would have funded a third Centralia project.

Scranton does not remember the Centralia mine fire being "a big item" while he was governor. Maysie Gutshall Mohney, executive deputy secretary of DMMI under Charmbury, says the Centralia mine fire was considered "very insignificant" in Harrisburg. The Cedar Avenue mine fire, Mrs. Mohney says, occupied much of the time, energy, and monies of DMMI. "There was just so much money spent. . . . It just sort of swallowed up all the money," she said, adding there were state and federal legislators with an interest in the Cedar Avenue mine fire.

It might well have been different for Centralia if its own corps of legislators had taken an interest in the village's plight. The problem was that U.S. Representative Herman Schneebeli, State Senator Zehnder Confair, and State Representative Amin Alley had no apparent appreciation for the special problems of a coal region community. Centralia was the only coal community in their largely agricultural districts. Confair lived in Montoursville, 70 miles to the north. Schneebeli lived in Williamsport, which is near Montoursville. Alley lived the closest, 40 miles to the north in Berwick. Centralia was as different from the rest of their districts as the Bronx would be to Oklahoma. Robert Burge and the Democratic-controlled Centralia Council aggravated the problem by their evident distaste for associating with these distant Republicans. Indeed, back in July 1962, when council was deciding how to get help in extinguishing the mine fire, a letter was prepared asking the help of U.S. Representative George Rhodes (D–Reading), who wasn't their representative but *was* a Democrat. Amin Alley, who served just one term, said it was always his belief the mine fire was being attended to.

Smith eventually prevailed on Charmbury to allow him a token sum of money to spend at Centralia on a third project, probably around $40,000. Smith then appealed to Charles Kuebler of the Bureau of Mines for a federally supervised project at Centralia. Federal mine fire projects, of course, required 50 percent state participation. If the Bureau of Mines had matched the money Charmbury was willing to spend, it would have been enough to fund Plan C, the flushing project. Kuebler told Smith his funds were committed to two other mine fire projects. He could not help him until the next federal fiscal year, which would begin on October 1, 1963.

Stymied again, Smith considered what he could do with the minimal amount Charmbury was willing to spend. He knew the mine fire was spreading quickly to the east, away from Centralia. The only thing he could do with the money was excavate a trench that would cut off the mine gangway in which the fire burned to prevent it from moving much further in that direction. He would gamble that the K&H flushing project had contained the fire on the north and west. To the south was the dump pit, and beyond that the Centralia anticline, a solid mass of rock.

There was a secondary reason for the trench, according to Daniel

Lewis, a Bureau of Mines inspector who worked at Centralia and who knew Smith well. Lewis believes Smith intended the trench to serve as a huge chimney, venting the deadly carbon monoxide before it could reach the homes of Centralia. It would feed air to the fire, true, but that would make little difference if the fire was contained behind the trench and flush barrier. Charmbury, though claiming not to remember any details about the Centralia projects, says Smith designed a trench for that purpose at Cedar Avenue.

Work began on July 9, 1963. Once again the contractor was Edward Bridy. The contract price was $36,225. A story in the Mount Carmel *Item* that day described the work to be done and the history of the fire, speculating that the garbage in the dump was set afire "by youngsters" and spread to the coal mines "several years ago." Already, the history of the mine fire had been distorted beyond recognition.

This project was prefaced by exploratory drilling to find the mine fire's eastern perimeter, but it did little good. The fire was simply moving too fast. George Potochney, the shovel operator on the job, recalls how they dug down and reached the main east-west gangway of the mine. The section of gangway they reached was hot, he says, but not on fire, although loose coal at the bottom was burning. "The timber wasn't [burning] until we opened it [the gangway] up. Then the timber started flaming, so it was like dry-rotted in there.

"The mine inspector came up and looked at it. We were kind of mad about it, you know, because he should have stopped us there and run around the fire. You know, you could see in there, and it looked like it [the fire] was in only ten more feet. We could have took it off that side, because there was no fire out to the east, or there before. . . . He said no, he insisted, he said just follow the stakes."

Gordon Smith personally supervised the work in the early weeks, before the diggers hit the hot gangway, recalls Potochney. Smith intended to supervise it to the end, but on August 13, 1963, he hurriedly left Centralia to design and supervise a rescue operation in Sheppton, about fifteen miles away, where three miners were trapped three hundred feet underground by a rockfall. Potochney says Smith did not return to Centralia after Sheppton.

One can only speculate whether it would have made any difference if Gordon Smith had been in Centralia when the diggers reached the hot gangway. If the trench had prevented eastward spread of the mine fire, later efforts to stop the fire might have been easier, or at least cheaper. The project was halted in October when the mine fire was detected on both sides of the uncompleted trench. That same month, a $775,000 federal-state antisubsidence project was approved for Wilkes-Barre by Charmbury and Secretary of the Interior Stewart Udall. There would not be another attempt to stop the mine fire at Centralia for three and a half years, and the mines closed in 1962 never reopened.

7
Too Long a Wait

President Lyndon B. Johnson delivers remarks before signing the Appalachian Regional Development Act on March 9, 1965, as Vice President Hubert Humphrey, lower left, and a group of public officials look on. At upper left is U.S. Representative Daniel Flood of Wilkes-Barre. To Flood's left is Governor William Scranton of Pennsylvania. (Photo: Johnson Library)

NO evidence can be found to show that the Pennsylvania Department of Mines and Mineral Industries gave serious thought to doing a fourth project at Centralia. Indeed, the third state project had been little more than a rear guard action to give Centralia citizens some protection from the deadly gases generated by the mine fire. Much later, this would become known in the village as an appeasement project. Once it was completed, DMMI washed its hands of the problem.

Secretary of Mines Charmbury intended to turn over the Centralia problem to the U.S. Bureau of Mines. He knew by April 1964 that the Appalachian Regional Development Act, a major legislative initiative of the Johnson administration, would contain millions of dollars in new federal funding to fight mine fires. There was every likelihood the money would be in hand by the fall of that year. Centralia could wait while DMMI attended to more politically pressing problems in the Scranton and Wilkes-Barre areas. Unfortunately for Centralia, the wait turned out to be longer than Charmbury anticipated. No further direct action to contain the Centralia mine fire was taken until May 1967.

■ ■ ■

President Lyndon B. Johnson received the report of the President's Appalachian Regional Commission on April 9, 1964, a year after President John F. Kennedy created the study group at the request of the Conference of Appalachian Governors. The report called for massive federal spending in Appalachia to end the economic underdevelopment that was the source of the region's legendary poverty. Among the many projects suggested was a cleanup of abandoned mine land problems, including mine fires and strip mining scars. Johnson, a great believer in the federal government's ability and duty to improve the lot of the average citizen, enthusiastically endorsed the report and prepared to submit it to Congress as legislation.

Governor William Scranton, pleased with the Appalachian report but unhappy that it recommended only $3 million for cleaning up abandoned mine land problems in the first year of the program, met with Johnson and presented him with compelling evidence in favor of additional funding. Johnson promised $13 million of the $20 million Scranton requested, and in return, Scranton did all he could to round up votes in Congress for the bill. He also gave extensive testimony in support of the abandoned mine land cleanup provision of the Appalachian Regional Development Act at a hearing on May 6, 1964.

"In Pennsylvania there are presently eleven mine fires in the bituminous region and sixteen others now raging in the anthracite area," Scranton testified. "It isn't just that they are there, but it's the fact they can do so much future harm that makes them so tremendously important." The governor argued that state governments in the Appalachian region had done what they could to clean up the problems, but "It is simply beyond their financial resources to do the entire job."

Scranton's efforts in this area did not end with his support of the Appalachian bill. Toward the end of his term, he proposed a $500-million state bond issue for land and water conservation projects, of which $200 million would go to DMMI for extinguishing mine fires and burning culm banks, preventing subsidences, and the like. Voters approved the bond issue on May 16, 1967, several months after Scranton's term expired. The $200 million for DMMI created a program called Operation Scarlift.

Scranton was the chief Republican proponent of greater federal funding for abandoned mine land work, and Congressman Daniel Flood of Wilkes-Barre held that distinction for the Democrats. Flood, a flamboyant former actor, represented the Eleventh District, which included Centralia after March 8, 1966. Flood's district was afflicted by all the problems the Appalachian Regional Development Act was designed to correct. He was a ferocious fighter for his constituents' interests, although he paid more attention to Luzerne County, his power base, than the outlying sections of his district.

Despite the efforts of Scranton and Flood, the Appalachian Regional Development Act did not pass the Congress in 1964, as many expected it would. Senate approval did not come until September 25, 1964, and House approval could not be obtained before the end of the Eighty-eighth Congress. Action on the bill had to begin anew in January after the swearing in of the new Congress. In the meantime, the mine fire at Centralia grew larger and the Scranton administration did nothing to stop it.

■ ■ ■

Secretary Charmbury's immediate worry in 1964 was the Laurel Run mine fire near Wilkes-Barre. Burning for over forty-five years, it had recently escaped constraining barriers and was moving under the village of Laurel Run only a few miles from Congressman Flood's house. Flood mentioned Laurel Run during his testimony for the Appalachian bill. If not stopped, this mine fire could spread up and down the heavily populated Wyoming Valley. DMMI announced on March 19, 1964, that a $1-million federal-state flushing project would begin at Laurel Run, of which the state would pay $500,000.

A press release announcing the project states, "This . . . project is in accordance with the Scranton Administration's program to assist in the control of mine fires at abandoned coal mines *in those instances where such work is in the interest of public welfare"* (emphasis added). It strains belief that Charmbury did not consider the Centralia mine fire to fall under this category. Deputy Secretary of Mines Gordon Smith clearly warned Charmbury in May 1963 that the Centralia fire could move beneath the village if prompt action was not taken. Centralia's fire, too, could spread up and down its valley and reach other communities. Laurel Run was about the same size as Centralia. The only discernable difference between the two communities was that Centralia was not defended by powerful legislators.

■ ■ ■

How far had the mine fire spread? Centralia Council had no idea where it had moved since it was detected in the dump two years before. Now the council had reason to wonder and worry, for late in the summer of 1964, it was approached by Penn Fuels Gas and told the company planned to lay a natural gas pipeline through Centralia. It would be part of a pipeline paralleling Route 61 from Leesport, near Reading, to Shamokin, and would follow Locust Avenue through Centralia. Penn Fuels already had State Department of Highways approval.

Centralia Council's first reaction was understandable concern about what might happen if the mine fire reached the natural gas pipeline, which would cross the Buck vein outcrop near St. Ignatius Elementary School. What if a subsidence, the danger of which is always greatest along an outcrop, ruptured the pipeline and the fire ignited the natural gas?

According to the minutes of a special council meeting held on September 24, 1964, Penn Fuels official Glenn Butler assured the councilmen that in the fire area "the pipe will be encased in a larger protective tube capable of withstanding temperatures up to 4,000 degrees Fahrenheit." No mine fire could burn that hot. Council consequently adopted and published an ordinance allowing Penn Fuels to run the line through Centralia. At the same time, it voted to send a letter to DMMI stating Centralia's concern over the pipeline and asking DMMI to "take measures to insure the safety of such a venture."

At the November 2 council meeting, council president Robert Burge directed secretary John Koschoff, Sr., to write a letter to Penn Fuels, "notifying them that the borough is aware that the pipeline installed in the fire area was not according to agreement. Borough should have been consulted about a change in pipe encasement." In a 1983 interview, Glenn Butler insisted that Penn Fuels lived up to the promises it made to Centralia Council, saying that the protective sheathing was installed "in front of the church [St. Ignatius] and any-place it crossed the highway. Wherever it was specified, we did it."

Whatever the truth of the matter, a natural gas pipeline now crossed the fire's path about 370 yards west of the former landfill. This episode should have made Centralia Council considerably more vigilant about the mine fire. Instead, it only seemed to leave council members with a vague sense that something was not right.

That winter, snow melted from an area of ground about one hundred feet west of the first row of houses in Centralia, and council worried this was evidence the mine fire was nearing the village. At their January 4, 1965 meeting, council members directed Koschoff to write another letter to DMMI requesting "tests and assurances of the mine fire status." Like the letter sent in September, it was not answered.

By the spring of 1965, from the edge of town Centralia citizens could see an unearthly glow at night over the pit excavated during the third state project. Those venturing to the edge saw active fire exposed on all its walls, blue flames, and red hot rock.

■ ■ ■

President Johnson signed the Appalachian Regional Development Act on March 9, 1965. Under the new law, projects could begin almost immediately. Charles Kuebler, now chief of the U.S. Bureau of Mines office in Wilkes-Barre, began planning a massive, multi-million-dollar project to eliminate the mine fire's threat to Centralia. Charmbury had already informed him that Pennsylvania wanted Centralia handled under the new program.

The Appalachian law required states to initiate mine fire projects but placed them under federal administration. Since federal funds would pay 75 percent of the Centralia project, it was only natural that the Bureau of Mines administer it. The state would pay the other 25 percent, and Columbia County would provide flushing material and obtain property releases.

Kuebler assigned the Centralia project to John Buch in the Schuylkill Haven field office. Buch was eminently qualified for the job, having tackled many mine fires in his career with the Bureau. It was Kuebler, though, who held Centralia's fate in his hands. He would be a key figure in the Centralia story for the next fourteen years.

Kuebler, raised in the Anthracite Region, held a bachelor of mining engineering degree from Lafayette College and a master's degree from the Massachusetts Institute of Technology. He was considered a good mining engineer by his peers, but once he decided on a course of action, that was it. He had little respect for opinions on mine fire control offered by anyone who was not, like himself, a professional mining engineer. His associates at the Bureau of Mines and engineers at DMMI who knew him called Kuebler "Ironhead," though not to his face.

Buch knew the Centralia fire was larger than when the state abandoned it in 1963. His two-phase project, which he was certain would protect Centralia forever if carried out properly, tried to take that into account. The problem was that Buch did not have hard data on the fire's location, data that could only be obtained by drilling. He used existing data and surface observations to determine that $2.5 million would be enough money to save Centralia. Unfortunately, that figure became written in stone.

According to "Centralia Mine Fire Control Project: History and Recommendations for Control," written by Buch in May 1965, Phase I of the project would begin with the backfilling of the dump pit where the fire ignited in 1962. Buch believed the pit was feeding air to the fire. Extensive exploratory drilling to find the boundaries of the fire would follow. Then they would encircle the fire with a flush barrier, the integrity of which was crucial to the success of Phase II.

Phase II would be the excavation of a huge trench between the fire and Centralia. The trench would be a staggering 2,500 feet long and would vary in depth from 100 to 200 feet. Once excavation began, the fire would have a tremendous new source of air. Buch intended the flush barrier to prevent the fire from accelerating past the projected trench location, which would be disastrous for Centralia, but he indicated in the report he did not believe a flush barrier could hold back the mine fire indefinitely. "The mined and caved conditions" in the area of the proposed barrier would be difficult to flush successfully, and the contractor would never know if the material filled all the myriad cavities. This was why the trench was needed.

Total cost of the project was estimated at $2,525,000, of which $300,000 was allotted for Phase I. The figure did not include the cost of acquiring homes that would be in the way of or dangerously near the trench. It was almost a tenfold increase over the $277,490 Gordon Smith said he needed in the spring of 1963 to encircle the fire with a trench, an increase reflecting the greater size and depth of the Centralia mine fire in 1965. Pennsylvania reaped no bargain by abandoning Centralia in 1963—the state's share of the new project came to $631,250.

A slightly different version of Buch's May 1965 report on Centralia that may have been a preliminary draft states: "It is recommended that the drilling and flushing phase proceed without delay. If this mine fire is permitted to continue uncontrolled, it will jeopardize the entire borough of Centralia."

■ ■ ■

Appalachian Regional Commission members approved the Centralia project on June 8, 1965, designating it project No. 7. On the same day it approved a new $4-million mine fire project at Laurel Run, and anti-subsidence flushing projects at Scranton and Coaldale. The Bureau of Mines told the commission that "groundbreaking" for the Centralia project would occur within sixty days and work would be completed within three years. Both estimates would prove wildly inaccurate.

An entire year was lost gathering property releases in Centralia and Conyngham Township, and Kuebler would not proceed until every release was in hand. The level of public concern about the mine fire was low, and the property owners were reluctant to sign the releases, which were written in difficult legal language. All but two were signed by October 5. Anthony Clover, a Centralia homeowner, simply refused to sign, and federal and county officials finally decided the project could proceed without his signature. The other holdout was Pagnotti Coal Company. Pagnotti had acquired surface and mineral rights to the mine fire site when it purchased Lehigh Valley Coal Company's extensive coal land holdings in October 1963. James J. Tedesco, chief executive officer of the firm at the time, did not sign until the end of February 1966, and then only after the Columbia County Commissioners sent two pleading letters.

Despite having all property releases in hand by March 1966, the Bureau of Mines did not act for months. Congressman Daniel Flood's chief aide, Eugene Hagarty, telephoned Joseph Corgan, chief of the Division of Anthracite, on April 28 and complained about the endless delay in beginning the Centralia project. Centralia had become part of Flood's district on March 8, 1966.

Corgan sent Flood a letter the same day Hagarty called. It explained, "Bureau of Mines engineers . . . are now in the process of evaluating property releases provided by Columbia County officials. When it is ascertained that the releases, and other appropriate legal documents are in order, the project will be submitted to the Secretary of the Interior for his approval. Once approved, a contribution contract will be submitted by the Bureau of Mines to Columbia County and the Commonwealth [of Pennsylvania] for their endorsement. . . . The Bureau is doing everything it can to expedite the Centralia project."

The Bureau of Mines feared Flood as it feared few other congressmen, but Flood, like most congressmen of the era, did not have the staff to independently investigate whether the Bureau of Mines was dragging its feet at Centralia. When he barked, the Bureau jumped— briefly.* In this case, he did not follow up, and the Bureau did not noticeably speed up the start of work to protect Centralia from the mine fire.

Secretary of the Interior Stewart Udall gave final approval to the Centralia project on June 8, 1966. Kuebler prepared to put the contract out on bids, but this could not be done until after the contribution contracts were signed on July 20. Bids were opened on August 19 and the low bidder was Empire Contracting Company of Old Forge at $281,215.

This was under the $300,000 allocated for the project, but not when the Bureau's 16 percent "planning and engineering" fee was added. The fee came to about $45,000, but the Bureau decided the amount allocated for Phase I should be increased to $360,000. An amended contribution contract was required, and it was signed September 12.

■ ■ ■

Lack of sufficient water, which had severely hampered the second state project in Centralia in 1962 and 1963, was one of the key problems faced by Empire Contracting Company, for enormous volumes of water would be needed for a major flushing project. The water company that served Centralia simply could not supply enough water through its gravity system.

There was an alternative supply, however. An enormous amount of water poured daily from the Centralia mine drainage tunnel's portal about one mile east of the village. The tunnel, cut through solid rock in the nineteenth century, prevented the mine water pool from rising above a certain level. The water was foul smelling and a yellow-brown color, heavily polluted with mine acid that would quickly corrode a

---

*The Bureau of Mines had experienced Flood's wrath the previous year, when through no fault of the Bureau, Senator Hugh Scott of Pennsylvania, a Republican, beat Flood to the punch in announcing the $4-million Laurel Run mine fire project. A lengthy Bureau of Mines internal memorandum, written June 9, 1965, the day of the offense, speculated that Pennsylvania's representative to the Appalachian Regional Commission, a Republican appointed by Governor Scranton, had leaked the news. The memorandum author worried that Flood's distress might be felt by the Johnson administration in general.

standard pump or metal pipe. Building a pump capable of withstanding the polluted mine water and laying more than a mile of pipe over the mountain to reach the job site would delay the project for eight months.

Kuebler allowed the exploratory drilling to begin on November 7, but halted it after only twenty-nine holes had been drilled, some into very hot ground. It made little sense to drill holes if the flush barrier could not be built for months. The data might well be useless because of the fire's movement.

Kuebler did permit Empire to continue backfilling the former land-fill and the pit excavated by DMMI in 1963. Buch, in his "Centralia Mine Fire Control Project: History and Recommendations for Control," implies both pits should have been filled long before 1965 to cut off some of the air feeding the fire. Gordon Smith was of a different mind—as noted in chapter 6, he believed a strategically placed pit could pull the deadly mine fire gases away from a populated area and vent them into the air. Smith won the argument this time. The Bureau of Mines completion report for Phase I states, "A small part of the open pit and trench were left open to serve as vents to the mine fire."

This was not the end of the argument, however. It would not be settled until after Smith's death in 1977. The pits were backfilled at Kuebler's orders in 1978, with tragic results. The gases began moving toward Centralia.

Empire Contracting got the go-ahead to resume drilling on May 8, 1967. Not long after the drilling began, the Bureau of Mines discovered to its dismay that the mine fire had moved farther north, toward the homes on Park Street, and west, toward the homes on Locust Avenue and Wood Street, than they ever imagined. In addition, the drillers were finding much larger mine chambers than anyone expected. When the flushing began, the huge underground rooms quickly swallowed up the flushing material allocated for the project. Moreover, the flushing material ordered by Kuebler was not adhering to the 35-degree slope of the mine chambers. Kuebler ordered a larger size be used, and that seemed to work. The flush barrier's projected final cost was rapidly escalating. There would have to be more money provided or a cutback in the scope of the project.

Congressman Flood sent letters in August to DMMI and the Bureau of Mines asking for reports on the Centralia project. Charmbury responded that 90 percent of the allocated flushing material for Phase I had already been dumped into the mines, "but a considerable additional cubic yardage of flushing will be needed because of encountering more voids and broken areas than originally anticipated." Charmbury said a change order increasing Empire's contract by $132,825 had been issued by the Bureau of Mines, "to provide for continued additional flushing without interruption of operations." The change order was never issued. The completion report for Phase I makes no mention of it, and the report's final cost for Phase I is the same as in the amended contribution contract signed by the three parties.

The response from Joseph Corgan of the Bureau of Mines makes no mention of the change order. It describes the problems with the flushing and reaffirms that Phase II of the Centralia project would be the excavation of a trench to contain the mine fire. Flood did not investigate further.

Kuebler, instead of asking for more money from the Appalachian Regional Commission and the state, changed the design of the flush barrier. Instead of encircling the fire, it would face it like a half-circle, preventing the fire from reaching Centralia but allowing it to burn unimpeded to the east and south.

Kuebler's problems were not over. The exploratory drilling showed the fire to have reached depths and areas undreamed of in 1965. At some locations, the fire was already 225 feet deep. The Phase II trench, as a result, would cost $4.5 million, $2 million more than expected.

Sometime in late September or October of 1967, a decision was made at the top levels of the Bureau of Mines to abandon the proposed trench and instead build expanded flush barriers. In so doing the Bureau of Mines went against its own belief that flush barriers would provide only temporary protection for Centralia. Why was no effort made to obtain additional funding from the Appalachian Regional Commission, which had plenty of money at this point? A $4.5-million project was certainly not out of the realm of reason. The Laurel Run mine fire project would cost $4 million.

The answer may be found in a memorandum written on August 2, 1978 by Thomas P. Flynn, a top assistant to Corgan in 1967 and in 1978 the Bureau's chief of the Division of Environment. He wrote the memorandum following a conversation with Rick Becker, an aide to U.S. Senator John Heinz (R–Pennsylvania). Flynn told Becker the trench concept had been abandoned because it simply was too costly. It would have meant spending almost $5 million to protect real estate with an assessed valuation of $500,000, Flynn said, quoting unnamed Columbia County officials. The cost-benefit ratio just wasn't favorable to Centralia. If only DMMI and the Bureau of Mines had not waited so long.

8
Sideshow

Exploratory drilling during first phase of Appalachian Regional Commission project in Centralia, circa 1967. (Photo: U.S. Bureau of Mines)

LOUIS Pagnotti sat in his West Pittston office and wondered why he ever let himself get in such a bind. It was December 1967 and he had just learned the Bureau of Mines planned to let his coal burn at Centralia. The flush barrier had been redesigned to temporarily stop the fire from moving west, under Centralia homes, and nothing would be done, at least for now, to prevent the fire from moving east and south, crossing Locust Mountain and setting afire the Conyngham Township coal Pagnotti really cared about, his reserves in the Byrnesville area.

Tom Long, a Pagnotti engineer, was the first to grasp the extent of the problem. Long feared the fire was moving toward the spoon-shaped mass of coal formed by the convergence of the north and south dips, or arms, of the Buck vein. This was east of the Odd Fellows Cemetery on the crest of Locust Mountain. Once the mine fire crossed the mountain, it would follow its air supply down the vein into the old mine workings in the south dip. From there it would travel west to the village of Byrnesville and the Pagnotti stripping operations around the village. If the fire reached his Byrnesville operation, it would not make mining impossible but would certainly make it difficult, miserable, and dangerous. Miners' lives would be threatened and much coal would be lost.

Long and Henry Ventre, Pagnotti's field manager, devised a proposal for escaping from the difficulty the company found itself in. If the Bureau of Mines was not going to take effective action to stop the spread of the Centralia mine fire, why not do it themselves? The company had a 10-cubic-yard shovel standing idle near Centralia and plenty of miners to do the work, which would be unpleasant but well within the abilities of Pagnotti Coal Company. They would strip mine the mine fire into oblivion.

It made sense to Pagnotti, but one serious obstacle stood in the way. It was the release his company signed in 1966 to allow the Bureau of Mines to trespass on Pagnotti property to carry out its Centralia plan. Pagnotti Coal was now obligated not to interfere with the Centralia project in any way.

Pagnotti had always cooperated with state and federal mine fire projects, for a long career in the coal business had taught him a mine fire is not to be trifled with. Any state mine inspector in an area where Pagnotti mined coal could tell stories of how he willingly helped extinguish mine fires that were not in any way his responsibility.

Neither was the fire at Centralia his responsibility. He had in-herited it from Lehigh Valley Coal Company in February 1964, when the holdings purchased the previous fall were actually transferred into his possession. One term of the sale was that the existing lease of sur-face rights for strip mining at the fire site would remain in effect. The lease ran until September 30, 1965. This prevented Pagnotti from taking any action against the Centralia fire at that time. By the time the lease expired, the Bureau of Mines had announced its $2.5-million Centralia mine fire project.

Because of the release the company signed in 1966, Pagnotti would need Bureau of Mines permission to strip out the fire that was burning his coal. Pagnotti did not imagine the federal engineers would raise many objections. He was certain they would welcome the chance to be rid of responsibility for a serious problem.

The only condition of the offer was that Pagnotti Coal be allowed to keep and sell any coal it recovered during the excavation. Long and Ventre had high hopes that a significant amount of coal could be re-covered in the spoon area. To be certain, they had a Pagnotti crew drill six boreholes there to see if the fire had already reached it. It had not. There would be no charge to the government, and relatively few out-of-pocket expenses for the company. As a final sweetener, they would do the project under Bureau of Mines supervision.

After leaving Pagnotti, Ventre and Long drove the sixty miles from West Pittston to Centralia. At the Bureau of Mines trailer, which sat near the Odd Fellows Cemetery, Ventre explained the company's pro-posal to John Buch, John Rosella, who was another engineer assigned to the project, and field inspectors Daniel Lewis and John Stockalis, emphasizing it would not cost the government anything and would be done under Bureau of Mines supervision. Not surprisingly, Buch and the others were very interested. Buch said he would have to telephone Washington. He went to the other room of the trailer, closed the door, and placed the call, which probably went to anthracite division chief Joseph Corgan. He returned after about twenty minutes, his face downcast, and told the others that "Washington"—he did not give any names—said it just wasn't possible. Pagnotti's offer had been re-fused, despite the huge prospective savings to the taxpayers and the near certainty the mine fire would be eliminated as a threat to Cen-tralia. What did Washington officials see in the gift horse's mouth?

Long, interviewed in 1983 along with Louis Pagnotti III, grandson of the late company president, said he never learned why the offer was refused. Daniel Lewis, interviewed separately, did not know either.

Lewis speculated that such an offer could only have been rejected by Corgan or somebody higher up than him. Because of the Bureau's strict chain of command, Lewis believes Buch's call went to Corgan.

Charles Kuebler could recall no such offer by Pagnotti, but Thomas P. Flynn, Corgan's deputy that year, did remember hearing about it, although he could not recall why it was rejected.

Wilbert Malenka, who became Kuebler's deputy around this time, believes that legal questions would have caused the Bureau officials in Washington to reject the Pagnotti offer. Malenka, while denying any direct knowledge of the offer, said he knew of no instance where the Bureau of Mines turned over a mine fire that threatened a community to a private contractor and walked away. He said there would have had to be limits on such a deal, that the Bureau could not simply allow a private contractor (albeit one who owned the coal) to continue excavating until the coal was exhausted. Malenka questioned, too, who would have paid for relocation of houses and roads under such an arrangement. Finally, he suggested the Bureau would have been accused of caring more about saving coal than saving people.

A somewhat similar plan, however, succeeded in extinguishing the Carbondale mine fire near Scranton in 1974. Carbondale Redevelopment Authority joined Glen Alden Coal Company on the fire project, according to Ivor Williams, who was vice-president of Glen Alden at the time and later joined the Bureau of Mines. "The redevelopment bought the homes [of people in the way of the excavation] and they built townhouses on the other side of Carbondale, where there is no coal. They moved the people there or wherever they wanted to move," Williams said. "They bought their homes out. We put two contractors on the job. The fire wasn't quite as big as this one [Centralia], but it was an immense fire. We stripped it all out and the contractors made money on the coal. We paid the redevelopment twenty-three cents [royalty] for every ton of run-of-mine coal. There wasn't any government involved. They were paying the redevelopment, they never bothered. They just took the homes away."

Malenka questions who would have paid for relocations if Pagnotti took over the fire work at Centralia, but the company did not believe any would be needed. There must have been a way the Bureau could have made the proposal work, since it had severe doubts about the feasibility of the flush barriers it planned to substitute for the intercept trench at Centralia, and since Pagnotti was willing to work under Bureau supervision. Perhaps to Corgan it seemed safer to use the money they had in hand to do the project their way, the bureaucratically safe way. There was less chance anyone would question why the Bureau had dawdled so long in starting the project.

To look at this incident today is to lament over what might have been. Pagnotti had the workers, equipment, know-how, and desire to dig out the Centralia mine fire. It appears that only the fears of bureaucrats prevented him from saving the village.

9
In the Fire's Grasp

A worker trains a cooling jet of water on a drag line shovel being used to excavate a trench through the Centralia mine fire in July 1969. The U.S. Bureau of Mines began this emergency project after mine fire gases invaded the three homes at right. Mrs. Marion Laughlin lived in the house closest to the pit, Mr. and Mrs. William Birster in the middle house, and Mrs. Anna Ryan in the third. They evacuated their homes before the project began. (Photo: U.S. Bureau of Mines)

RESIDENTS of East Park Street were the first to suspect the grave danger the nearby mine fire posed to their lives and properties. In late November 1967, a group of them asked Councilman Joseph Tighe to request the Bureau of Mines to monitor their homes for carbon monoxide. Tighe wrote a letter to Charles Kuebler on November 24 that noted, "With cold weather prevailing, which will cause home owners to keep their windows closed, we are concerned with the dangers of explosion or asphyxiation."

Kuebler dismissed Tighe's request, stating in a November 29 letter, "The Bureau of Mines does not have the personnel or funds to provide this service." He suggested Tighe contact Gordon Smith at the Department of Mines and Mineral Industries, which Tighe did.

Smith agreed to send an inspector to Centralia, and early in December, carbon monoxide was discovered in one of the houses. Available documents do not identify the owner, but they do state the "trace" of carbon monoxide was officially attributed to the house's furnace, not the mine fire. No carbon monoxide was found on a second visit to the house.

In a letter to Congressman Daniel Flood dated January 5, 1968, Secretary of Mines H. B. Charmbury virtually ruled out the possibility mine fire gases would ever enter Centralia homes "because of the extremely heavy cover and massive rock strata intervening between these homes and the fire." Although the letter was signed by Charmbury, a memorandum strongly implies the letter was written by Gordon Smith, who should have known and probably did know how fractured the rock strata were below Centralia. It was an answer, however, that could easily fool a layman.

Centralia Council, particularly Tighe and council president Robert Burge, was increasingly concerned about the way the Bureau of Mines was handling the mine fire. They had not learned of the decision to scrap the trench until December 12, 1967, the day of the final inspection of the Phase I work. They also learned that work on the flush barriers that would replace the trench would not begin until January or February of 1969, over a year hence. Burge wrote to Flood, "We are concerned that a delay such as this could result in the fire continuing north [toward East Park Street] and then possibly turning west again beyond the flushed area toward our community."

Ideally, the Bureau could get a project like this under way in about two months. It had apparently learned nothing from its delay in beginning the Phase I work, delay that contributed to the decision to abandon the trench plan. It had rejected Louis Pagnotti's offer to take over the project and now showed no urgency in beginning a grade B plan that Centralia officials were begging it to hurry along.

In October 1968, an exasperated Centralia Council wrote to Flood asking him when work might be expected to begin. Flood wrote back that "some action" was expected by November 15. Nothing happened, and the silence from the Bureau of Mines continued.

The chief cause of the delay was a decision by the Bureau of Mines to change the design of the flush barriers planned for Phase II. During the summer of 1968, Kuebler attended a conference which Malcolm Magnusson, who was in charge of the Bureau's mine fire work in western Pennsylvania, also attended. Magnusson briefed Kuebler on a promising new mine fire control technique he and others had developed at the Bureau lab in Bruceton. They had determined that fly ash, a light, powdery waste product of coal-burning power plants, could be used to build a far better flush barrier than ever could be built with sand, clay, or other materials. Fly ash could be blown into the mines by pressurized tankers. It was so fine and free flowing that it would fill up small cavities in collapsed mines much better than sand or clay. No water was required to place the fly ash, but when mine water came in contact with the ash, the barrier became almost as solid as the rock itself. Bureau scientists in the Bituminous Region were excited. The main test had taken place on July 19, 1967 and had been judged an overwhelming success.

Kuebler, who vividly remembered the problems the Bureau had building a flush barrier at Centralia in 1967, was immediately interested and arranged for himself, Wilbert Malenka, and others to witness a fly ash demonstration at Bruceton. Malenka recalls being impressed by the results. Kuebler arranged for further tests in the sloping mines of the Anthracite Region—those at Bruceton and elsewhere in the Bituminous Region are flat—and became firmly wedded to using fly ash at Centralia.

Kuebler gained approval for fly ash from his superiors in Washington, but he had a tougher time selling the concept to DMMI, and particularly to Gordon Smith. Smith, Malenka recalls, did not like fly ash. Its chief disadvantage, which even Magnusson conceded, was that it tended to slide down mine chambers with a pitch of greater than ten degrees—and at Centralia, the pitch was as great as 35 degrees. Malenka said the Bureau believed that it could blow fly ash into a 200- to 300-foot wide barrier area at Centralia and depend on fly ash's compactability to hold it in place. Once it came in contact with mine water, it would become all the more stable. Another disadvantage, which the Bureau discovered only through experience, was that the success of fly ash depended greatly on how badly caved the mines were. "That's a hard thing to determine in advance," Malenka said.

After considerable thought, the Bureau decided to construct a 1,200-foot underground fly ash barrier just east of the first row of homes. It would extend from the Buck vein outcrop near the Odd Fellows Cemetery down to Main Street. The fly ash would be supplied free of charge by the Metropolitan Edison power plant at Reading. When this barrier was completed, a second one would be built east of the fire, "in the boondocks" as some would say later, in order to stop the fire from crossing Locust Mountain and entering valuable coal deposits there and further east, toward Girardville. It was a beautiful plan, on paper, and Congressman Flood announced on April 3, 1969, that a contract had been awarded to Stearns Service Corporation of Nanticoke in the amount of $518,840.

To the public, particularly the Centralia public, fly ash was presented as the ultimate in mine fire control. A Bureau of Mines press release that spring stated, "Personnel have monitored the boreholes and data have been analyzed in an effort to design *the most effective method to contain the fire*" (emphasis added), adding that this would be "pneumatic injection of approximately 80,000 cubic yards of fly ash. . . . The light, powdery fly ash forms an effective barrier by penetrating voids more completely than sand and water, thereby excluding air from the fire." It was a somewhat misleading press release—everyone at the Bureau knew that excavation was the best way, by far, to effectively contain the fire—but one the general public would find quite reasonable and credible. In private, and even to some persons in Centralia, the Bureau men referred to the use of fly ash as an experiment, or "demonstration project."

Stearns Service Corporation began the Phase II work on May 5. One of the first things it did was backfill several mine openings a few hundred feet due east of three houses on Wood Street. The houses were occupied by Anna Ryan, a widow who had lived there sixty-two years, William and Janet Birster and their three children, and Marion Laughlin, mother of Mrs. Birster. When the mine openings, which had vented some of the gases generated by the fire, were closed, Wilbert Malenka believes, the flow of mine fire gases westward toward the three houses and others in the neighborhood suddenly increased.

■ ■ ■

Unexplainable illnesses had afflicted the Birster family and Marion Laughlin since February. They now suffered headaches, nausea, and extraordinary drowsiness almost daily. When they left their houses they felt much better, but when they returned home the ailments returned, too.

One night late in March, Janet Birster went next door to her mother's and rapped on the door. There was no response, but Mrs. Birster could hear the television set blaring. Worried, she pushed open the door and found her mother in a deep sleep on the living room couch, oblivious to the racket around her. Mrs. Birster roused her only with difficulty. Marion Laughlin complained of stiffness in her arms and legs and wondered aloud if she was about to "take a stroke." She vowed to see a doctor, but changed her mind in the morning after leaving the house and feeling fine.

Then it was the plants. Mrs. Laughlin received a large flower as a gift on April 5, the day before Easter. The next day it was drooping, and by day's end it was quite dead. In succeeding days the other plants in her house died, which distressed her greatly.

When the project began on May 5, matters seemed to worsen, although none of the affected citizens made the connection. The houses smelled musty, even with a window open, and their nausea, headaches, drowsiness, and now shortness of breath grew worse. None of them sought medical attention, unsure what a doctor would say about come-and-go symptoms.

On May 15, Janet Birster's coal furnace went out and she was unable to relight it. Match flames died before she could light the kindling paper. She knew there was not enough oxygen in the basement to support a flame, for she had heard around town that mine fires could rob oxygen from people's homes. William Birster notified a state mine inspector, George Gallagher, the following morning. Gallagher advised Birster and the others to keep windows open to vent the gases. He could not test the atmosphere in their homes without permission from Gordon Smith, nor could he order them to evacuate.

Evacuation, though, was the last thing they wanted. Their homes were their pride and joy; it was unthinkable to leave if it might be possible to wait until the proper authorities took corrective action. Besides, none of them could afford to stay in a motel or apartment for very long, nor did they wish to burden relatives who were no better off than themselves.

That Friday evening, May 16, Marion Laughlin invited the man she was dating, Albert Lewullis, in for a cup of coffee after an evening at the American Legion. She had scarcely stepped into her kitchen and removed her jacket than she felt ill, more ill than she ever felt before, and began to dry retch violently. "I got deathly sick, it just hit me like a ton of bricks," she would say. When the attack finally stopped, she went into the living room and lay down on her couch. Lewullis stayed until 3:30 A.M., but she did not know he was there. He left the kitchen door open when he left, to give her air.

Mrs. Laughlin was awakened around 6 A.M. by a pounding on her kitchen door. It was George Gallagher, the state mine inspector. "You know, I didn't sleep all night worrying about you," he said. "I still can't tell you to leave, but if you were my wife I wouldn't let you stay here." Fearing now for her life, Mrs. Laughlin called her mother in Ashland and asked if she could stay there for a few days. There would be no more nights in this home.

Mr. and Mrs. Birster were in anguish. Should they leave or try to stay for a few more days? The following morning, Sunday, May 18, the Birsters felt more nauseous than ever before, and their canary, who had been so lively the night before, lay dead at the bottom of its cage. It was the traditional sign of bad air to generations of miners. Only a fool would ignore this warning. They made arrangements to stay temporarily with Mrs. Birster's brother in Centralia, still hoping the problem could somehow be made to go away.*

William Birster spent the next week trying to obtain some kind of aid for his family and mother-in-law. His problem was compounded by the fact that the three houses, while considered part of Centralia, sat on the Conyngham Township side of the line. John Yokemick, chairman of the Conyngham Township Board of Supervisors, was sympathetic when Birster called but had no idea how the supervisors could help. Birster then called Joseph Tighe. Tighe, too, was sympathetic and concerned, but said Centralia Council could not become directly involved until the fire was proven to have crossed the Centralia line, which ran in front of Birster's house. Tighe did offer to notify the Columbia County Commissioners.

The neighborhood around the three houses was in a state of near panic. Directly across Wood Street were the homes of Mrs. Anne Maloney, who still heeded her late husband's warning to leave one window open because of the mine fire, and Tony and Mary Lou Gaughan. Down South Street from the Gaughans lived Carl and Helen Womer. Mr. and Mrs. Frank Jurgill, Sr., lived next door to Mrs. Maloney.

---

*Mrs. Ryan presumably suffered the same symptoms as Mrs. Laughlin and the Birsters, because she eventually abandoned her home. She declined to be interviewed for the book.

When a worried Bureau of Mines drilled boreholes near the three houses and behind the Gaughan and Womer houses, the results did not calm the neighborhood one bit. While relatively low temperatures—65 to 128 degrees Fahrenheit—were found 25 feet from the Laughlin house, boreholes drilled 120 and 150 feet southeast showed temperatures of 760 and 900 degrees. The boreholes drilled behind the Womer and Gaughan houses gushed steam but did not show fire temperatures. Kuebler ordered a speedup of the start of the fly ash barrier work, telling Stearns Service it must begin work near the three abandoned houses on Monday, May 26. The hot holes were too close for comfort.

County Commissioner Richard Walton visited Centralia at Tighe's request on May 22. By this time, the South Street residents had decided they wanted nothing to do with the planned fly ash barrier. Excavation of a trench was all they would accept. Almost fifty persons gathered on the street a few minutes after Walton arrrived. A story in the Mount Carmel *Item* said "most of the men and women" present told Walton they did not want fly ashing, but rather preferred an excavation "to save their properties." In a mining town like Centralia, many of the men and women were familiar with the techniques of controlling mine fires and how well each could be expected to work. Walton inquired of Stearns Service whether the method of fighting the mine fire could be changed. He got a firm no in reply. There was a contract, Walton was told, and it must be followed. Kuebler told Walton the same thing when he and Joseph Corgan met with Walton and Commissioner Carl Canouse in Centralia the following day. "Mine officials plan to go ahead with the fly ash plan despite protests from residents who favor a trenching project," the *Item* reported.

The county commissioners offered to pay the lodging expenses for the displaced Centralians for ten days to two weeks or until the gases cleared from their homes. Walton, however, must have thought the gases would not clear; he and Stephen Phillips, head of Columbia County Redevelopment Authority, began searching for a government agency that would purchase the three houses.

The South Street residents despaired over the strange inaction of Centralia Council. Council president Robert Burge told Richard S. Harriman, a correspondent for the *Sunday Patriot-News* of Harrrisburg, that council members could only be "observers" until the fire crossed the Centralia line. Burge blamed the present problems on the seventeen-month delay between Phase I and Phase II.

Helen Womer, with the support of her neighbors, wrote to Congressman Flood and asked him to meet with them in Centralia so they could explain why a trench was needed. Flood already knew how bad things were; Corgan wrote to him on May 27 stating, "This is an extremely difficult mine fire to control."

Unknown to the residents, Bureau engineer John Rosella, who was in charge of the Phase II work, agreed with the need for an excavation. The temperatures being reported by the Stearns workers alarmed him, and he became convinced the fire would move rapidly beneath the South Street homes if something was not done. Daniel Lewis, the project inspector for the Bureau and a close friend of Rosella's, said Rosella "fought his head off" to get a trench at Centralia.

Probably he would have failed if not for Flood. This was a problem tailor-made for the congressman's personal touch. Unlike the people in Centralia, Flood knew the Phase II contract could be rewritten through the change order process. He also knew the Bureau, like any government agency, could be pressured into doing things it did not really want to do.

Flood had become one of the more powerful members of Congress two years earlier when he was made chairman of the new Subcommittee on Labor and HEW of the Appropriations Committee. Many of the Johnson administration's Great Society program budgets passed through this subcommittee. He was also a member of the Defense Appropriations Subcommittee. No one crossed him unnecessarily.

Always the showman, Flood breezed into Centralia late in the afternoon of Friday, June 13, for the requested meeting at the house of Helen Womer, the unofficial leader of the South Street residents. According to Malenka's memorandum describing the meeting, Flood expressed his concern about the state of the mine fire and grandly announced that plans for Phase II had been changed to permit excavation of that part of the mine fire closest to the homes. "Congressman Flood assured the residents that Mr. Corgan, Mr. Kuebler [who was present] and engineers in charge of the project were the most capable and dedicated mine fire experts in the world," Malenka wrote. Clearly, Flood and Corgan and probably Kuebler had conferred prior to the June 13 meeting. No memorandums could be located describing this session, but Flood convinced the Bureau of Mines to give the residents their trench.

Kuebler's stony insistence that the contract could not be changed masked a private conviction that it should be. A memorandum he wrote to Corgan on June 13 suggests he was firmly convinced the fly ash barrier plan was unworkable, at least as a means for protecting the South Street residents and others whose homes were in the path of the mine fire.

> An emergency situation has developed in the southwest corner of the project, where the fire has spread at a rapid rate through an extensively mined, unmapped underground area near the Buck Mountain Bed outcrop. Recent drilling for fly ash injection has disclosed the mine fire progress in the bed and in the subsurface refuse from the mining operation.

> This is a critical area in the mine fire control work that was planned, as it is adjacent to the built-up section of the borough, a school and a church, and at present three families have been evacuated from two houses because of oxygen-deficient atmosphere seeping through the ground into their basements from the underground mine workings.

> The unsystematic [bootleg] mining created numerous voids not shown on the mine maps, subsidence and fissures to the surface which provide oxygen to the fire, making it difficult to contain with the injection of fly ash. It is imperative that this area be excavated as soon as possible to eliminate the fire and to prevent its westward advance to the populated area of the borough.

Many of these conditions were uncovered during Phase I of the Centralia project. Extensive drilling was done in the area Kuebler describes for the Phase I flush barrier and for exploratory purposes. Indeed, field inspector reports from 1967 give a graphic picture of the tortured subterranean world Kuebler describes in his memo to Corgan. Kuebler saw the Phase I field reports, and so did Corgan. Knowing all this, why did the Bureau of Mines abandon the intercept trench planned for Phase II and replace it with a flush barrier? As noted at the end of chapter 7, the only likely explanation is that top officials of the Bureau in Washington did not believe Centralia was worth the expense of properly protecting it from the fire.

Former Columbia County Commissioner Richard Walton, who had extensive dealings with the Bureau of Mines in 1969 over Centralia, believes cost-benefit factors heavily influenced Bureau decisions on the mine fire. He stated in an interview:

> One of the things they [BOM] felt is that it [fly ash] was a cheaper way of doing it. Definitely. It is hard to tell people in a community that. You have to look at the cost-benefit ratio when any money is spent from

the federal government. On any federal grants we had, for any type of construction, flood prevention or anything else, it was all based on a cost-benefit ratio. In other words, you have to give a dollar benefit for a dollar of cost. And of course, when you look at that community over there, why I think the whole thing was, that to do that thing the way they should do it would be worth more than the entire town.

Walton denied ever expressing this opinion on the worth of Centralia to Bureau officials.

Corgan alluded to the unfavorable Centralia cost-benefit ratio in a June 16 memorandum to Bureau of Mines director John O'Leary, who had been appointed that year by President Richard Nixon. "This is a critical fire," Corgan wrote, "located too deeply underground for complete excavation. The circumstances surrounding this fire could eventually require the evacuation of more homes." Too deeply underground? The phrase implies it would be physically impossible to excavate a fire that deep, which Louis Pagnotti certainly did not believe in 1967. More likely, Corgan meant the depth of the fire made the project too costly for the Bureau's liking.

The trench they would excavate in the summer of 1969 was a much smaller one than that envisioned in the original 1965 plan for Centralia. The original trench was to be 2,500 feet long and vary in depth from 100 to 200 feet. Some 750,000 cubic yards of earth were to be removed during the project. The original cost estimate for the big trench was $2.5 million, but this jumped to $4.5 million after the discoveries of Phase I.

The little trench of 1969 was to be 240 feet long, 140 feet wide, and 50 feet deep at its deepest point. Only 48,000 cubic yards of earth were slated to come out of this trench, and the estimated cost was also less—$82,250. Where the trench ended on the north, the fly ash barrier would begin. Bureau engineers designed the barrier to protect the bulk of Centralia, but eight houses on East Park Street would lie beyond the barrier's eastern limit, exposed to the fire, a fact not publicly discussed at the time.

There was no guarantee that those persons living behind the trench would remain safe from the mine fire gases. If the fly ash barrier leaked, the gases could go around the backfilled trench through the old mine network and reach the supposedly safe houses. Charles Kuebler says that he told the people at Helen Womer's house no mine fire project was ever guaranteed to work and that Flood agreed. Many people of Centralia, particularly the ones living away from the front line, listened only to the reassurances that fly ash was their savior. They wanted to believe the government knew what was best for them.

Work on the trench continued through the summer of 1969 and into the fall, far longer than the 30 days predicted. Digging began near the Gaughan and Laughlin houses and moved south toward the ballfield, then east along the outcrop toward the cemetery. DuPont Corporation sent a technician with special dynamite that could withstand temperatures up to 2,000 degrees. Regular dynamite lowered into 900-degree holes would have quickly detonated.

When the fire was uncovered, the people marveled at the sight. As the digging moved east, away from Centralia, the shovel turned up the main fire. Brilliant pillars of satanic red coal lit up the sky at night.

John Rosella knew that without more money he had no hope of defeating the fire. Even if they could not give him the funds to dig the fire completely out of the ground, perhaps they would give him enough to dig out a big enough chunk to minimize the threat to Centralia. Fly ash *had* lowered temperatures in the areas at Centralia where it was used; perhaps it would work as planned, or at least be sufficient in tandem with a larger trench. Stearns had already taken out 60,000 cubic yards, 12,000 more than originally planned. Why stop now? Rosella pleaded with Kuebler for more money, and Kuebler, recalls Daniel Lewis, was sympathetic. The bureaucrats in Washington and Harrisburg were not. Early in October, the order was given to begin backfilling the hole.

"Then when he got to the massive fire, the massive burning pillars, and we ran out of money, and he couldn't get no more money, then orders were we had to backfill that. He cried," Lewis said. "Johnny Rosella cried. And we had the fire [in our grasp]. There's no question about it. I'll stand on that till the day I die. We had the fire."

The story has a cruel twist. Late in the spring of 1969, DMMI decided to take over funding of the Kehley Run Mine Fire Project at Shenandoah, using Operation Scarlift monies. In July, Joseph Corgan wrote to the Appalachian Regional Commission asking for permission to reallocate the almost $2 million freed by the state decision. Corgan wanted to apportion the money among mine fire projects at Centralia, Carbondale, and Swoyersville, and an antisubsidence project at Scranton. Centralia was to get $440,000. The twist is that Appalachian Regional Commission documents give no indication the money was to be used for enlarging the excavation at Centralia. Rather, the documents suggest Corgan asked for the money simply to prevent the ARC from reallocating the funds to projects outside his bailiwick. Gordon Smith quotes Kuebler to that effect in an October 3 memorandum to Secretary of Mines Charmbury. Bureau of Mines protests that there was no money available to dig the big trench at Centralia pale in the light of these documents.

Charmbury had his own plan for the Kehley Run money, and it did not involve Centralia or any other mine fire project. After hearing of Corgan's attempt to grab the $2 million, he fired off an angry letter on September 17 to William Schmidt, Governor Raymond Shafer's representative to the ARC, protesting that he withdrew the Kehley Run project from the ARC only on the condition the $2 million be used for backfilling strip mines in Pennsylvania. He did not want the money diverted to Centralia and Carbondale. "We hope this will not be done," he concluded.

It was not. Perhaps it never occurred to Charmbury and Corgan that the $2 million no longer needed at Kehley Run, if added to the almost $2.2 million remaining of the original Centralia allocation, would have funded the big trench at Centralia—and ended this story here. Clearly, the decision had been made long before this that Centralia was not to get a major trench.

10
Lonely Battle

Mary Lou Gaughan displays carbon monoxide reading on her husband Tony's colorimetric CO gauge. A gas reading of 0.1 percent—a lethal amount—was taken at the mouth of the uncapped borehole (lower right) in November 1976. (Photo: David DeKok, News-Item)

IN 1976 I knew nothing about Centralia, which seemed to be just another obscure village among many along Route 61. I had worked as a Shamokin *News-Item* reporter for only a year and had read nothing about the mine fire. On November 1, 1976, however, I was asked to fill in for the reporter who regularly covered Centralia Council meetings.

There was no indication that anything but routine municipal business—streets, sewers, and police matters—would be discussed at the meeting, and only two members of the public—a tired looking couple who appeared to be of late middle age—were present. At 10 P.M., three hours into the session, council president Francis Goncalves asked wearily if any citizens had anything to say, looking at the couple in the audience.

"Yes I do," Tony Gaughan said.

In a rising voice, Gaughan complained that several boreholes near his house were emitting deadly levels of carbon monoxide. He said the Centralia mine fire was the source of the gas, adding that the fire was moving toward his property. It would move beneath his house fairly soon, Gaughan predicted.

Mary Lou Gaughan said steam rising from some of the boreholes drew the curiosity of neighborhood children. Her husband said carbon monoxide in one of boreholes had been measured at "point one," sufficient to kill a person in two minutes. The Gaughans worried the deadly gas would find its way into their home and kill them while they slept.

I had been half asleep when Tony Gaughan's harangue began but was wide awake now. A fire beneath a house? Holes in the ground spewing carbon monoxide? It seemed beyond belief. I questioned the Gaughans after the meeting, and they responded with a torrent of words about trenches, flushing, fly ash, and betrayal.

Their words meant nothing to me, but I decided to look into the story further, promising the Gaughans I would stop by to visit them soon. I was the first of many journalists to find in the Centralia mine fire a story of endless fascination.

■ ■ ■

The Centralia mine fire was almost forgotten in 1976, even by the people of Centralia. As if to an angry god, the village had sacrificed three houses during the summer of 1969. The Bureau had provided the underground fly ash barrier that was supposed to hold back the fire, like a dike holding back the sea from the Netherlands, and then resumed an air of complacency. Most Centralia residents believed the problem solved. Some mocked the Gaughans for their Cassandra-like concern.

Council president Francis Goncalves, who would become bitter enough toward the Bureau of Mines to call for certain former officials to be stripped of their pensions, says he was repeatedly reassured by the Bureau that the fly ash barrier was working and would continue to work. That was not quite the truth.

Indeed, the first breach of the fly ash barrier occurred before work was even completed. In the spring of 1972, as work on the eastern barrier neared completion, the fire broke through at two locations near the Centralia anticline. Although this barrier was far from any populated area, the breach would allow the fire to cross Locust Mountain and reach the mines under the village of Byrnesville.

There was not enough money left in the $2.5 million budget to repair the breach, so Bureau officials requested an "emergency" $250,000 appropriation from the Appalachian Regional Commission. It was approved by the ARC on September 22, 1972 but did not clear the Interior Department bureaucracy until February 1973.

Not all the $250,000 was used to repair the fly ash barrier. About $50,000 was used to drill 53 monitoring boreholes on the cold side of the barrier. These early-warning devices of failure had not been part of the original plan. Had the Bureau, despite its public statements, lost faith in the permanence of the underground barriers? Charles Kuebler insists they never had absolute faith, that Centralia residents were told in 1969 the fly ash barrier would not carry a guarantee. The public, however, heard only Daniel Flood's flowery praise of the Bureau and the fly ash barrier. "The completion of the Centralia mine fire [project] marks another landmark achievement for our environmental protection, and at the same time relaxes the fears of Centralia area residents from the awful possibility of devastation by uncontrolled underground fires . . ." Flood said at completion ceremonies at Centralia on February 15, 1974. "It is an outstanding example of how the taxpayers' dollars can be put to work for the betterment of the community in which they live."

■ ■ ■

I found the Gaughan house—an unpretentious bungalow that Tony Gaughan had built himself in 1950—at the eastern end of South Street. Almost before I had my coat off, the Gaughans began telling the story of the Centralia mine fire, beginning with its origin in the dump near the Odd Fellows Cemetery in 1962.* They told me about the trench the Bureau of Mines dug in 1969 to stop the mine fire, and how the Bureau ordered the pit to be halted and backfilled before all the fire had been ripped out of the earth. I was told about the fly ash barrier, and what a failure they believed it to be.

Tony Gaughan's voice had a distant sound of Ireland, though his family had been in Centralia for decades. His voice rose and fell as he remonstrated about the Bureau of Mines and its "lies." Unhealthy and tired looking, he had retired on disability from his mining job in 1973 after suffering a heart attack. His poor health he blamed in part on tension and anxiety brought on by the mine fire. Both Gaughans were in their early fifties, but Tony Gaughan looked much older.

Daniel Lewis, a Bureau inspector, was one of the few government men they trusted. It was Lewis who alerted them in late 1975 to the higher temperatures and high carbon monoxide levels he was finding in the boreholes between their house and the fly ash barrier. With deadly carbon monoxide gas so close to their home, the Gaughans worried it might find its way inside. Lewis told them he would begin monitoring the boreholes more frequently. The Gaughans assumed that meant he would check the air in their house, too. Not until March 1976 did they learn their house could be inspected for gas only by a state Department of Environmental Resources (DER) inspector, and then only if they made a personal request to James Shober at the DER office in Pottsville.**

Weekly visits by DER inspector Leonard Rogers did little to calm the Gaughans, however. They knew how capricious a mine fire could be. Just because Rogers found no carbon monoxide during his visit didn't mean they were safe. The Gaughans could hear water running beneath the house's crawl space and reasoned if water could find its way down there, so could the gas.

Then there was the fire itself. Although the Bureau told them in April 1976 that the fly ash barrier was still holding back the mine fire, temperature data collected by Lewis in the monitoring boreholes near their house indicated otherwise. One of the boreholes, No. 7, had been measured at 76 degrees in 1972. Now it was up to 180 degrees. Lewis told them when the temperature reached 300 degrees, the mine fire was there. If not there now, it certainly appeared to Gaughan to be

---

*The Gaughans did not appear to know how the fire in the dump really started.

**The Department of Environmental Resources was created in 1970 from the Department of Mines and Mineral Industries and several other state agencies. This James Shober is the son of the James Shober in chapter 3.

headed in that direction—and the borehole was only 27 feet from their front door.

John Rosella, the Bureau engineer, had told him in April that the fly ash barrier had settled, allowing gases to escape over the top. That admission had been made out of earshot of his superiors. None of them would confirm what Rosella said.

The Gaughans had written twenty letters to Congressman Flood or the Bureau of Mines, pleading for better protection from the gases. The responses, all from the Bureau of Mines, were simply restatements of what the Bureau had done in the past to protect Centralia. "They have to put out the fire sometime," Mrs. Gaughan said sharply. "Why not do it before they have to move the whole town? I don't want to leave here. I've lived here all my life."

Both Gaughans believed there was a conspiracy to rob Centralia of its coal.* It was the only explanation that made any sense to them. Why else would the fire have continued to burn for fourteen years? Why else would such idiotic bungling have occurred? They had seen projects come and go. Their anger boiled over when telling how the Bureau of Mines backfilled the trench in 1969.

The Gaughans knew nothing of the cost-benefit ratio, or of the cold-hearted calculation in Washington that Centralia was not worth saving. They saw only the end result, a fire lapping at the bounds of their home. Once they and other Centralians were forced to abandon their village to escape the mine fire, the Gaughans believed, big corporations would come in to exploit the coal.

Tony Gaughan was adamant that the fire had to be dug out of the earth if it ever was to be controlled. The Bureau, he said, wanted to reinforce the fly ash barrier with additional fly ash, but he did not believe that would help.

It was time for a demonstration, and we went outside. I watched as Gaughan unscrewed the metal cap on borehole No. 7 and stepped back. The steaming hole was hot to the touch, not merely warm. Mrs. Gaughan produced a device that resembled a water pistol. It was a colorimetric carbon monoxide detector that Tony had obtained somewhere. The device measured both the presence and concentration of carbon monoxide by drawing a gas sample through a tube of white chemical. If the gas was present, the powder turned a deep, sickly yellow. She held it to the mouth of the borehole, and almost instantly

---

*As noted in chapter 2, the coal under Centralia belongs to the village. The conspiracy theory was popular in Centralia in the late 1970s and 1980s, but its proponents tended to ignore the sad state of the anthracite market. Who would buy the Centralia coal?

the powder became the color of urine. "Point one," Gaughan said with odd satisfaction. "It's enough to kill you." He referred to a level of 0.1 percent, or 1,000 parts per million.

As they turned to walk back to the house, I gazed at the houses on either side of the grey valley and wondered why this family was the only one raising hell.

■ ■ ■

The more I investigated the mine fire problem, the more unsettling it became. No one in government wanted to take responsibility for doing anything to help Centralia. Both the Bureau of Mines and the Department of Environmental Resources seemed perfectly willing to let bureaucracy take its leisurely course. The money to patch the fly ash barrier would come, eventually.

Wilbert Malenka, a deputy to Charles Kuebler, explained that money for the project would have to come from the Appalachian Regional Commission in Washington, not from the Bureau of Mines budget. Malenka and Kuebler insisted there was no source of money in the Bureau budget that could be tapped to help Centralia.

Kuebler declared the fly ash barrier was in fine shape, though he admitted it was leaking carbon monoxide. "This is to be expected," he said. No gases had been found in the Gaughan house.

Malenka said the earliest the ARC could approve any money for Centralia was February 1977, when the ARC Board of Governors would hold its annual meeting. It was his understanding, although he was not certain, that Pennsylvania would ask for funding to patch the fly ash barrier at that time.

The ARC, however, revealed that the state had *not* submitted an application. The staff was under the impression there would be no application, which was confirmed by the official in Governor Milton Shapp's administration in charge of applications for ARC funds.

The Bureau of Pennsylvania Appalachian Development, it seemed, had turned down the Centralia project in favor of two acid mine water projects aimed at making streams more hospitable for trout. A rumor, which was never substantiated, suggested that the acid mine water projects would benefit a private fishing club patronized by friends of Governor Shapp, a Democrat.

"As you know, federal funds have become less and less," lectured James Grim, an official at the state office.

Grim said DER had appealed the denial of funds for a Centralia project and had even offered to pay the entire cost of the acid mine water projects from its own budget. He said it was "a possibility" the

Centralia funds would be restored. If not, the project would have to wait an entire year until the next round of ARC funding was made available.

■ ■ ■

The *News-Item's* story about the Gaughans and the mine fire was published on December 8, 1976. Headlined "Lethal Gases Cause Concern at Centralia," the story had immediate impact. Centralia Council, which until now had taken a rather restrained, if concerned, approach to the mine fire problem, held stormy meetings to demand action. State Senator Franklin Kury, a liberal Democrat who represented Centralia but never showed any previous interest in the problem, dashed off a letter to DER strongly supporting the Centralia project. Bureau of Mines director Thomas V. Falkie, a native of Mount Carmel, made a hastily scheduled visit to Centralia on January 5, accompanied by his chief deputies for mine fire projects, Thomas P. Flynn and James Paone. Falkie went to Tony Gaughan's house and assured him that federal action against the mine fire was imminent. Clifford McConnell of DER assured Gaughan the Centralia project had been restored to the list of projects to go before the ARC Board of Governors in February.

One might have assumed that because government was showing so much interest in Centralia, a solution to the problem was around the corner. That assumption could not have been more wrong.

11
Awakening

Charles Kuebler (left), chief of the U.S. Bureau of Mines office in Wilkes-Barre, and Wilbert Malenka, Kuebler's deputy, confront an angry crowd of Centralia residents at a meeting in Centralia Municipal Building on September 7, 1978. (Photo: David DeKok, News-Item)

FIFTEEN years had passed since that fateful day in 1962, and the Appalachian Regional Commission was preparing to authorize yet another feeble swat at the Centralia mine fire. At the ARC's annual Board of Governor's meeting on April 12, 1977, delayed from February by bad weather, funding for the new Centralia project was approved without problem.

No one from the Bureau informed the Centralia public why so much time had elapsed since Falkie's visit without anything being done to patch the leaky fly ash barrier, however, and the Bureau of Mines gave Centralia Council no information because it preferred to leave local leaders in the dark. "There is much anxiety in Centralia," wrote John L. Moore in a March 3 story in the *Wall Street Journal.* Moore was the first reporter from outside the Centralia area to cover the story since 1969. "Townspeople worry particularly about carbon monoxide, the lethal gas produced by burning coal. Others are concerned about their homes catching fire."

The Bureau, in response to repeated criticism from Centralia citizens and questions from journalists about the reliability of the fly ash barrier, which their own internal reports called into question, began providing misleading or simply untrue answers to questions about the fly ash barrier, which in turn fanned public suspicion all the more.

An example of this occurred March 8 when Gary Sheppard of *CBS News* came to Centralia. He interviewed Wilbert Malenka and John Rosella; afterward, Malenka wrote a memo to Kuebler that attempted to reconstruct as much of the interview as possible.

Malenka admitted to Sheppard the fire could someday pose a serious threat to Centralia but added, "Gases as detected are dangerous, but these gases are only obtained through cased boreholes and *are prevented from reaching the surface by competent rock strata"* (emphasis added). Had Malenka already forgotten that three Centralia families were driven from their homes in 1969 by mine fire gases that reached the surface without apparent difficulty?

Rosella chose to describe the mine fire problem as "possible leakage of mine gases through the fly ash pillar." Sheppard asked Rosella if he would live in Centralia, "knowing this mine fire is burning so close?" He answered, according to Malenka's memo, "Centralia has some beautiful homes. I would not be afraid to live in this town." He apparently had forgotten his tears of frustration in 1969 after his Bureau superiors ordered him to backfill the trench.

A *News-Item* reporter telephoned Malenka later that day to inquire about a small subsidence that had opened about two hundred feet east of the Gaughan house. Despite the clouds of steam puffing out of the hole, Malenka insisted it was the result of "water leaking into mine workings."

An *Associated Press* reporter wrote a story on the mine fire in late March, centering the story around the Gaughans. "It's going to wipe out the whole town," Tony Gaughan predicted with chilling accuracy.

Gaughan had become the Bureau's chief antagonist, and it is likely that had he not been there, the mine fire problem would not have received nearly the attention it did, either from the Bureau or from journalists.

Gaughan was a particular irritant to Kuebler, who had little but contempt for the former miner's views on what should be done about the mine fire. It was an attitude he extended to anyone in Centralia who offered him advice. Nothing Kuebler did endeared him less to Centralia, or caused more hatred of the Bureau, than this lordly attitude.

Always a management man, both in his long service with the Lehigh Navigation Coal Company and his later work with the Bureau, which he joined in 1959, Kuebler was an efficient administrator, but seemed to have little appreciation of the human cost of Bureau policies at Centralia. He believed Anthracite Region people should expect to endure a certain amount of danger and discomfort from mine fires, and was fond of telling how persons living near a Scranton mine fire endured dangerously low oxygen levels in their basements without public complaint, happy for whatever small aid the Bureau could offer. To Centralians he must have seemed like one more coal baron from out of their past. To Kuebler, who defended the fly ash barrier, of which he was so proud, with all the fight a sixty-seven-year-old man could muster, Centralians must have seemed like ungrateful children.

There was one other factor that colored Kuebler's attitude toward Centralia citizens. He blamed the village itself for the mine fire. It is unclear whether he knew exactly how the fire started, but he blamed feuding between Centralia Council and Conyngham Township Board of Supervisors over who was responsible for fighting the fire for allowing it to propagate through the summer of 1962. Only he has mentioned this supposed feud, which could well have occurred. Whether it did is immaterial. It was illogical and unfair for Kuebler to collectively blame all of Centralia for the actions of a few. The degree to which it colored his actions is unknown.

■ ■ ■

The Bureau's new plan for Centralia would have two phases. Phase I would be the drilling of a dozen boreholes in an attempt to pinpoint where the fly ash barrier was leaking. Phase II would be the repair of the barrier by blowing down additional fly ash. No one at the Bureau warned Centralia residents that if the fly ash barrier had failed once for natural reasons, it certainly could do so again.

There was another section of the plan for Centralia that was not made public at the time. The Bureau planned to backfill two pits east of Centralia that had vented the deadly mine fire gases for fourteen years. One pit was a remnant of the landfill where the fire started in 1962. The other was a remnant of the pit excavated by DMMI in the summer and fall of 1963 to vent the mine fire's gases.

The Bureau had hoped to backfill the pits during the first federal-state project in 1967, but Gordon Smith's objections stood in the way. A small portion of each pit was left open for the same reason Smith envisioned in 1963—to vent some of the gas that would otherwise be drawn underground toward Centralia by natural mine ventilation. Now Smith was gone, purged by the Democrats—Pennsylvania was still a spoils system state—after Milton Shapp was elected governor in 1970. Officials of the Shapp administration did not oppose closing the pits.

Of the two, the more important by far was the one excavated in 1963. It lay astride an east-west mine gangway that led directly west under South Street past the Gaughan and Womer houses to the heart of a heavily populated neighborhood along Locust Avenue. It was Kuebler's firm belief these holes were feeding air to the mine fire.

■ ■ ■

Delay followed upon delay. The project was supposed to begin on July 1, 1977, but state and federal officials could not agree on the wording of a cooperation agreement. The Bureau wanted DER to agree to a clause that exempted the Bureau from any responsibility if the project had bad results. DER refused to sign such an agreement.

In mid-June, when it appeared the cooperation agreement was still distant, the Bureau decided to begin Phase I of the project with its own funds. Ten boreholes were drilled "to relieve public pressure, allay fears and anxieties of local residents, and to determine if the mine fire had breached the barrier," according to a July 27 memo to Kuebler from Malenka. "This limited amount of drilling indicates there is a part of the fly ash barrier that is permitting a seepage of gases and the barrier has not been breached by the fire."

Some boreholes hit tightly packed fly ash, but others hit wide openings on top of the fly ash or no fly ash at all. Relatively low temperatures were found, leading the engineers to conclude in the report that the main fire was 360 feet east of the underground barrier. It meant the barrier had never been intact, that the fire eventually could pass through.

In September, the cooperation agreement was concluded to DER's liking and the contract went out on bid. When the bids came back, the lowest was $429,550, pushed well above the $385,000 authorized for the project by inflation. This meant the project had to make a new round trip through the bureaucracy. Not until February 1978 was the extra money approved, and not until May did the work begin.

Backfilling of the two pits occurred early in Phase II, and South Street residents didn't take long to figure out what was going on. Frank Jurgill, Sr., who lived across the street from the Womers, cornered Kuebler one day and demanded to know why the pits were being filled. Kuebler told him both pits were drawing air into the fire. Jurgill argued to no avail that the pits pulled much of the gas away from his neighborhood. "You could look directly over and see it," Jurgill said of the 1963 pit. "It was drawing up the fumes and the vapors were always coming up, which means it's an updraft."

Kuebler and Malenka told Centralia residents the deadly gases could not harm them because of the thick bed of rock—seventy feet was the usual figure cited—between their homes and the fire. Kuebler and Malenka knew that the rock was riddled with fissures and that gases had easily reached the three homes in 1969 and could just as well reach the others.

The frontline residents began demanding, in ever more strident tones, that a trench be excavated to stop the fire. They believed all that needed to be done was to extend the uncompleted 1969 trench. Ironically, the project to strengthen the fly ash barrier was working, although its effects would prove temporary. Vapors no longer rose from the boreholes near the Gaughan home, and temperatures would soon begin to drop. Centralia residents were told this, but by this time they distrusted the Bureau to such an extent the report was virtually ignored.

Growing demands for a trench led Centralia Council to schedule a town meeting on June 13. It was the first town meeting held in the new Centralia Municipal Building, built with a federal public works grant, and it was the first of countless town meetings that would be held there in coming years to discuss the mine fire. It is difficult to imagine the Centralia story unfolding in the manner it did without the spacious public forum this building provided.

Someone in the audience said he heard a rumor the fly ash barrier would fail again in a few years, and Kuebler stunned them by admitting it was true. Nevertheless, he opposed any plan to excavate a trench. The newly reinforced fly ash barrier was sufficient to protect Centralia, Kuebler insisted, and could be reinforced once again when the time came. The vertical distance between the fire and the homes, he said, would provide sufficient protection from the gases, and exposing the fire by ripping open the earth risked having it run away far beneath the village. Kuebler predicted a trench would cost more than $8 million and take years to complete.

"Somebody made a mistake up there and they're not man enough to stand up and admit it," snapped Mayor Joseph McGinley.

"Hindsight is easier than foresight," Kuebler shot back.

A few days later, in a move aimed at appeasing its more vocal critics, the Bureau announced it was drilling more boreholes and injecting additional fly ash along Wood Street, which ran parallel to the fly ash barrier past the Gaughan and Maloney houses.

By late July, however, public sentiment was firmly behind an excavation project, despite Bureau assurances the fly ash barrier could be made to work and that it had no money for a trench. Funding indeed *was* a problem, but no one made a serious effort to tap into that great reservoir of money, the U.S. Congress. Dr. George Gensemer, a Columbia County commissioner, contacted U.S. Senators John Heinz and Richard Schweiker to see if they could help. Both senators assigned aides to look into the problem but in reality provided little but the lip service Centralia had come to expect from its politicians.

At another town meeting on July 27, residents repeated their call for the Bureau to "strip out the fire." They added a demand; now they wanted to know the exact boundaries of the mine fire, something the Bureau could not tell them. Many worried the gases might invade nearby St. Ignatius Elementary School. "We don't get any satisfaction from the Bureau of Mines," thundered Mayor McGinley. "They say it [fly ash barrier] works, but it doesn't. We can't get anything out of them."

That same day, Kuebler and Malenka met at Schuylkill Haven with Robert Oberman and others from DER to discuss the worsening Centralia situation. Kuebler and Malenka blamed their problems on Centralia's retired miners, as well as the news media. Malenka's minutes state, "Recent meetings and conversations with residents of Centralia, together with press and radio coverage, show that a majority of residents apparently want an isolation trench excavated. The magnitude, cost and dislocation that an isolation trench would entail is not understood by the residents. Residents who have mining experience become experts in advocating remedial action. Their concern is appreciated."

The DER man begged Kuebler to consider three options for "positive control" of the mine fire. One was a trench; the second was grouting, a sophisticated form of flushing, and the third was subsidizing a commercial strip-mining operation for isolation of the fire and removal of the coal. He agreed to give it some thought.

It didn't take Kuebler long to decide—the pressure from the people, media, and finally, to some degree, the politicians, was becoming intense. The Bureau agreed to excavate a small trench if funding could be obtained from the Appalachian Regional Commission.

DER considered the mine fire to be a much greater threat to Centralia than did the Bureau. Clifford McConnell, in an August 7 letter to Susan H. Gahres, director of the state Bureau of Appalachian Development wrote:

> The estimated total cost of controlling the fire as it is understood at the present will be in the nine to ten million dollar range.
>
> However, in order to stop the seepage of lethal gases into the residents' homes, it is necessary to act immediately to install a portion of this trench. We feel that an increase of $400,000 in construction money, coupled with $75,000 remaining in the original contract, will allow us to install the initial trench with a great time saving, which at this point is most necessary. . . . Time lost at this stage of the game could result in greatly increased project costs and loss of a significant portion of the borough of Centralia and/or fatalities from carbon monoxide poisoning.

This warning, which regrettably would be proven almost entirely correct, did not reflect the Bureau's opinion. The Bureau indicated privately it was only agreeing to the trench to quiet public outcry. In public, it planned to announce the trench was made necessary by a recent discovery that the fire had breached the fly ash barrier. The breach had been repaired, but clearly the fly ash barrier could no longer be trusted—or so the story went. There is no evidence any fire passed through the barrier in 1978.

Goncalves announced on August 8 that Congressman Flood had promised to seek emergency federal funding for the trench if he could obtain valid cost figures from the Bureau. On August 9, Goncalves and most other members of council attended a meeting in Bloomsburg called by the Bureau of Mines. They were briefed on the Bureau's new plan for a limited trench, a "dragline trench" it was called at the time. Support was strong for the trench, particularly after Kuebler stated— erroneously, as it would turn out—that no homes would have to be acquired and demolished to make way for the trench.

The Bureau was clearly still opposed to the trench. James Paone in the agency's Washington headquarters told the *News-Item* the next day that the dragline trench would only be one part of a much larger trench that would require relocation of many families. He compared it to a "Panama Canal project" and predicted the environmental problems created by the trench would be staggering. "If they think they have problems now," he warned, "just wait until this happens."

On Sunday, August 13, an Air Force reconnaissance jet made several passes above Centralia, causing considerable commotion in the village. It took infrared pictures of the mine fire area at the demand of Flood, who saw the photos as a good first step toward helping Centralia. He had been surprised by the turn of events there, by the failure of the fly ash barrier, and was at a loss as to what he should do. Council told him Centralia residents very much wanted to know the boundaries of the fire.

"We showed Flood the pictures and he said, 'good,'" said former aide Thomas Makowski. "It gave us an idea of the extent of the fire, something they never really knew. It looked like it encompassed the whole damn town, but I didn't know how to read those darn things because all it showed was the heat rising."

Flood's staff gave the pictures to the Bureau after providing copies to Centralia Councilman Ronald Tanney and the *News-Item*. "We assumed that now they had an idea how bad the fire was down there, they would come up with some sort of alternative or plan," Makowski said of the Bureau. "They were already talking about evacuating the people."

Funding for the dragline trench was quickly approved by the Appalachian Regional Commission, prompted by gloomy predictions from Pennsylvania officials. The trench was to be 415 feet long, picking up where the 1969 trench left off and extending north to the center of Poplar Street, an alley between South and Park streets. It was to be 155 feet wide and 140 feet deep at its deepest point, although upon completion it would be backfilled with clay and other incombustible material so the fire could not pass.

No homes lay in the path of this trench. Several were very close, however, and the Bureau decided it needed a safety zone around the trench. At an August 21 meeting of Bureau and DER officials, it was determined that sixteen houses and SS. Peter and Paul Russian Orthodox Church would have to be removed before the trench excavation could begin. It was not that living near the trench would put the families or churchgoers in direct physical danger—there was no safety zone for the 1969 trench—but the Bureau worried that insurance for the project would be prohibitively expensive if the homes were still there.

At a town meeting on September 7, emotions ran wild. Kuebler and Malenka were repeatedly called liars. Mayor McGinley stormed out of the meeting after Kuebler denied telling him at the Bloomsburg meeting that no homes would have to be taken for the trench. The number of homes had jumped to twenty-five, allegedly because the Bureau had used faulty maps to calculate the previous number.

Five families, among them the Womers, announced they would not move under any circumstances. Helen Womer accused the Bureau of wanting to dig the trench so it could grab Centralia's coal and questioned whether the trench would do a better job than the fly ash barrier. She said her family never had a mortgage to worry about and did not intend to get one now.

In the coming years, many outsiders would profess astonishment that people like the Womers would choose to live with the mine fire rather than start anew somewhere safe. Indeed, even those in Centralia who saw a necessity to leave greatly regretted what they had to do. They had endured much to live in Centralia—the perils of mining work, the years of deprivation when the mines were closed—and their inclination was to stand and fight, not run. Some persons chose to stay, it should be noted, because they could not afford to leave.

Helen Womer, who worked at the Centralia office of Pennsylvania National Bank, became the leading opponent of any plan to fight the mine fire that involved taking houses—hers would be one of the first to go before any trench was dug. Very articulate, she had an unfortunate gift for twisting facts to back her arguments.

Tony and Mary Lou Gaughan, surprisingly, were among the five families who vowed not to move. Despite their frequently voiced fear of the mine fire gases, they had decided against moving because of their age and ill health. They would join the Womers in calling for a solution to the mine fire that did not involve relocation, a solution that would become more and more elusive.

Five families at the September 9 meeting said they were willing to leave, and thus was born the tragic conflict in Centralia that would grow increasingly bitter as the years passed. Joan Girolami, a mother of two who lived on East Park Street, was in this group. She was becoming a leader of the families who wanted drastic action to stop the fire.

Mrs. Girolami, 37, had first become worried about the mine fire in 1976, when traces of carbon monoxide gas were found in homes further east on her street. When the Bureau built the fly ash barrier in

1969, she had signed a property release after being assured, she said, that the barrier would prevent the mine fire from reaching her home. The Bureau had pumped fly ash into the mine voids beneath her home, which was on the very edge of the barrier. This year the Bureau had discovered a 746-degree temperature in a borehole a few feet behind her swimming pool.

Centralia was in turmoil that summer, and no one knew it better than the six men who sat on Centralia Council. Paid only a token salary, more used to dealing with sewer and vandalism problems than the fate of a community, they begged Kuebler to find some way to protect the village that would not require destroying so much of it. They asked for a meeting with Paone to sort things out, and Kuebler arranged it for October 5 in Wilkes-Barre. When word of the meeting spread, East Park Street residents sent a letter to Malenka demanding that one of their number, Mrs. Eva Moran, a fiery former council member, be invited to the meeting as their representative. In the end, they all got to go, along with Helen Womer.

Unknown to anyone, Columbia County Redevelopment Authority executive director Stephen Phillips was having little luck securing a source of funds—he needed $1 million—to purchase the twenty-five homes and the church. Pennsylvania Department of Community Affairs had given tentative, very reluctant approval to paying half the cost if it could be spread over a three- or four-year period but said the county or local government would have to come up with the rest. Phillips knew that was out of the question. His best remaining hope was to obtain all of the money from the U.S. Department of Housing and Urban Development. He telephoned Flood's staff to sound out the possibilities.

The biggest shock of the October 5 meeting was an admission by both the Bureau and DER that the mine fire was under "four or five" houses on East Park Street. Paone named it the 300-degree zone, for the temperature at which the Bureau considered a mine fire to be present or relatively near. Much higher temperatures had been found, like the 746 degrees behind Joan Girolami's house. Houses in the 300-degree zone were all east of the fly ash barrier, completely unprotected from the mine fire. None of the Bureau's plans for fighting the fire, either the big trench envisioned in the original 1965 plan or the fly ash barrier, ever offered any protection for these homes. The fire was not in this part of Centralia when the barrier was built, so the design had raised no protests on East Park Street.

Paone laid out seven options for consideration by Centralia Council. The first—and this was heavily favored by Kuebler—was to set aside funds so additional fly ash could be pumped into the barrier when leaks developed. The second was to pump more fly ash into the barrier now, followed by a hydraulic slurry that might fill some of the cavities the fly ash would surely miss. The third option called for hydraulically injecting some incombustible material other than fly ash. The fourth proposed adding cement grouting to the underground barrier, which presumably would make it even more impermeable, and fifth was the dragline trench already proposed. Sixth was an "intermediate" trench costing $3.5 million, and seventh was a major trench, the "Panama Canal project," that would cost $9–$10 million and destroy seventy-eight homes.

Only the last option carried any sort of guarantee from the Bureau, but Paone said the Bureau had no way to fund it at present. "They pressed us for a recommendation," Paone recalled later. "We weren't prepared to give a recommendation. . . . There was still study needed."

Council members left the meeting in a state of confusion. McConnell from DER wanted them to endorse the dragline trench, which he believed was desperately needed. If the Bureau couldn't make up its mind, the councilmen wondered, how could nonengineers like themselves be expected to make an informed decision.

Over the next two weeks, council members agonized over what to do. They sent a letter to Paone on October 14, asking once again, "What, in your opinion, is the best way to deal with this catastrophe?" Council secretary Thomas Cook added, "Everyone involved respects your opinion, and if you would offer a possible concrete solution it would help immensely to calm down the hysteria that is becoming worse with the advent of the cold weather."

In the absence of any further word from the Bureau, Centralia Council voted unanimously in late October to endorse the dragline trench. "It was a difficult decision, a decision we did not enjoy making," council president Francis Goncalves told the *News-Item*. "We realize there will be a great inconvenience to the families involved, and we are concerned where the relocation funds are going to come from."

Paone responded to council's letter on November 2, after council had endorsed the dragline trench. He said the Bureau believed a large trench to be the most certain means of controlling the mine fire but was concerned about the length of time it would take to begin the digging. In the meantime, Paone said, the dragline trench was the best option. "This trench, plus the nearly completed fly-ash barrier reinforcement, will provide temporary protection to area residents and at the same time will also permit us to thoroughly explore other options."

If council members thought that the matter was settled, that the only remaining question was where to get the money to buy the twenty-five homes and the church, they were about to receive a rude shock. The Bureau, having looked once again at the cost-benefit ratio at Centralia, was about to pull the rug out from under council. After council members had staked their reputations on their decision and endured public and private criticism from the Womers and other anti-relocation families, the Bureau decided it did not want to excavate a trench at Centralia. The public reason for the change of heart was the one to two years the Bureau believed it would take to begin digging the dragline trench, even if relocation funds could be obtained. Phillips had applied to HUD for an emergency grant on November 17 but was not optimistic it would be approved.

Paone and Kuebler summoned Centralia Council and the same group of citizens back to Wilkes-Barre on December 19 to tell them the trench would not be excavated—if council approved, of course. "As we studied the situation and we looked at the land values here, and the displacement of the citizens, we felt that the indirect method had more and more promise to us," Paone said at the meeting. This was Paone's only public reference to the cost-benefit issue, and no one at the meeting realized its significance.

The "indirect method" was a $6-million plan to create a "super flush barrier," one that would supposedly fill up every nook and cranny under the thirty-five acres where the mine fire burned, or soon would burn, with incombustible material, fly ash, and concrete grout. It was, Paone said, the Bureau's most advanced technique for mine fire control. The mine fire would burn out for lack of air "one or two years" after completion of the project, which he estimated would last four to five years, and no properties would need to be acquired. The $464,000 appropriated by the Appalachian Regional Commission for the dragline trench could be applied to the first phase of the new project, drilling about 250 boreholes to determine where the fire was.

Robert Oberman of DER said the state no longer thought a trench was needed or feasible. Kuebler said the new project might provide even better protection than a trench. It remained only for Centralia Council to withdraw its endorsement of the trench and transfer it to this new project.

Kuebler said the Appalachian Regional Commission told the Bureau it would not pay for the entire project. Most of the funding, he said, would have to come from the U.S. Office of Surface Mining (OSM), which was organized in 1977 and had a special fund, the Abandoned Mine Lands Fund, for work of this sort.

Since the actual measures to control the fire and gases would not begin for many months under this new plan, the Bureau proposed to protect a few Centralia houses with in-home carbon monoxide detectors. When the carbon monoxide level reached fifty parts per million, an alarm would sound to alert the family. Manufactured by Energetics Science Incorporated, a division of Beckon-Dickson Corporation of Hawthorne, New York, the Ecolyzer 2000 was originally developed for use by the Occupational Safety and Health Administration in factories.

"How many places in the country do people have to live with an indicator like that?" the meeting transcript states one unidentified resident asked.

"You would, if the Bureau supplies them," Kuebler snapped.

"If you had put the fire out when it started, you wouldn't have this," the resident rejoined.

"I don't want to argue with you," Kuebler said. "As I previously told this group, this is your fire and not the Bureau's." The statement went unchallenged by Paone.

And so it went for much of the long meeting. They were not demanding anything more than had been given Scranton, Laurel Run, and other affected communities—effective and meaningful protection from a mine fire that threatened their lives and property.

Kuebler's long tenure with the Bureau was coming to an end. He would retire in 1980 at the age of 69. His opinions on Centralia and the fly ash barrier never changed, so far as anyone knows.

Centralia Council met in special session on December 21, 1978, and approved the Bureau's new plan. The next move was up to the U.S. Office of Surface Mining.

12

Infighting

John Stockalis (left) and Daniel Lewis, inspectors for the U.S. Bureau of Mines, test the temperature in the dirt floor of John Coddington's cellar on December 7, 1979. The temperature, elevated by the mine fire, was 136 degrees. Coddington's station was closed by state police that day after the temperature of gasoline in the underground storage tank began rising. (Photo: David DeKok, News-Item)

TIME was fast running out for Centralia, although none of the characters in the drama could know it at the time.

With the vent pits sealed, gases had no safe exit east of Centralia and were drawn toward the fly ash barrier by air currents within the mine. The barrier was beginning to settle again, and as openings in it widened, small breaths of the gases began flowing through. Though the gases were almost imperceptible at first, the ten Ecolyzer carbon monoxide detectors installed by the Bureau during the first month of 1979 soon came to be seen as lifesavers.

A bureaucratic war over the Centralia mine fire was brewing in Washington between the Bureau and its new rival, the U.S. Office of Surface Mining. Both were agencies of the Interior Department, but that seemed to make the infighting all the more bitter.

OSM was established as a result of a long battle in Washington to enact a federal law regulating, but not banning, the strip mining of coal. Bitterly opposed by the coal industry, the law was needed to end the widespread practice of leaving open pits and refuse piles for the public to worry about after a mine was closed. Vast areas of the nation's coal lands lay despoiled and useless. Among the states, only Pennsylvania had anything approaching effective regulation of new strip mines.

Environmentalists like Louise Dunlap of the Environmental Policy Center in Washington, D.C., longed to bring the industry under federal regulation. Dunlap and a friend, Ernest Preate, enlisted the aid of Walter Heine, who headed Pennsylvania DER's Bureau of Mine Reclamation. Preate and Heine drew up a model strip mining control bill that provided for federal regulations but eventual state enforcement. Heine believed federal enforcement of the regulations, particularly in the case of smaller mining companies, would prove onerous and insensitive.

After much debate and amendment by Congress, the bill was passed in late 1974. To the dismay of environmentalists, President Gerald Ford killed it with a pocket veto. Congress passed the bill again in 1975, and this time Ford vetoed it outright. Congress enacted the Surface Mining Control and Reclamation Act a third time in 1977, and President Jimmy Carter signed it into law on August 3. Walter Heine became OSM's first director.

In addition to regulating coal operators, the bill funded a mammoth effort to clean up the old scars of coal mining. All strip-mined coal was to be taxed at 25 cents per ton, while deep-mined coal would be taxed at 15 cents per ton. The resulting Abandoned Mine Lands Fund would be available to backfill strip mines, prevent subsidences, and fight mine fires.

Billions of dollars were expected to flow into the AML fund during its fifteen-year lifespan. Each coal mining state was alloted a portion of the 50 percent of the fund reserved for the states. Twenty percent was reserved to OSM for its own abandoned mine land projects. Another 20 percent went to the Department of Agriculture's Rural Abandoned Mine Lands Program, and 10 percent was set aside for small operator assistance.

The Appalachian Regional Commission agreed to fund the exploratory drilling phase of the Bureau's proposed new Centralia project, using the money that would have funded the dragline trench. It told the Bureau it must apply to OSM for the rest, about $5.5 million. The Bureau didn't like that one bit.

Walter Heine had never forgiven the Bureau for its active opposition to the federal strip mining bill. He was particularly incensed that the Bureau had helped President Ford find reasons to justify his second veto of the bill—after the veto had taken place. Bureau officials, on the other hand, believed OSM and its environmentalists wanted to ban as much mining as possible and abolish the Bureau.

The crux of the matter was simple: each agency believed the other was infringing on its turf. OSM expressed its displeasure with the Bureau by subjecting its new plan for Centralia to close and skeptical scrutiny. The Bureau, in a fit of pique, withheld many of the documents and data OSM needed to evaluate the proposed project.

■ ■ ■

Five families on East Park Street—Joan and Louis Girolami, Agnes Owens, William and Helen Frye, Martin and Rosalyn Kranzel, and Charles Molnar—wanted nothing more to do with the Bureau. Some of this group had attended the Wilkes-Barre meetings in October and November 1978. All of them had lost confidence in the Bureau's mine fire control schemes.

Relocation to a safer place was their ultimate goal, and to that end they began a letter-writing campaign to persuade the federal government to buy their homes and move them out. For the short term, they waged their own campaign to gain effective protection from the mine fire's deadly gases. They didn't believe the Bureau could be trusted for that, either. In addition, they told the Bureau they might not allow drilling on their property when the new project began, because the Bureau would not guarantee that any damage to their homes would be repaired.

The ten Ecolyzer carbon monoxide detectors that had been distributed to these five families and others were also a concern. The Bureau had decided, in the interests of economy, not to purchase as many of the $2,000 devices as there were families needing protection. As a result, each family was told it could have the device for thirty days at a time, after which it would be given to another family. In addition, the alarms were not loud enough to be heard on the upper floors, or to wake a sleeping parent if the devices were placed in the basement, where gases would first enter a house.

Letters from the five families went to President Carter, Secretary of the Interior Cecil Andrus, U.S. Senators Richard Schweiker and John Heinz of Pennsylvania, and Pennsylvania's governor, Dick Thornburgh, who was elected the previous November. One of the mythical figures of American life is the citizen who, incensed by some great wrong, successfully petitions his elected leaders to set matters right. In real life, such a citizen can more often expect to be ignored, receive a form letter from the agency responsible for the problem, or worse, be treated as a dangerous crackpot.

President Carter, the two senators, and Governor Thornburgh took no action after receiving the letters from Centralia. It is doubtful, given the procedures of political offices, that they even saw or knew of them. The only replies the Centralia families received were from the Bureau or DER, a seeming snub that mystified and angered them. Mrs. Girolami wrote back to Schweiker on behalf of all of them on February 15: "We the taxpayers and property owners of East Park Street are pleading with you for help. We have written several times before about the Centralia mine fire, but we had no response. We are inviting you or one of your aides to come to Centralia and look at the way we are forced to live because of the mine fire."

There was no response to that letter either. One reason is that whenever Schweiker or Heinz passed along a letter from Centralia, the Bureau wrote back to the senator stating all the things it had done or was planning to do for Centralia, implying that these families were malcontents. Another reason is that Centralia was simply not a problem that interested Heinz, Schweiker, or Thornburgh. It involved relatively few people and was not yet receiving press coverage in the larger newspapers. This is particularly unfortunate, because timely intervention in 1979 might have saved much of Centralia from the mine fire.

Congressman Daniel Flood was physically unable to do anything about Centralia in 1979. He had become embroiled in legal problems at the end of 1978 after a former aide, Stephen Elko, linked him to several kickback schemes, and his health deteriorated rapidly during 1979. Former aide Thomas Makowski says Flood spent 188 days in the hospital that year, his last in Congress. His only votes were pairings. Although Makowski is sure Flood could have done something for Centralia had he been healthy, the fact remains that Flood's record of helping the village was a poor one indeed. His power base was Luzerne County, and problems outside the county like the Centralia mine fire interested him little. He would respond to them if pressed but did not follow up on complaints to make sure the problem had been solved.

The Bureau eventually installed louder alarms on the carbon monoxide detectors but refused for a long time to end the practice of rotating them from family to family. Joan Girolami, in one of her less temperate letters to Schweiker, referred to this practice as "Russian Roulette."

■ ■ ■

One of Walter Heine's first appointments as OSM director was Dr. Charles Beasley, a mining engineer who taught at Virginia Polytechnic Institute. Beasley organized the corps of OSM mine inspectors and was now acting director of the Region I office in Charleston, West Virginia. Heine had great confidence in Beasley and turned to him late in the spring of 1979 when others at OSM could not decide what to do about the Bureau's Centralia plan.

Beasley grew up in Sprague, West Virginia, a small coal mining village, and appreciated the problems that mine fires, burning culm banks, and the like caused for people who lived nearby. His chief virtue with respect to Centralia was that he could look at the problem with new eyes, unencumbered by any need to cover up or justify what had been done—or not done—in the past.

When he examined the data the Bureau was willing to provide, Beasley became increasingly doubtful that the Bureau's plan for a super flush barrier had any real chance to stop the mine fire. Backfill technology is an inexact technology when used for roof support in abandoned mine lands, he said, but is even less credible as a fire control measure. Explaining further, Beasley said he doubted that a barrier could be made to rest on the steeply pitched coal veins under Centralia. Even if it could be built, it would neither extinguish nor contain the mine fire because it was impossible to construct an airtight barrier in the broken, twisted rock beneath Centralia. The hot gases could bypass the barrier through cracks and fissures in the mine roof and could even set the roof on fire, it being "near coal" material.

In a June 27 memo to Heine summarizing his opposition to the Bureau's proposed Centralia project, Beasley wrote, "The technology for extinguishing the fire may not be available. Extinguishing the fire by known techniques could be impossible and at the very least prohibitively expensive. . . . I recommend the project not be funded at this time."

"To me it just looked like . . . it was just feeding pablum to those people up there," Beasley said. "Just getting their hopes up, knowing it wasn't going to be the final effort."

Beasley's memo did not become public until August 8, when its findings were published in the *News-Item*. Until then, OSM officials had suggested publicly it was opposition to the project by the five Park Street families that might sink the project, which was nonsense. OSM would prove just as adept as the Bureau in lying to and misleading the Centralia public.

■ ■ ■

Daniel Lewis may have been the best friend Centralia had in the Bureau. Lewis had worked on the Bureau's Centralia projects since 1965 and had become a friend of many in the village. Greatly disturbed by the Bureau's failure to take adequate steps to protect Centralia, Lewis would become a whistle-blower, going over the heads of his immediate superiors to plead Centralia's case with higher-ups, elected officials, and journalists. He paid the price of most federal whistle-blowers—ostracism or severe reprimands from his superiors. His political connections—among other things, he was the son-in-law of an influential former congressman—protected him from worse treatment.

What particularly irked Bureau officials was Lewis's firm belief that the Bureau's closing of the pits east of Centralia was responsible for mine fire gases coming into Centralia. Lewis and John Stockalis were responsible for checking temperatures and gas levels in the hundreds of boreholes the Bureau had drilled in and around Centralia. When Lewis found carbon monoxide in borehole M-2 in April 1979, he knew trouble lay ahead. M-2 had been drilled on the cold side of the fly ash barrier in July 1978, midway between Tony Gaughan's house and SS. Peter and Paul Russian Orthodox Church. No carbon monoxide was found in the borehole when it was drilled. Presence of the deadly gas now meant the fly ash barrier was no longer intact. Lewis observed that M-2 lay along the gangway that led west to the pit the Bureau had backfilled the previous spring.

In June 1979, carbon dioxide and oxygen-deficient atmosphere were detected in the homes of former mayor John Coddington and David Lamb, a young father who ran a motorcycle shop in Centralia. Both homes were in the 100 block of South Locust Avenue. Coddington's Amoco station and apartment lay just off the crucial gangway, but Lamb's house was over a hundred yards south, which indicated the gangway was feeding gases to other mine tunnels.

The problem at the Coddington home came to light when Joseph Coddington told his father he smelled a strange odor in the service station's basement, which he used for a television den. John Coddington placed a call to the Bureau's office trailer in Centralia and got Wilbert Malenka on the line. Malenka told Coddington the odor must have come from his sewer. He finally agreed to send Lewis to check the basement air with his testing equipment, and that is when Lewis was able to confirm his suspicion that the mine fire gases had spread far beyond the fly ash barrier.

The official verdict, however, was that the sewer was to blame, and Coddington took Malenka at his word. He had the fire company flush the sewer line from St. Ignatius Church down to his gas station, but the gases did not go away. Malenka tried to convince him there was no trap on his sewer line to prevent gases from coming into the house. Coddington knew there was. Malenka told Lamb the same after Lewis found unusual carbon dioxide levels in his basement.

Lamb's basement harbored a secret that neither the owner, who had lived there only since 1977, nor Lewis knew at the time. The house's former owner had been a bootleg miner, and the location of his mine was his cellar. Lewis later learned the miner had sunk a shaft from the basement down to the bottom rock, then tunneled laterally to the coal pillar that supported Locust Avenue. He suspects the miner made it through the pillar and beneath a large yard between Rita Kleman's house and that of Eleanor Tillmont before running out of coal or deciding for some other reason to stop mining. The shaft was backfilled, but only loosely, giving the mine fire gases relatively easy access to the Lamb house and perhaps to other houses in the neighborhood as well.

In 1980, Lewis courageously sent a memo to John Murphy, research director of the Bureau office in Pittsburgh, outlining how the mine fire gases invaded Centralia homes only after the pit east of Centralia was backfilled. For this he was reprimanded and ordered to follow the chain of command. Charles Kuebler, Wilbert Malenka, James Paone, and Thomas P. Flynn all scoff at the idea that the pit closing could have caused the gas influx, but the fact remains that when the pit was open and the fly ash barrier was leaking in 1976, the gases did not find their way into Centralia homes. When the barrier failed again in 1979, the gases gradually entered first one house, then another.

■ ■ ■

Almost without anyone noticing, the mine fire had crossed the Centralia anticline to the south side of Locust Mountain. It was now in the mines that ran beneath the village of Byrnesville.

An abandoned strip mine on the Byrnesville side of the mountain was steaming profusely, a phenomenon caused by the mine fire vaporizing ground water.

Lewis and Stockalis had observed a jump in temperature in several boreholes on the south side of the mountain. They reported this to Malenka, but the Bureau made no effort to inform either Centralia Council or the Conyngham Township Board of Supervisors until Robert Lazarski of Centralia Council demanded a status report on the fire in late August 1979.

A *News-Item* reporter ran into Lewis on one of his periodic visits to Centralia, and the Bureau inspector insisted on showing him several other disturbing phenomena he had found. Chief among these was a dangerous mine opening one hundred yards west of Route 61 and one hundred feet south of St. Ignatius Cemetery. Lewis had detected a deadly flow of carbon monoxide at the opening, which was easily accessible to children. He said air coming out of the mine the previous winter had been hot—110 degrees. He had also found carbon monoxide coming from a crack in the rock just off the shoulder of Route 61 south of Centralia. On cold days, Lewis had seen brief bursts of steam come out of the rock fissure and roll across the highway.

■ ■ ■

The hue and cry that arose when Beasley's damning memorandum became public in August had forced OSM to make a strategic retreat. The Bureau fought a spirited war in defense of its proposed project, although OSM considered this to be motivated less by concern for Centralia than a desire to make work for the Bureau's Wilkes-Barre office. Centralia Council members feared if this project was not undertaken, nothing would follow in its place.

Beasley, who had been recalled to Washington, was now OSM's assistant director for abandoned mine lands. He insisted that the Bureau, if it wanted to fight the Centralia fire, undertake a comprehensive study of all possible ways to extinguish or contain the fire. This study was to include so-called alternative technologies, that is, methods never tried by the Bureau in its previous mine fire control work. In addition, he wanted recommendations on how to protect the health and safety of Centralia residents until such time as a mine fire project could begin.

Councilman Lazarski was becoming increasingly frustrated with what he correctly perceived to be a bureaucratic war between OSM and the Bureau. In a long letter to Heinz on November 25, he described the worsening mine fire situation and bemoaned the seeming inability of OSM or the Bureau to decide what to do about it. "I certainly hope we are not being used as a pawn in a personality or power struggle between these two agencies," Lazarski wrote. "We are only a small community, but we are definitely united in our determination to have this fire taken care of. One can only stand by for so long and watch an inadequate bureaucratic force at work."

When the Bureau submitted its proposal to Beasley at the end of November, it mentioned for the first time the possibility of federal purchase of Centralia homes. It was none too soon.

■ ■ ■

When John Coddington came down to open his gas station the morning of November 21, he was surprised to see a thin plume of steam rising from a small hole in the vacant lot between the station and David Lamb's house. It had not been there the day before.

Lewis hurried over as soon as Coddington called. He found no carbon monoxide in the steam, and its temperature was only 66 degrees, but two days later the temperature jumped to 122 degrees, prompting fears the mine fire was moving toward the underground gasoline storage tanks at Coddington's station and the natural gas pipeline under Locust Avenue.

The Lamb family was having problems of its own. David and Eileen Lamb began suffering severe headaches whenever they stayed too long in their basement. They did not understand why this was happening, although Lamb later linked it to the mine fire gases coming up from the old shaft.

OSM district manager Robert Biggi visited Centralia in early December to assess what appeared to be a rapidly worsening situation. Malenka assured him the temperatures found in the hole, now up to 126 degrees, did not pose any threat to the gasoline tanks or the natural gas pipeline under Route 61.

On December 5, Joe Coddington observed a wisp of steam rising from the dirt floor of his television den and found the north wall warm to the touch—quite unusual for December. Stockalis, sent by

Malenka to investigate, dug a small hole in the floor and inserted a temperature probe. It measured an astonishing 102 degrees. He reported back to Malenka, who telephoned Lewis that night and told him to keep checking the temperature in the cellar.

DER inspector Leon Brass checked the cellar floor temperature on December 6 at the request of Lewis and Coddington and found it had jumped to 132 degrees. Coddington asked Brass to check the temperature of the gasoline. It was 58 degrees, about 8 degrees above normal and an indication the mine fire's heat was beginning to warm the underground tank. Brass returned on December 7 and found the cellar temperature had risen to 136 degrees and the gasoline to 64 degrees, which they all agreed was ominous. The gasoline level in the tank rose a foot when Brass removed the cap to insert the temperature probe.

Coddington, with a heavy heart but no reluctance, notified Centralia fire marshal Michael Kogut, who in turn notified Pennsylvania State Police fire marshal Joseph Ducaji in Hazleton. As a precautionary measure, Ducaji ordered the 9,000 gallons of gasoline removed and the tank filled with water. The boiling point of gasoline is 194 degrees.

The closing of Coddington's station was the biggest story to come out of Centralia since 1969. The *News-Item* ran it at the top of page one under a six-column headline. It was picked up by *Associated Press* in Philadelphia and sent out on both the state and national wires that evening and the following day.

The *News-Item* reached Beasley on December 12 and found him unaware of the incident at Coddington's station. He defended OSM's long delay in deciding what to do about the mine fire, blaming it on the Bureau's failure to provide him with necessary information. OSM planned to have the Bureau study all available options for fighting the mine fire, while at the same time ensuring that steps were taken to better protect Centralia residents from the fire's poison gases. Beasley did not reveal that OSM had decided to relocate eight to eleven families in the 300-degree zone.

A December 21 briefing paper and a December 27 memorandum from Beasley to Walter Heine said OSM planned to purchase additional carbon monoxide monitors and, if necessary, reinforce the fly ash barrier. The Bureau would "positively delineate the total fire area," but with infrared photography, not by drilling boreholes, and then "determine the most feasible and effective way to permanently control or extinguish the mine fire."

These plans had been in existence before Coddington's station was closed. The incident did not seem to imbue OSM or the Bureau with any new sense of urgency. They would follow their own agenda and seek no citizen input.

OSM's increasing reliance on electronic devices to protect Centralians from the poison gases while it pondered the options was a risky gamble. Everything depended on the proper functioning of these machines, and honest recording and interpretation of their findings. It would have been far better for Centralia Council and the affected citizens to have pushed hard now for a comprehensive solution to the fire; instead they accepted halfway measures. Council was so desperate for the federal government to do *something* that it eagerly accepted anything OSM offered. The affected citizens were too disorganized to mount an effective challenge to government policy. OSM would have its way, and the results would be disastrous.

13
Increasing Danger

Robert Lazarski (left), vice-president of Centralia Council, and Edward Polites, president. (Photo: David DeKok, News-Item)

OSM briefed Centralia residents on the new plan at a packed meeting in Centralia Municipal Building on January 4, 1980. Because the meeting was held so soon after the Coddington incident, community expectations were high. Many assumed that OSM was planning to do something serious to stop the fire.

There was some grumbling when Dr. David Forshey, one of the Bureau representatives at the meeting, said that results of the mine fire study would not be available until September, but when Beasley promised OSM would implement the best option presented by the Bureau in September, "whatever it is," residents were relieved to hear such a direct promise after years of bureaucratic double-talk from the Bureau. Waiting nine months then seemed entirely reasonable. The problem, of course, was that the usual paperwork and review process would delay the start of an actual *project* until probably the spring of 1981. Relatively few people knew about the developing gas problem in the area of Coddington's station and the immediate action it required.

Residents should also have paid more attention to Beasley's statement that financing would not be a problem if the amount proposed was "reasonable and realistic." He said $100 million would be unreasonable, but $6 million "does not scare me." He was limiting the project to one with a relatively low price tag, given the effect of inflation on construction costs during the 1970s.

Helen Richards, an OSM real estate specialist who would oversee the relocation of families, said eight houses in the 300-degree zone were being considered for purchase; families outside the zone might be considered for relocation later. She did not say which houses she meant, but most residents were aware that the 300-degree zone included houses at the end of East Park Street.

This relocation plan would do nothing to protect people in the area around the Coddingtons. These families were supposed to be protected by the fly ash barrier, which the Bureau could not bring itself to admit had failed. Even after OSM discovered how leaky the barrier had become, internal policy disputes would prevent the relocation of families in real danger.

■ ■ ■

OSM believed that Pennsylvania should participate in funding any future Centralia project. Beasley recalls that Deputy Secretary Clifford McConnell of DER was at the January 4 meeting. Afterward he introduced himself to McConnell and told him, "I'm looking forward to a cooperative venture on this to see what we can do." To his dismay, McConnell answered, "You're on your own"; the Thornburgh administration had no intention of helping to fund any Centralia project.

Whether this came as a real surprise to Beasley is open to question. The correspondence file on Centralia at OSM's Region I office in Charleston, West Virginia, contained a letter of January 30, 1979, in which McConnell outlined DER's position on Centralia to James Gilley, OSM deputy regional director for abandoned mine lands: "Since this has, over the years, been a federal [USBM] project, we strongly believe that the U.S. Bureau of Mines should continue the project to completion. . . . It is obviously a very high priority [for DER], although we cannot categorize it among the state projects since it has been, and is a federal project."

Gilley replied, "A solely federal effort at Centralia may contravene present policy established during the infancy of the Office of Surface Mining."

McConnell shot back, "For any other agency than the U.S. Bureau of Mines—after the many years the Bureau has been in there—to step into the picture would be a gross waste of time and money."

McConnell implied that DER would expect OSM to pay the entire bill at Centralia even after Pennsylvania received its sizable share of the Abandoned Mine Lands Fund. "After the states obtain primacy, there are still federal projects authorized," he reminded Gilley. Thornburgh administration policy on Centralia was still being made by DER at the start of 1980.

Governor Dick Thornburgh took no notice of the Centralia mine fire during 1979 or 1980, his first two years as governor. Later, when he moved Centralia policymaking into the Governor's Office, he would largely adopt the existing policies of DER. Nothing, not even the health of Centralia residents, would be allowed to push the Thornburgh administration into a situation where state funds might have to be used to save Centralia. Even the Pennsylvania Department of Health, headed by Dr. Arnold Muller, willingly subordinated the health of Centralia residents to the policy goals of the Thornburgh administration.

Denials by state officials that sufficient money was available to help Centralia have a hollow ring. While it is true the state did not have access to its share of the AML Fund in 1980, and would not until 1982, it did have over $40 million remaining in the Land and Water Conservation bond issue of 1967 that could have been used.

Given the appalling neglect of the Centralia fire by the Scranton administration in 1963 and 1964, and state acquiescence in the Bureau of Mines' mishandling of the mine fire between 1965 and 1969, it seems somewhat fatuous for DER to imply it was all the Bureau's fault.

The people of Centralia would never understand why they did not merit help from the governments they helped elect and pay for. They could not understand the value the bureaucracy placed on avoiding risk, not straining a budget, avoiding dangerous precedent, and not antagonizing key political leaders.

Something was lost here in the endless corridors of the bureaucracy, and it was respect for human dignity. Only the people of Centralia could stop the dull ranks of officialdom from concluding, with suitable expressions of regret, that nothing could be done to save their village. From 1980 onward, Centralians would be pawns in a struggle between the Thornburgh administration and the Interior Department over who would pay for Centralia. If they thought government was for the people, they would find reason to change their mind.

■ ■ ■

OSM planned to purchase the East Park Street homes of Joseph Moyer, John Lokitis, Edward Dempsey, Patrick Garrity, Marie McDonnell, Martin Kranzel, and William Frye, as well as a vacant and dilapidated house next to the Fryes owned by the Arcus brothers of Bloomsburg.

The decision to purchase these eight houses was based on a November 29 memorandum from Wilbert Malenka to Thomas P. Flynn. There was no mention of the 300-degree zone in the memo. Rather, Malenka's reason for concern was that the fractured rock beneath the houses might "permit the seepage of gas, which is a real threat to the residents."

He did not need to mention to Flynn that the houses lay outside the fly ash barrier. Indeed, the barrier's eastern limit was a few feet east of Joan Girolami's house, between her house and that of the Arcus brothers. No one ever mentioned the fly ash barrier as a reason for the Park Street relocations in 1980. Certainly the Bureau did not, for that might have led to questions why seven homes were left without even limited protection from future movement of the fire when the barrier was constructed. Lokitus, the eighth owner, had built his house several years later.

The Bureau knew by the time this memo was written that a gas problem was developing at the Coddington and Lamb houses, but it formed no plan to help those families. The houses on East Park Street had no gas problem at that time, although the Bureau had good reason to believe one was coming. Having OSM buy the eight houses eliminated an embarrassing deficiency in the fly ash barrier plan on which the Bureau had staked so much.

The relocation plan split up the five East Park Street families who had swamped federal officials with angry letters the year before, demanding to be relocated. The Kranzels and Fryes would be allowed to leave; the Girolamis, Molnar, and Mrs. Owens had to stay. There was no rhyme or reason to the plan, so far as the families could see.

Joan Girolami was particularly perplexed. She knew the Bureau had found a 746-degree temperature when it drilled a borehole behind her swimming pool in 1978. Helen Richards now said her house was not in the 300-degree zone. Mrs. Richards did assure her, however, that her house was in a second group of six properties to be acquired later, a group that also included the Murray, Owens, Darrah, Womer, and Gaughan houses.

Federal agencies must apply the terms of the Uniform Relocation Act when acquiring property. OSM planned to pay the seven families and the Arcus brothers the fair market value of their houses, as determined by two independent assessors. The seven families would also receive up to $15,000 in relocation assistance to make it possible to buy homes comparable to the ones they were leaving. Since the Arcus brothers did not occupy the house they owned, this benefit did not apply to them.

Beasley laid down a special directive in a February 25 memo to Stephen Phillips, executive director of Columbia County Redevelopment Authority, whose staff would administer the relocation on the local level: "It has been decided that compensation for the properties should not include any detraction from value which may exist as a result of the mine fire. Therefore, the adjusters should be instructed to make no downward adjustments nor apply any economic depreciation because of the mine fire."

Despite Beasley's memo, within OSM debate still raged whether the Centralia purchases were strictly legal under terms of the Surface Mining Control and Reclamation Act, a key section of which was open to a variety of interpretations.

Beasley obviously thought the purchases were legal. Heine agreed, adding that they were vital if OSM was to carry out its mandate to protect the seven families from an abandoned mine land hazard. This was the purpose of the AML Fund. Others in the department argued the law forbade any property purchases not directly necessary to the success of a project to eliminate a hazard.

Assistant Secretary of the Interior Joan Davenport was the final arbiter. She did not approve the $225,000 Centralia relocation plan until April 18, weeks after the seven families assumed it was final. Although she agreed with Heine, she was skeptical about any plan to extinguish the Centralia fire. She ordered Heine to provide cost-benefit statements for each of the options the Bureau submitted in September and directed him to "invite" Pennsylvania to agree to do any further work at Centralia with its own money.

■ ■ ■

Helen Richards was the first OSM employee to discover the gas problem at the Coddington and Lamb houses, but she didn't find out from the Bureau. According to an OSM chronology of the Centralia gas problem during the first half of 1980, Mrs. Richards visited the houses on January 9 and was informed by Coddington and Lamb that carbon dioxide levels in their respective basements "were high and rising each time samples were taken."

Samples collected by Malenka on January 2, she would later learn, showed carbon dioxide levels of 2.53 percent in the Lamb cellar and an astonishing 10.53 percent in the Coddington cellar. The normal level for this gas is 0.03 percent. Oxygen in the Coddington cellar that day had dropped from its normal level of 20.95 percent to 11.02 percent, and a trace of methane was detected.

Mrs. Richards, who periodically stepped outside her real estate role, reported the situation to Robert Biggi at the OSM Wilkes-Barre office on January 11. During their telephone conversation, Malenka called to propose emergency drilling and flushing around the Coddington and Lamb houses.

No effort was made until June to explain to the Lambs and Coddingtons the degree of danger they faced from the gases. Neither OSM nor the Bureau considered that to be its responsibility, and neither agency is known to have made an attempt to enlist the aid of the U.S. Department of Health and Human Services or some other federal agency with expertise on the question. There is no record at this stage of any involvement by the Pennsylvania Department of Health, which should have taken the lead in helping the Centralia public cope with this dire public health threat.

One of the more pitiful aspects of the Centralia mine fire story was the almost frantic effort by the affected families to find out the exact nature of the danger they faced from the gases, particularly carbon monoxide. They knew carbon monoxide was fatal in large volumes, but what about the lesser amounts they were breathing? They pleaded for information at the public meetings with state health officials, and more often than not faced smiling indifference or patronizing lies. Eventually, they were forced to do their own research.

■ ■ ■

Pennsylvania's Health Department treated information about the effects of carbon monoxide as a state secret, and it is not hard to imagine why. If the affected families had been told what even small amounts of carbon monoxide could do to them, the outcry might have forced the Thornburgh administration to take serious action to stop the mine fire, or at very least to move the endangered families to safety. Millions of state tax dollars were at stake.

Carbon monoxide kills by combining with hemoglobin in red blood cells to block the flow of oxygen to the brain. When a human is exposed to nonfatal volumes of carbon monoxide, a series of symptoms resembling those of influenza occur. These are, in order, a throbbing headache and irritability, dizziness, weakness, impaired vision, ataxia, nausea, vomiting, heart failure, and eventual unconsciousness.*

Persons with heart or lung disease, particularly angina pectoris sufferers, and pregnant women and their unborn babies are much more susceptible to carbon monoxide than healthy males, for example. Environmental Protection Agency (EPA) standards allow exposure to 9 parts per million over a twenty-four-hour period, or 25 ppm over a one-hour period, *one time per year*. These standards were designed to protect angina sufferers. Angina pain occurs when too little oxygen is delivered to heart muscles, and EPA decided upon the standard after studies showed angina patients experienced pain at 9 ppm while not at rest and at 13 ppm while at rest.

The United States Navy sets a 15 ppm standard for submarine crews on extended voyages, and NASA has a 25 ppm standard for flights of the space shuttle. At the upper end of the scale is the 50 ppm standard set by the Occupational Safety and Health Administration (OSHA) for workers on an eight-hour shift.**

Studies showed that asthma sufferers and others with chronic obstructive lung diseases, like black lung, experience a one-third reduction in the time they are able to exercise before experiencing shortness of breath at the EPA level, according to Dr. Wilbert Aronow, chief of cardiovascular research at the University of California at Ir-

---

*Edward Rubenstein, M.D., F.A.C.P., "Carbon Monoxide and Smoke Inhalation," *Medicine* 2, edited by Rubenstein, (1984): 8 :IV:1–2 (a publication of *Scientific American*).

**"Are Kerosene Heaters Safe?" *Consumer Reports* 47 (October 1982) : 499–507.

vine. "There's a big difference between a healthy individual at these low levels and a susceptible person. This is the key," he said.*

That indeed would be the key at Centralia. Healthy adults in the mine fire impact zone, as it came to be called, would be able to cope with the lower volumes of carbon monoxide, if not with the higher ones, but many residents of the zone were not healthy. A good number were elderly, some with heart or lung problems. Among the children, a fair number suffered from asthma, and so did some of their parents. Some of the younger wives planned to have more children.

The effects of carbon monoxide exposure have been established by many studies, but these studies have involved only relatively short-term exposure to the gas. No one has studied the effects of long-term exposure to low levels of the gas. Given the ill effects of short-term exposure, long-term effects of this poison cannot be very salutary.

Carbon dioxide is considerably less dangerous than carbon monoxide, and probably as a result, it is less studied. OSHA sets a standard of 5,000 ppm, or 0.5 percent, as the maximum allowable exposure for a worker on an eight-hour shift. The American Society of Heating, Refrigerating, and Air Conditioning Engineers sets a lower standard, 2,500 ppm, or 0.25 percent. The U.S. Navy standard for submarines is 8,000 ppm, or 0.8 percent. Increased illness has been noted among sailors exposed to 5,000 ppm (0.5 percent) to 10,000 ppm (1.0 percent) carbon dioxide over the long term.** The chief danger of carbon dioxide at Centralia was that it drove out oxygen from a building, reducing the oxygen below its normal volume of 20.95 percent.

■ ■ ■

OSM drilled a borehole a few feet north of Coddington's gas station in late February 1980, hoping to draw heat and gas away from the building. They inserted a 12-foot steel pipe in the hole to lift the gaseous discharge above the heads of passers-by. Steam gushed from the top of the pipe, and the temperature in the cellar floor dropped 20 degrees almost immediately—to 116 degrees. Coddington talked of reopening his gas station. By early March, however, it was evident that OSM had only created a curiosity. Carbon dioxide and oxygen returned to previous levels, and the temperature did not drop any further. The gas station remained closed.

Bureau inspectors installed five more carbon monoxide monitors on March 11, and installed recording devices on all the monitors, in-

*Conversation with the author, March 1981.
**Op. cit., *Consumer Reports.*

cluding the ones at the Coddington and Lamb houses. The devices recorded the time, level, and duration of carbon monoxide incidents, marking the information on a paper tape that was checked every month. All the monitors were set by the Bureau to sound an alarm at 50 ppm.

On March 12, simultaneous gas alarms sounded at the Coddington and Lamb houses. Bureau inspectors decided that a citizen's band radio in a passing car set off the alarms. They installed an aluminum shield on the monitors that prevented any further interference, according to Bureau records.

Coddington, whose sense of humor would help carry his family and neighbors through the difficult months ahead, decorated the borehole pipe with red ribbon, like a barber pole. The pipe was hot to the touch, and children stopped to use it to warm their hands while walking to and from nearby St. Ignatius School.

■ ■ ■

St. Ignatius Elementary School provided a Catholic education for about eighty-five Centralia children. It was staffed by two nuns of the Immaculate Heart of Mary order, who were supervised by the parish priest, Father John Suknaic. Standing over him on school matters was Monsignor Francis Taylor, vicar for education in the Diocese of Harrisburg.

The school was located across Locust Avenue from the church and, like the church, was believed to rest on solid rock. It is true that mine maps showed no tunnels beneath the school, but mine maps in the Anthracite Region often do not show bootleg mines or rock tunnels. Either of these, or natural fissures in the rock, could allow mine fire gases to enter the school.

Late in the winter of 1980, children at St. Ignatius School began complaining to their parents of unusual headaches. Their parents reported the problem to Father Suknaic and members of Centralia Council, who in turn informed the Bureau, which in turn informed DER. DER inspector Leonard Rogers visited the school in early March and discovered above-normal levels of carbon dioxide. Bureau officials ordered five boreholes drilled near the school.

Copies of gas analyses obtained from OSM under the Freedom of Information Act show that mine fire gases—carbon monoxide, carbon dioxide, and methane—were found in the school and in the boreholes drilled around the building. If the gases had been found only in the building, the Bureau might have found a plausible reason for their presence unrelated to the mine fire. Finding the gases in large volumes in the boreholes left only the mine fire as the source of gases inside the school.

Samples collected on March 20 showed a high level of carbon dioxide in the school basement, 2.08 percent, as well as 2 ppm carbon monoxide, an insignificant volume. The level of carbon dioxide was actually higher at the school that day than it was at the Coddington home. Borehole X-23 on the east side of the school showed 0.59 percent carbon dioxide, only slightly above normal, but a very high 341 ppm carbon monoxide.

The *News-Item* received a tip the next day that gas had been found at the school. A reporter telephoned Malenka, who stated, "We have detected carbon dioxide, but we cannot attribute it to the mine fire in any way. There's no coal there. We drilled three holes at the rear and east of the school. We drilled two holes to the south of the school. We intersected no coal beds. It's all on solid rock."

Malenka did not mention the large volume of carbon monoxide found in borehole X-23. In trying to explain away the carbon dioxide in the school, he tripped up, saying the gas might have been generated by oxidation of deteriorating mine timbers or coal, an odd occurrence if the school indeed rested on solid rock. Reverting to his favorite explanation, he then stated, "We're checking the sewers more closely." Malenka also said a carbon monoxide monitor had been placed in the basement of the school, an expensive and seemingly needless precaution if the school indeed rested on solid rock.

The reporter telephoned Sister Frances Xavier, principal of the school, but she would not answer his questions. She referred him to Father Suknaic, who declined comment.

The problem did not go away, and children at the school continued to suffer from headaches. Council member Edward Polites, whose children attended St. Ignatius (but remained healthy), said the nuns and priest did not want to take a chance on the health of the children but also did not want to become involved in finding a solution to the problem. "They did take the monitor," he noted.

Polites wanted the state Health Department to do tests to see if there was a relationship between the gases in the school and the headaches suffered by the children. "They wouldn't do it," he said. "I didn't know what the effect was of exposure to it over a long period of time. I had nothing scientific to go on. I had nothing medical I could use to get the Health Department to do the study."

At a March 27 meeting in Philadelphia of members of Centralia Council and officials of the U.S. Department of Housing and Urban Development, Polites raised the gas problem. Stephen Phillips had arranged the meeting to discuss funding for relocation of Centralia families, which he expected would be recommended by the Bureau's study. After the meeting, Helen Richards wrote: "Borough officials reported that OSM is doing better in its efforts to keep them better informed. They maintain that the school is in danger from CO [carbon monoxide] and that CO_2 levels at the school have increased and children are getting sick."

Perhaps coincidentally, a Bureau inspector arrived at St. Ignatius School the following day to collect gas samples. The findings were similar to the earlier ones, with one important exception. A low, non-explosive volume of methane was found in the gas mixture. It was one more piece of evidence linking the gases to the mine fire.

Why did the Bureau refuse to admit this? And why did church officials play down the danger and allow students to be exposed to the gases for another school year after this one?

The Bureau went so far as to omit the March 20 and March 28 gas analysis reports from "Problems in the Control of the Centralia Mine Fire," a booklet detailing its findings in its study of the mine fire. All other gas analysis reports were included in the booklet, which was distributed to Centralia families in September of that year. Perhaps the Bureau worried that full disclosure of the gas threat to the school would prompt public demands for a major project to stop the mine fire. This might have turned congressional scrutiny toward the failed fly ash barrier and the failure of the Bureau efforts in Centralia in general.

The attitude of church officials is more difficult to comprehend. Former Bureau inspector Daniel Lewis suspects Father Suknaic was misled by the Bureau into believing there was no mine fire gas problem at the school. Father Suknaic was dedicated to his calling and tended to ignore earthly annoyances like mine fire gases. His attitude may have led Monsignor Taylor to believe there was no problem.

Centralia is predominantly Catholic, and the church plays an important role in the lives of Catholics there. They were taught to obey church authority and were reluctant to challenge the church over the threat to the school, no matter how much they might have worried privately about it. Polites recalls that a number of parents were very upset about the gas danger that year but knows of none who pulled their children from the school.

14
Scattered Leaves

Christine Oakum tells members of the state House Mines and Energy Management Committee at a hearing on March 12, 1981 in Centralia about her fear of gases from the mine fire and what they might do to her children. She was one of eight Centralia residents to testify before the panel. (Photo: David De-Kok, News-Item)

One mother who had a child at St. Ignatius was Christine Oakum, a Kulpmont native who moved to Centralia in 1975 with her husband Thomas and infant son Sean. They bought a spacious house at 110 S. Locust Avenue, adjacent to the house where the Lambs now lived and a half-block from the school. The Oakums knew Centralia had a mine fire when they purchased the house, but did not believe the fire could reach their street. The neighbors, she recalled, never discussed it.

By 1980 that had changed. Mrs. Oakum, now a mother of four boys, had read about the mine fire in the *News-Item* and Shenandoah *Evening Herald* in 1978 and 1979 and was well versed on the problem. It did not prepare her for the shock of learning her house had been invaded by the gases.

She and her husband had gone to Kulpmont two days earlier after the death of her mother. When Thomas Oakum returned to the house on March 26 to pick up some extra clothing for the family, he saw that his wife's favorite house plant had shed its leaves and appeared to be dying. He told her when he got back to Kulpmont. It was a mystery to him, but not to her. She had heard mine fire gases could do that to plants. Mrs. Oakum called DER after returning to Centralia the following morning and opened every window and door in the house, despite the cold. By the time Malenka, Lewis, and DER inspector Leonard Rogers arrived that afternoon, she was near panic.

They found an unusually high volume of carbon dioxide on all three floors of the house. It was not a dangerous volume, but she did not know that. Her first thought was to ask Malenka for a carbon monoxide monitor. If there was carbon dioxide in the house, she reasoned, carbon monoxide could not be far behind. Malenka told her no monitor was available, but promised to place her name on a waiting list.

A waiting list? Mrs. Oakum remembered that Lew Walcoski, Centralia's only barber, sold canaries to the few remaining miners working in the area. As soon as the three men left, she hurried downtown to the barber shop to buy one.

■ ■ ■

David and Eileen Lamb, neighbors of the Oakums, had a very sick daughter on their hands. Five-year-old Rachel Lamb had been asthmatic since birth, but as the months passed in 1980 her condition got worse. Her breathing at night grew so labored and painful that Lamb, at the suggestion of his family doctor, rented an oxygen machine to make it easier for her to breathe, and thus sleep. At first her parents did not blame the worsening of her condition on the mine fire gases, but after talking to Joan Girolami, who told them about the gases, they began to connect Rachel's problems to the carbon dioxide that came into their house from the mine fire. It made sense that an asthmatic child who has trouble breathing even a normal level of oxygen would gasp for breath when that level is reduced even a small amount.

■ ■ ■

John Coddington had been certain that after all the commotion in December about the mine fire and its threat to his gasoline, someone would do something to end the fire threat once and for all. He knew now he had been wrong.

Coddington found it hard to understand why his house was affected by the gases but houses across the street were not, since they were closer to the mine fire. Now it seemed the carbon dioxide levels were rising every day. His wife, Isabelle, was diabetic and he worried about her. His son Joe still lived at home, and his daughter Colleen would be home from Penn State in a couple of months. All the Bureau would do was monitor the gases.

Coddington telephoned John Murphy, the top Bureau official in Pennsylvania, on April 11. Murphy was on another line and had Ivor Williams, chief of the Bureau office in Wilkes-Barre, return the call. Coddington told Williams he was worried about the accumulation of carbon dioxide in his cellar and wanted it checked over the weekend. Williams, who privately was very worried about the Centralia situation, promised someone would come.

■ ■ ■

When Christine Oakum was told by Lewis that an old heating vent in the wall was acting as a chimney, sending carbon dioxide through a floor register into her sons' bedrooms upstairs, she devised a radical solution. The entire family would sleep in the living room on the first floor, where the gas volumes, so far, had not been very high. They thought about moving out, but realized it would bankrupt them. Besides, they preferred to fight for their home, which they had worked hard to make nice.

Mrs. Oakum wrote the first of her many letters on April 11, this one to the Environmental Protection Agency office in Philadelphia. She reasoned, wrongly, that EPA might have help to offer because the air inside their home was polluted by carbon dioxide. "We think it is a shame that children are not even safe in their own house," she wrote. "It appears that the government is willing to spend billions of taxpayers' dollars to aid foreign nations who hate this country, but is reluctant to take action to prevent the loss of lives and property of loyal American citizens and taxpayers."

■ ■ ■

Of them all, Lamb was the most radical. During April, his daughter was in and out of the hospital. The inspectors who came to his house would tell him nothing and often would not give him copies of the gas test results. He was seething. Though his ferocious temper was not easily provoked, the Bureau was pushing him to the limit.

One day in mid-April, Bureau inspector Jack Delaney walked down Lamb's cellar steps and staggered back up a few minutes later, his face white, obviously ill. He was rushed to a hospital by other men from the Bureau, and a doctor reportedly told him never to go into the cellar again. The incident did not leak out to the press, but many in Centralia heard about it.

Lamb called Robert Biggi at the OSM office in Wilkes-Barre on April 24 and demanded to know why nothing was being done to help the affected families. He asked if political considerations were involved. Biggi, stammering, told Lamb he was certain that was not the case. Biggi offered to place calls to Ivor Williams and Earl Cunningham, who was Biggi's superior at the OSM office in West Virginia. Cunningham, who was deputy regional director for abandoned mine lands, told Biggi there was nothing OSM could do to help the families. Cunningham told Lamb the same when Lamb called on April 29.

Rachel Lamb had been taken to the hospital the previous day with a pneumonia-like condition. It was the worst she had ever been, and her doctor recommended that she never go back to the house because of the oxygen-deficient atmosphere.

"I was so mad, because my daughter was in the hospital for the fifth or sixth time and I wasn't getting anywhere," Lamb recalled. "I made about ten calls that day. I finally got through to Beasley. I was on the phone all morning. I wanted some action. I was sick of this nonsense. They were going to do something."

Lamb let out an impish chuckle. "So I kind of flew off the handle, and I said, I'll tell you what. If there's not somebody there tomorrow at eight o'clock, I'll guarantee you'll either feel my hands around your neck or you'll be looking down the end of a double-barrel shotgun. I'm sick of watching my daughter, night after night, suffer and in the hospital all the time. I said, I'm damn sick of this bureaucracy, and I'm sick of you and everybody else involved. Now get your ass up here and do something. The next morning they were there! It was eight o'clock in the morning and everybody was there! I couldn't believe it!"

OSM declared an emergency at Centralia on April 30 after examining the gas readings at the Oakum, Lamb, and Coddington homes. The official "Finding of Fact" for the emergency revealed that gas levels in the homes were worse than anyone outside the Bureau had been led to believe. The oxygen volume in the Coddington cellar dropped as low as 7 percent near the floor, and volumes at the Lamb and Oakum houses ranged from 11 to 20 percent. Carbon dioxide volumes in the three homes ranged from 1 to 7 percent. "Emergency reclamation and abatement or control measures are necessary to prevent an imminent catastrophic event," the document noted.

Lamb telephoned Sally Williamson, a nurse at the state Health Department office in Williamsport, and told her what was happening to Rachel. A staff nurse went to examine the little girl, and the nurse's findings prompted Williamson to make a hurried phone call to Dr. Evan Riehl in Harrisburg.

He was the first Health Department doctor to examine the gas problem of Centralia, an action long overdue. At first Riehl seemed genuinely interested in the problem. In an interview on May 2 with the *Morning Press* of Bloomsburg, he seemed determined to get to the bottom of the gas crisis. "There are two dangers that have to be investigated," he said, "the possibility of asphyxiation and the presence of explosive gases."

Riehl offered a remarkably candid assessment of the carbon dioxide risk. "A high concentration of carbon dioxide can cause hyperventilation—it can make you short of breath." He said little about carbon monoxide, probably because at this point the chief threat *was* carbon dioxide and oxygen-deficient atmosphere. Although that would change, the Health Department and the Thornburgh administration would pretend it had not.

■ ■ ■

OSM proposed to protect the three houses by injecting sand, fly ash, cement, and water into the mine cavities beneath them. The idea was to block the gases from entering the homes. The problem, as always, was to fill all the cavities and make the fill material stay in place.

The Bureau never told OSM that St. Ignatius School, too, was affected by the gases. OSM did not find out about the problem at the school until May 5, when a parent telephoned Dick Leonard, public affairs officer at the West Virginia office. Leonard passed the information on to Biggi.

Biggi discovered the Bureau had not drilled its boreholes at the school deep enough to provide conclusive evidence of whether mine tunnels extended beneath the school. He ordered two new boreholes drilled along the north wall of the school, and told the Bureau to deepen borehole X-35. The Bureau's conclusions did not change after the additional work was completed, yet the gas incidents at St. Ignatius School continued without interruption. Lewis told a *Morning Press* reporter that one day the carbon dioxide volume in the school basement was 3.5 percent and the oxygen volume 16 percent.

Drilling and flushing around the Lamb and Oakum houses initially aggravated the gas problem, then seemed to ease it. Bureau inspectors tried to enter the Lamb basement on May 13 while a drill rig was sinking a borehole in the yard between the Lamb house and Coddington's. They hastily retreated after detecting 17 percent oxygen on the third step, and 16 percent on the fourth.

Other families in the neighborhood worried that the drilling and flushing would send the gases into their homes. Eight families appealed to Centralia Council for carbon monoxide alarms. Lazarski telephoned Biggi, who told him money was available. Malenka, on the other hand, told Lazarski on May 13 that Bureau policy forbade purchase of more gas monitors. "I stated to Mr. Lazarski that the Bureau effort is directed toward resolution of the overall mine fire problem, and not the acquisition of additional instruments or temporary measures such as flushing," Malenka wrote in a memo to Ivor Williams on May 14.

At Coddington's, nothing went right. Flushing material erupted through the cellar floor on May 28, depositing a half-ton of the messy mixture before the machine could be shut off. Coddington's carbon monoxide alarm sounded twice that day, first at 1:30 P.M. and again at 8:30 P.M. "It is apparent that grouting is forcing greater quantities of mine atmosphere containing carbon monoxide into the basement," Malenka wrote to Williams on May 29. That was probably true of the first incident, but what about the second, which occurred over three hours after work ceased for the day? Malenka's memo labeled the carbon monoxide incidents "the first recorded and confirmed quantities of the gas (+50 ppm) attributable to the mine fire."

The flushing at Coddingtons would end in June when flushing material was seen washing out of the mouth of the Centralia mine drainage tunnel, over a mile east of the house. ■ ■ ■

Centralia's new congressman, Raphael Musto, was receiving many letters and phone calls from the Centralia public asking for his help. Musto won a special election earlier in 1980 to replace Flood, who resigned after his health and legal problems became too much to bear, and already Centralia was occupying more of his time than almost any issue.

Musto arranged a meeting in Centralia June 3 so representatives of OSM and the Bureau could tell the public "the progress of the Office of Surface Mining and the Bureau of Mines in dealing with the fire problem," according to an OSM letter of June 26. The meeting offered Centralia citizens an opportunity to vent publicly the frustration toward OSM and the Bureau that grew with each turn of events that spring.

The families on East Park Street who had been promised relocation wanted to know why the process was taking so long. Mrs. Oakum demanded of Riehl that he explain the carbon monoxide exposure limits for young children. He did not have an answer but promised to get back to her. One man demanded that OSM reopen the 1963 trench east of Centralia to vent the gases. "I think it's important that you understand we're not going to abandon you," Cunningham of OSM told the sizable crowd. None of the serious questions were answered at the meeting, but it seemed as if they were. The people looked forward to the day in September when the Bureau would announce what could be done to save Centralia.

Something had to be done soon. On the morning after the meeting, the carbon monoxide alarm sounded at St. Ignatius School. It rang until 8:10 A.M., when it was unplugged by one of the nuns.

Joan Girolami had no illusions about the Bureau's study. She was bitter that her house had not been included in the relocation and wrote an angry letter to Cunningham on June 5. In the letter, Mrs. Girolami reminded Cunningham of the statement Helen Richards made in January that the Girolami house would be included in a second phase of the relocation. Mrs. Richards denied to her superiors that she said that. Mrs. Girolami had no way to prove her version of events.

■ ■ ■

Christine Oakum was not satisfied with the information on the mine fire gases that Riehl gave her at the June 3 meeting. He had been helpful about the exposure limits for carbon dioxide and oxygen, but he said little about carbon monoxide. She never received a satisfactory answer to her question about carbon monoxide exposure limits for small children. Therefore, she and some of the other women sought facts about carbon monoxide from other sources. They traveled to the State Library in Harrisburg and found medical textbooks that gave them some information. Mrs. Oakum also wrote to Patricia Harris, Secretary of Health and Human Services in the Carter cabinet, and asked her for information. Mrs. Harris referred her letter to the Center for Disease Control in Atlanta. The doctors were shocked at the gas volumes at Centralia that Mrs. Oakum described in her letter.

They couldn't believe the readings [for oxygen] . . . were so low. Some of the readings I sent them were from the Coddingtons. At the time, he was getting 12 percent oxygen. I showed their letter to DER officials, Bureau of Mines officials, and there was a light stirring here. So somebody from DER called up CDC and said the readings were at the source, not in the ambient air . . . like if they took a reading in a crack in the wall.

To me it was whitewashing! Because I could only assume they didn't want CDC involved. . . . The only good thing that came out of it was that CDC did decide that the safety standard for adults was 35 ppm. In a working situation for eight hours. At the time, the carbon monoxide monitors were being set to go off at 50 ppm. So because I got that letter, showed it to the Bureau of Mines, they got permission to lower that setting. . . .

I didn't care who had the responsibility to put out the mine fire, I just wanted the safety standards to know what levels my kids were safe at. All I got out of this was that children were more susceptible to the gases than adults. Or the older people—this I got out of a medical textbook—older people were more susceptible than young people because of the physical changes with old age. Their breathing becomes more difficult, their circulatory system—the gas is retained in their blood faster than young adults.

In early summer, the Oakums finally received a carbon monoxide monitor. It was a gift from the Frank Jurgill, Jr., family on South Street. The Jurgills, who did not yet have the gases in their house, gave up their monitor and went back on the waiting list. The Oakums also obtained an oxygen-methane monitor. It was yellow and made a chirping sound, so the boys named it Tweetie-Bird. Their canary thought it was another bird and sang to it.

At the July 7 meeting of Centralia Council, Mary Lou Gaughan condemned Ivor Williams' decision to open a borehole near the home of Helen Womer, her neighbor, for three days to see if this would lower gas levels in nearby homes. The gas alarm in the Gaughan house sounded on July 6 at 3 A.M. Mrs. Gaughan became so upset that she feared a heart attack was imminent. Examination of the machine showed that 58 ppm of carbon monoxide had entered the house and did not clear for three hours.

■ ■ ■

The Centralia women may have thought their increasingly severe criticism of the Health Department was falling on deaf ears. It was not, but this did not mean the Health Department was prepared to become their advocate in finding a solution to the problem. Riehl scheduled a meeting on August 5 at the DER office in Pottsville. He wanted OSM and the Bureau to explain the mine fire problem to the Health Department and tell the doctors what they might do to deflect the mounting criticism.

No one from Centralia Council was invited to the meeting, but Joan Girolami found out and informed council at the August 4 meeting. Council members were outraged, particularly because Malenka was there that evening but had told them nothing about the meeting. Malenka told them it would have been "inappropriate" to inform council, since the meeting had been called by the Health Department. It was too late for council to do anything about the closed meeting. Centralia citizens in general and council members in particular would be excluded from all meetings of state officials at which the mine fire was discussed.

One can only speculate why the Thornburgh administration chose to act in this manner. The simplest answer, and the one that springs most quickly to mind, is that they had something to hide from the Centralia public. The Thornburgh administration, it would become evident, lacked any real compassion for the men, women, and children of Centralia. This problem was viewed as simply a question of dollars and cents.

One of the key points stressed by Riehl at the August 5 meeting was that *all* the high carbon dioxide or low oxygen readings gathered to date had been measured near cracks in the basement floors of the three houses. This was not true. The May 13 oxygen readings in the Lamb basement that sent Bureau inspectors scurrying outside to safety had been measured midway down the cellar stairs. The minutes show no discussion of the carbon monoxide threat, despite the incidents at the Coddington and Gaughan houses and at St. Ignatius School.

Dr. Gordon Allen suggested it might be wise to examine "the subject of possible psychological stresses associated with the current situation." This would be the Health Department's whispered explanation for what the department considered Centralia residents' unreasonable fear of the gases.

OSM, Bureau, and DER officials discussed three short-term actions that could be taken to ease the Centralia situation while the Health Department continued "its review of the data on gas levels" and presented "its recommendations to the other agencies involved and to the Borough Council of Centralia." These were, according to the minutes, "drilling of large vent holes into the burning areas in the vicinity of the old strip mines in order to relieve underground pressure and vent gases into the atmosphere," constructing a gas drainage system around one of the homes to draw off the gases before they entered the house, and an old standby—checking heating systems "for possible gas leakage."

■ ■ ■

It was a small subsidence near the Odd Fellows Cemetery that first interested OSM in reopening the old pit to vent the fire gases. Bureau inspectors who examined the subsidence noticed it was blowing out fire gases "under pressure," according to the first briefing paper prepared by OSM for the project. OSM did not have to defend the Bureau's ill-fated decision to close the pit in 1978.

Neither did Ivor Williams. Unlike Kuebler, Malenka, and Flynn, he was not tied to the failure and deceptions of the past. He enthusiastically agreed with the OSM idea, urging the subsidence hole be deepened thirty or forty feet and surrounded by a fence with a lockable gate.

By the time OSM approved the project on August 8, it had metamorphosed into a creature of quite a different appearance. Instead of enlarging the subsidence hole into a pit, OSM drilled six boreholes north of the cemetery. Work was completed in September. Heavy steel pipes protruded eight feet from the nine-inch-diameter holes, and on cold days steam gushed out of the top. The pipes did not stop the coming onslaught of gases, however, and one can only speculate how much worse the crisis might have been without them.

Some in the Bureau point to the failure as proof that closing the old pit did no harm to Centralia. That is disputed by others, among them Frank Jurgill, Sr., the miner who complained bitterly to Kuebler when he saw workers closing the pit in 1978. Jurgill says the original pit had dimensions of 150 by 300 feet and provided a much stronger updraft than the six boreholes ever could.

■ ■ ■

Of the seven families on East Park Street who were to be relocated, only two—the Kranzels and Fryes—had left Centralia by mid-September. Lengthy bureaucratic delays within OSM were responsible, caused in part by a requirement that requests for funds to pay the families be channeled through an OSM office in Colorado.

Edward Dempsey, who lived on East Park Street, complained that Columbia County Redevelopment Authority could give him no reason for the delay other than "that's how OSM works." "My wife died because of this mine fire," he said. "It worried her to death."

John Lokitis, who began building his house on Park Street after the fly ash barrier was completed, believed the mine fire did not pose enough of a threat to warrant his moving and decided to remain where he was.

■ ■ ■

No one could accuse the Bureau of being lazy. After receiving orders from OSM to find the best and most cost-effective method of extinguishing or containing the mine fire, the men and women of the Bureau wasted little time.

Key members of the team met in Centralia April 15 and 16 to view the terrain and review the failures of the previous eighteen years. Led by Dr. Robert Chaiken, a chemist, the group included Malenka, Robert Brennan, Williams, and Robert Conway.

"The fire at Centralia is definitely widespread (Malenka estimates 150 acres) and exists in both the north and south dips of the coal seam(s)," Chaiken wrote in an April 23 memorandum to John Murphy. "There seems to be a general impression that a dig-out will be required if one is to obtain a solution to the problem."

Many of the Bureau's field engineers had believed that from the beginning. It was the administrators, the men who stayed attuned at all times to the whims of Congress, who made it appear that a fly ash barrier was the best way to save Centralia, when they knew very well it was not. All it would do was save money.

Freed by OSM's new hegemony from the burden of politics, the Bureau dared to proclaim the truth about Centralia. It would use this study to tell all who cared to listen that flushing was an abject failure, that it almost never stopped a major mine fire in this part of the Anthracite Region. Only a frontal assault with steam shovels would ensure the eventual death of the great fire at Centralia. To protect the Bureau, though, the writers of the study neglected to criticize the Bureau's own use of the technique at Centralia or explain why it had been used.

The odd result of this was the Bureau assumed the good-guy role at Centralia, and OSM became the heavy. OSM had the money and responsibility to help Centralia, but now it had to contend with the politicians. OSM officials proved just as willing as those in the Bureau to sacrifice Centralia when self-preservation or preservation of OSM so demanded.

OSM so distrusted the Bureau that it would never accept the desperate need for a huge and costly trench at Centralia. It wanted the Bureau to explore "new technologies" for mine fire control, although few of these existed. The Bureau dutifully examined the new methods and rejected them in favor of the old ways. Beasley, a forward-looking technocrat, never forgave the Bureau for this. He seemed certain that a dispassionate look at all the options would uncover one that would be both cheap and effective. It would prove to be an impossible dream.

Centralia citizens were briefed on the findings of the study at public meetings on September 29 and 30. OSM printed 650 copies of "Problems in the Control of the Centralia Mine Fire," enough so every family could have its own.

It was a magnificent report, embodying everything about anthracite mine fires that Bureau scientists had learned since the agency was founded in 1910. The report had chapters describing the many and odd characteristics of anthracite mine fires, the history of the Centralia fire (as seen by the Bureau, of course), mine fire control techniques, the physical effects of mine fire gases, and a lengthy exploration of options for controlling the Centralia fire. Ten options were examined. Four would use total excavation or cut-off trenches to stop the fire, one would use flushing, one would attempt to flood the mines, and four would use techniques labeled unconventional.

The first excavation plan called for total excavation. The study predicted this mammoth effort would cost $84 million and take as long as ten years to complete, but had the best chance to extinguish—not simply contain—the fire. The other three excavation options employed cut-off trenches, which would entail digging out the coal and rock in the path of the fire and backfilling with incombustible material. Much of the fire would be allowed to burn behind the filled area, unable to reach the village. Costs for the cut-off trenches were predicted to range between $22.1 million and $42 million.

The study predicted at least 109 homes and possibly as many as 136 would have to be acquired and demolished. Much of southeast Centralia would be destroyed to save the rest of the village, and life for those who remained would not be pleasant while the digging progressed. Blasting, the rumble of heavy trucks, choking clouds of red dust (a peculiar characteristic of anthracite mine fires), and a strong odor of sulfur would be everpresent.

One of the more intriguing options in the report, flooding the mines, was dismissed as a waste of time and dangerous. Some of the old mines under Centralia were already flooded; indeed, the Bureau counted on the mine water pool to prevent the fire from crossing to the north side of Centralia. The report concluded the mine water level could be raised 140 feet by damming the water tunnels that drained the mines, but this would extinguish only a tiny percentage of the fire and would risk a catastrophic flood in the valley. Pressure would build in areas of uncertain stability. The water could come cascading out the side of the mountain with little warning, and the Swamp, as the lowest neighborhood in Centralia was known, could be swept away.

Of the hydraulic flushing option, little more need be said. Flushing had a certain seductive appeal; it was relatively inexpensive, did not require destruction of homes, and in theory seemed foolproof. Unfortunately, it simply would not work at Centralia, for reasons already discussed at length.

Many persons who read about the Centralia mine fire wondered why it could not be extinguished by pumping water down into the mines. It was a logical question, and one addressed in the report in a section about the water curtain barrier option. The main reason it would not work was the great residual heat in the Centralia mines after eighteen years of burning. Anthracite coal retains heat well, and Bureau scientists estimated twenty years of continuous pumping would be needed to cool the rock enough so the fire would not spontaneously reignite when the spigot was closed.

This was one of the unconventional options presented in the report. Another was burnout control, which received relatively favorable treatment, perhaps because the Bureau was researching this technique at its field laboratory at Bruceton near Pittsburgh. Burnout control would accelerate the mine fire by injecting large volumes of air until all the coal or burnable rock had been consumed. The report listed only one drawback—that it had never been tried on a large scale.

A third unconventional option called for construction of an underground barrier by underground mining. It was rejected (although it was an old method from the days when mine fires started in active mines) because of the extreme danger it would pose to the miners.

The last alternative was complete relocation of Centralia and Byrnesville, wiping both villages off the map. Once the people were removed, the theory went, government could step back and allow the fire to burn over an area of about fifteen hundred acres. "As applied to Centralia, this option would result in the fire's lasting many years, propagating to the extent of the natural fire barriers," the report said.

"Public health and safety considerations would make it mandatory to relocate all affected residents and businesses. . . . The maximum extent of the fire area is about 1,500 acres, which contains about 310 surface structures. . . . It is clear that a 'do nothing' approach would require relocating the *entire* communities of Centralia and Byrnesville."

OSM wanted the Bureau to consider one other technique, an old method used successfully to fight mine fires in the flat coal beds of western Pennsylvania. Called surface sealing, it attempts to extinguish a mine fire by cutting off its surface sources of air. Surface sealing was discussed in the report, but was so ridiculed that it was not even included on the list of options. The Bureau believed it would not work at Centralia because of the geology of the Anthracite Region. Here the subterranean strata were shattered and twisted, and many of the steeply pitched mines ran almost to the surface. Even if a surface seal was temporarily successful in cutting off the fire's air, the Bureau believed there was every likelihood that subsidence and erosion would create new openings.

Beasley, who had taught a course on mine ventilation at Virginia Polytechnic Institute before coming to OSM, was particularly enamored of this plan. Despite the Bureau's adamant rejection of surface sealing, OSM officials would not drop the idea. They came to believe the Bureau had rejected surface sealing because it *was* so simple. A trench, they reasoned, would keep many Bureau engineers and inspectors employed for years. It would be a dandy pension plan.

Over three hundred Centralia residents jammed the municipal building for the September 29 meeting, which was chaired by John Murphy of the Bureau and Earl Cunningham of OSM. Cunningham told the gathering a decision on an option would be made by Secretary of the Interior Cecil Andrus or his successor, there being a presidential election in November. OSM would make a recommendation to the secretary shortly after January 1, 1981.

A briefing paper prepared before the meetings clearly states OSM had a well-defined plan for consideration of public opinion on the options, the opinion of its own staff, and the opinion of an outside consulting firm that would be hired to assess the social and economic impact on Centralia of a project to stop the fire. "All essential data should be available to OSM by late November, 1980. By late January 1981 an issue paper and decision document should be completed. Assuming 30 days for decision, six months for developing engineering design and bid specifications, and 60 days for solicitation of bids and contract award, [work] could not commence until the summer-fall of 1981 on site construction activities," the briefing paper says.

15
The Big Picture

Evelyn and James Buckley and their five-year-old daughter, Shannon, in March 1981. Shannon suffered from asthma and other respiratory problems that were aggravated by the mine fire gases in their house at 202 South Locust Avenue, Centralia. Her problems began in fall 1980 and continued into early 1981, when her family doctor ordered her removed from the house as much as possible. (Photo: David DeKok, News-Item)

OSM's plan for careful selection of a Centralia option was certainly reasonable and might well have succeeded. The problem was that top officials of OSM, including director Walter Heine, were horrified by the cost estimates presented by the Bureau for stopping the mine fire.

Heine was from Pennsylvania, had worked for DER, and was sympathetic to the plight of the people of Centralia. So were Beasley and many of the other people who worked for OSM. It did not prevent them from deciding that spending many millions of dollars to save Centralia presented too much political risk to OSM. They would have decided to go ahead, Heine recalled, "if we knew it was going to work, even if what we proposed was going to cost 50 or 75 million bucks." But Heine feared for the very survival of the Abandoned Mine Lands Fund if a costly trench failed to stop the mine fire. This might cause the big coal producers—who bitterly opposed the $200-million annual tax on their coal that fed the AML Fund—to put pressure on Congress to repeal the tax. It might be years before the damage could be undone, if ever.

"We always had to look at the big picture," Heine said. "You've got to make the program survive if you're going to help the whole nation. It's not an easy decision." Whenever an agency of government talks about the need to look at the big picture, one can be certain that little people somewhere have been left to suffer. Centralia was no exception.

With the return of cool weather in September, the gases came back with a vengeance. It was a pattern that would repeat itself over the next several years. The gases would largely disappear during the warm summer months, although the seeming improvement was due only to the houses being better ventilated. When doors and windows were closed in the fall, the gases could not escape as easily and the levels rose.

Carbon monoxide was found in more homes, and more people began to show symptoms of carbon monoxide exposure. Monitors were placed in the homes of Mr. and Mrs. Tony Andrade, who lived in the first house north of the Coddingtons, and Mr. and Mrs. James Buckley, next-door-neighbors of the Andrades. One also went to the trailer home of Mr. and Mrs. Terry Burge on Peach Street, northwest of the Coddingtons.

DER assumed sole responsibility for gas monitoring on September 20 under contract to OSM. OSM paid the entire cost of the monitoring out of the AML Fund, right down to the salary and expenses of Edward Narcavage, the DER employee who became chief gas inspector in Centralia.

Narcavage, who lived in nearby Mount Carmel, quickly won the respect and affection of the gas-stricken families. He was almost a neighbor and, more importantly, had a reputation for telling the truth, which endeared him to the families but not to his bosses at DER. By the end of September he was working seven days a week, doing daily gas inspections at seventeen homes and weekly inspections at seven others. Narcavage was always willing to go the extra mile. If a resident suspected something was amiss with the gases, Narcavage would visit the house to check the air, even if he had already been there earlier, even if it was hours after quitting time.

The problem with the daily and weekly gas inspections was they recorded gas levels for a particular moment of the day, not the entire day. Sometimes a carbon monoxide incident would last for hours, other times only minutes. If Narcavage happened to arrive between bursts of gases, or on a day when none occurred at all, the testing result might lead an untutored observer, or an intellectually dishonest one, to conclude no concern about the gases was warranted.

Narcavage knew better, because he saw the monthly tapes from the Ecolyzers. The tapes often told a very different story than the daily testing results. Every carbon monoxide incident appeared on the tapes, providing a more accurate picture of the level of danger in a particular house. As we shall see, the Health Department would choose to emphasize only the lower, daily results.

At that time, the Health Department was not taking carbon monoxide into account at all in determining whether a house was unsafe, according to Dr. Riehl. The department had to have been aware of the growing number of carbon monoxide incidents, yet it based uninhabitability only on high volumes of carbon dioxide (greater than 0.5 percent) or low volumes of oxygen (less than 19.5 percent).

Gas testing policy was approved at a September 3 meeting in Harrisburg of representatives of the Health Department, OSM, and DER. It was agreed that DER would measure the gas levels, the Health Department would review them, and OSM would temporarily or permanently relocate any family whose house was deemed uninhabitable.

Carbon monoxide was fast becoming the premier public health problem in Centralia, but it was just as fast becoming unmentionable at the Health Department. The doctors maintained the pretense that there was no problem and even extracted a promise from John Murphy of the Bureau that any questions that Centralia residents asked the Bureau inspectors about the health effects of the gases would not be answered. All such questions were to be referred to Dr. Riehl. Bureau inspectors were scheduled to be pulled off the job on September 24, but the Health Department was taking no chances. Murphy's memo outlining the new policy went out on September 15.

At the September 29 meeting in Centralia, Deputy Secretary for Public Health Dr. Donald Reid went so far as to tell the people that carbon monoxide had not been found in any houses. He described the Health Department standards for carbon dioxide and oxygen, but said nothing about standards for carbon monoxide.

Earl Cunningham said OSM definitely would purchase any house the Health Department decided was no longer safe. He was not supposed to reveal this, but he saw no reason to keep the approved policy secret.

Later in the meeting an argument developed over whether gas data collected in the houses and the school would be available for public inspection. An OSM lawyer argued that the Privacy Act, a federal law, forbade release of this information unless authorized in writing by the homeowner. Joan Girolami insisted the data be made available to all residents. Anne Maloney said neighbors of any family whose house had been invaded by the gases had a right to know that fact. OSM and DER eventually backed down.

The plan to relocate families in houses that gases rendered uninhabitable, limited as it was, all but collapsed after two unexpected events within the OSM bureaucracy. The first was Heine's decision to scuttle the plan to pick an option by January 1981 for controlling the mine fire. Second and even more important was a ruling by John Woodrum, a lawyer for OSM, that AML Fund monies could not be used to relocate Centralia families. How was this lawyer in the regional office in West Virginia able to destroy the policy, after OSM's role in the plan had been approved by officials at several levels, including Christopher Warner, a lawyer in the Washington office?

After the September 29 meeting, John Coddington had approached OSM and challenged the agency to fulfill its promise to buy endangered homes. He was fed up with living in a house full of poison gas. A few days later, the Health Department quietly declared the Coddington house uninhabitable, informing Cunningham at OSM but not the Coddington family.

Cunningham prepared a letter on October 16 authorizing Coddington to move his family to temporary quarters at government expense while OSM decided what to do about the house, according to a November 8 memorandum from Region I director Patrick Boggs to Heine. "However, when that letter was [circulated to] the regional solicitor for surname, Mr. John Woodrum took issue with the approach and rendered an informal decision which essentially says that Public Law 95-87 does not contain the authority we intend to exercise," Boggs wrote.

Woodrum's memo to Boggs of October 31 is short and to the point:

> Please be advised that this office cannot at this time concur in expenditures of monies for relocation to Mr. Coddington, the Yokums [*sic*] or Lambs. We are of the opinion that Title IV does not envision or authorize such relocation expenses unless the property in question must be taken or vacated as an integral part of the reclamation and/or abatement process. The fact that the dwellings may have been declared uninhabitable would not in itself give us the authority to purchase the property or pick up the relocation expenses of the occupants.

Boggs was worried about the safety of the Coddington family and embarrassed that a public promise had been made by Cunningham that could not be kept. He wrote a memo to Heine the same day he received the bad news from Woodrum, urging a speedy resolution of the dilemma. When he received no response, he sent another memo on November 8.

> I urge you to study the position paper in the context of our dilemma and give us a decision in writing as soon as possible in order that we may abate this very serious problem in, and about, the Coddington residence. The levels of carbon dioxide in Mr. Coddington's home are excessively high. He refuses to leave without some assurance from OSM that we will finance the relocation. If he stays, there is a strong possibility that he and his family may be seriously harmed.

The relocation policy was dead. OSM officials in Washington seemed more concerned that Cunningham had compromised them by speaking forthrightly at the September 29 meeting. Cunningham was made the scapegoat; his career at OSM was finished. He transferred a few weeks later to the U.S. Geological Survey and accepted a posting to Casper, Wyoming. Cunningham's departure marked the end of a brief period in which OSM seemed sincerely committed to finding a solution to the Centralia problem. Henceforth the agency's goal would be to prevent itself from becoming entangled in a costly solution to the Centralia problem.

Despite the opposing legal opinion within OSM, Woodrum's interpretation of the surface mining law became OSM policy. This may have been by default. The Carter administration was coming to an end, and federal agencies become conservative at the change of administrations, preferring to let the new leadership resolve any controversial problems.

A few months is but an instant to the federal bureaucracy. In Centralia, time was counted in days, even hours, as the families endured a winter of illness, fear, and clanging gas alarms.

■ ■ ■

No one on Centralia Council had any inkling that OSM had broken most of the promises of September. Council was waiting patiently, even eagerly for January, certain that OSM would then announce what it planned to do to stop the mine fire.

The Health Department, pursuing its containment policy, did not inform the Coddingtons until December 4 that their home had been declared uninhabitable. Terry Burge also got his notice that day. No help of any kind was offered to either family, however. The official notice merely listed the telephone numbers of Earl Cunningham—who no longer worked for OSM—Walter Vicinelly of DER, and Elizabeth Eicherly of Pennsylvania Emergency Management Agency (PEMA), and none of these agencies had any plan to help the families.

Coddington needed no piece of paper to tell him the house was unsafe. The carbon monoxide alarm was sounding with ever more frequency, often in the wee hours of the morning. "Sometimes I just let it ring once," Coddington said. "But when it's going off and on, it's not just me that jumps out of bed. My wife and boy jump out, too. You actually don't know what you're going to meet."* Always it was the gases that triggered the alarm, but they knew a house fire could do it too.

Then it was time to call Narcavage, who never failed to roll out of bed and hurriedly drive to Centralia with his testing equipment. There was little he could do other than check the air, reset the monitor, and tell the Coddingtons to open their windows wider, but his presence mattered greatly to the Coddingtons and the other families who

---

*Quotes from John Coddington in this chapter come from an interview conducted on March 19, 1981, a day more fully described in Chapter 1. Coddington looked and sounded ill during the interview.

were in similar circumstances. They did not believe their homes were safe after an alarm until Narcavage said they were safe. Knowing this, he did his best to help them in any way he could. Beginning in November, the gases began to affect the Coddingtons noticeably. "Sometimes my wife gets headaches and can't hold anything in her stomach," said Coddington, speaking of the long winter of 1980–81. "Then I know there's something wrong and we have to open the windows a little wider.

"We have a lot of experience that way. If you sit up there in that apartment with the windows closed—I don't care what time of the night it is. You're watching TV. You're sitting in one of those lounge chairs. You wake up an hour later and you don't know what time it is. That's when you realize you have to open the door."

It was bitterly cold on Christmas Eve of 1980, but the windows of the Coddington apartment were wide open. Outside, the temperature was 18 degrees below zero, and inside, the furnace roared as it struggled to keep the home warm. Colleen Coddington awoke on Christmas Day and found the pipes in the house had frozen. Many evenings that winter the Coddingtons huddled in blankets to ward off the cold that, indirectly, was caused by the heat of a monstrous fire.

■ ■ ■

Some Centralia residents were asking for help from State Representative Robert Belfanti, a Democrat from Mount Carmel, even though he was not their legislator. The people felt estranged from their own representative, Ted Stuban, who lived thirty-five miles north of Centralia in Berwick and was doing virtually nothing to help his Centralia constituents. Belfanti was one of their own; he knew many of them from high school or social clubs, and he empathized with their plight. He began making calls to the Governor's Office in December and discussed the Centralia problem with members of the governor's staff. Belfanti believed Centralia could still be saved, although some families would have to relocate.

By mid-December, Centralia Council knew OSM had broken every promise it made in September. News accounts told council it would be at least eighteen months before OSM began a plan to stop the mine fire, not January as Cunningham had promised. OSM would not even consider a mine fire plan until it had completed a lengthy, painstaking study of the environmental impact of extinguishing the Centralia mine fire. It seemed not to matter to OSM that Bureau lawyers had never required the Bureau to do an environmental impact study before any of its later Centralia projects. In 1978, the Bureau had filed an environmental assessment, a much simpler and quicker undertaking, before beginning the project to close the vent holes and reinforce the fly ash barrier.

Council believed there was nothing it could do to change OSM policy. It felt helpless, cornered by matters beyond its control, and it took out its rage on Wilbert Malenka at the January 1981 meeting. Joan Girolami was unwilling to let council place all the blame on Bureau. She chided the men for not working harder to find a solution to the mess. Edward Polites, who now was president of council, protested that council was doing all it could. No one listened to them in Harrisburg or Washington, he said. Nobody cared.

An OSM team arrived in Centralia on January 8 to begin fieldwork for the environmental impact study. The visit was notable only for a strange incident that occurred late in the day, after team members, including Malenka, had returned to the municipal office. Helen Womer suddenly stormed into the room and began shouting at Malenka that he was not going to rip apart Centralia with a trench. Mrs. Womer considered Malenka the embodiment of all that Centralia had suffered at the hands of the federal government. Although Malenka was only doing the bidding of his bosses, he was the face of the Bureau in Centralia. She attacked him vehemently for almost ten minutes, then left as suddenly as she had arrived.

Once Helen Womer had wanted a trench, when three of her neighbors were forced from their homes by gases in 1969. Now she opposed it, knowing it would claim her own house first of all. It did not seem to matter to her that others might be endangered by her stand against a trench. She would proclaim her right as an American not to be moved from her home against her will.

Once Mrs. Womer had feared the gases, but no more. In August 1980, Narcavage recalled, she asked that bottle samples of air be collected in her house and tested for mine fire gases at the Bureau lab in West Virginia. When the results came back showing a 0.5 percent volume of methane, Mrs. Womer insisted her house be checked twice a day for gases. It was an unusual request, but it was granted.

One day in November, she told Narcavage to remove the gas monitor from her house and to stop his daily visits. He was stunned, because he was finding 6 percent carbon dioxide in the cellar almost every day. James Shober, who was Narcavage's immediate superior, asked Mrs. Womer to sign a statement to end the gas inspections, which she did. She gave no reason for her decision.

■ ■ ■

When the researchers hired by OSM to study the social and economic impact on Centralia of extinguishing the mine fire concluded their work, they knew they had been in a very special community. "There is a strong value system with a deep sense of roots," they wrote in their report. "Many of the families have lived in the same house either all their lives or at least 30 years, and have invested heavily in property improvements. . . . The community is a strong community in its sense of coherence and roots."*

They had spent six weeks the previous fall conducting 430 interviews in Centralia and adjacent sections of Conyngham Township. Virtually every household was surveyed. The report went far toward explaining why people like the Coddingtons and Womers were so reluctant to abandon their homes, even in the face of danger.

At the same time, it painted a muddy picture of how Centralia citizens believed OSM should stop the mine fire. Over half the households surveyed—including households that were not close to the fire—accepted the need for drastic action, action that might make Centralia temporarily unlivable and force many of them to relocate. Total excavation of the fire—the $84-million option—was favored by 36.7 percent and deemed acceptable by 39.8 percent. Total relocation of the community was preferred by only 16.3 percent but considered acceptable by 40.8 percent. The remaining options the Bureau presented the previous fall, including flushing, drew at least some support, but none so much as total excavation or relocation.

"Discounting for those expressing no opinion, Centralia can be termed a town divided," the report said. Although it should not have surprised anyone that the community could not achieve greater unanimity on such a serious question, federal and state officials would seize upon that statement as an excuse for denying aid to Centralia.

■ ■ ■

During the last two weeks of January and the first week of February, the number and severity of gas incidents rose sharply. Narcavage, who now had two assistants, Wayne Readly and Jeff Stanchek, had a plan he hoped would reduce the ferocity of the fire. Narcavage wanted to seal off most of the cavelike entrance of the Centralia mine drainage tunnel, leaving only a small opening at the bottom for water to escape. When he and another inspector entered the tunnel during the fall of 1980 to measure the volume of air being sucked in by the fire, they set

---

*Robins and Associates, "Socioeconomic Impact Analysis, Centralia Mine Fire Abatement Alternatives," Final Report, December 12, 1980.

up an anemometer and were astonished to find that 44,000 cubic feet of air per minute flowed into the tunnel, creating a wind that would "blow your hat off," Narcavage said.

It was a huge fire, and its need for oxygen was enormous. To Narcavage, it seemed only logical that cutting off this major source of air would retard the fire. It certainly could not hurt Centralia residents. He compared the burning mines to an old-fashioned coal stove. "If you open the bottom, you create a draft and it pulls up and in through the chimney," Narcavage said. "And that's similar to that fire there." The tunnel was 230 feet below the fire.

When he presented the idea to his bosses at DER and to Biggi at OSM, Narcavage met what he judged to be indifference. The inspector's sincere interest in solving the problem did not fit into the DER (and now Thornburgh administration) policy of rejecting any proposal to help Centralia that was not primarily funded by the federal government. But he misjudged Biggi; his idea would find favor at OSM, although in the end this would mean little.

OSM officials at the regional level—particularly Patrick Boggs— Bureau officials, and the technical staff at DER knew something had to be done but as usual could not agree upon what. Boggs told Biggi to organize a task force of federal, state, and local officials to discuss some ideas.

OSM wanted to drill about 10 boreholes between Locust Avenue and Wood Street to see if the fire had broken through the fly ash barrier. It also proposed to seal the Centralia drainage tunnel and to backfill the mine gangway beneath South Street that was believed to be the main conduit for poison gases from the fire to the homes. The latter project would be risky. If successful, it might end the gas threat to the families. If not, it could easily force more gas into the homes, including some not presently endangered.

The Bureau and DER wanted a full-scale exploratory drilling program of up to ninety boreholes that would map the fire boundary—or boundaries, since no one was certain anymore if there was one fire or several. OSM's drilling proposal would find only a section of the fire boundary, and David Simpson, chief of the Bureau's Wilkes-Barre office, believed a complete mapping was necessary before the fire could be properly fought.

The Bureau, in fact, already had $750,000 earmarked for the drilling, part of a $16-million appropriation for such work it had won from Congress the previous fall over the strenuous objections of OSM. Nevertheless, Simpson and Robert Oberman of DER gave qualified approval to the OSM proposal in early February when the Centralia Mine Fire Advisory Group chaired by Biggi held its first meeting.

None of the proposals would do anything to protect the families who were endangered by the mine fire's poison gases. OSM lawyers remained adamant that no money could be spent to acquire property in Centralia and relocate families.

Congressman James Nelligan hoped to do something about that. Nelligan, who lived near Wilkes-Barre, was the first Republican to represent the Eleventh District in many years. Aided by a split in the Luzerne County Democratic Party, and by the Reagan landslide, he had unseated U.S. Representative Raphael Musto the previous November.

Council members were quite surprised when Nelligan telephoned late in January and asked if they would meet with him in Centralia. They were accustomed to having to plead with their congressmen to come to Centralia and were more than happy to cooperate. The meeting was set for February 14.

Nelligan's uncle, who lived in northern Columbia County, had told him about the Centralia mine fire during the fall campaign—and warned him to stay away from the problem if he valued his political life. Similar warnings came from other Republican officials in Columbia County, including at least one member of the Board of Commissioners. This only intrigued him. He drove to Centralia one cold day in October, saw the steaming vent pipes, and decided then and there that if these people needed his help, he, Jim Nelligan, was not going to run away. It would become evident to those who came to know him that Nelligan had a monumental ego, but his cocksureness led him to eager acceptance of a challenge that others shunned.

■ ■ ■

It was in September that Tony Andrade, who was retired on disability from a state job, his wife Mary, and their daughter Diane had first experienced the extraordinary drowsiness described by Coddington. Narcavage tested the air in their house on South Locust Avenue and, to their dismay, found carbon monoxide. Their real difficulties, however, began in December. "My only problem was drowsiness and a few headaches," Andrade said. "But my wife and daughter—their eyes bothered them and they had headaches. They got very nauseous at times. They wouldn't be able to hold their food down." In the last two weeks of January and the first week of February, their carbon monoxide alarm rang over a dozen times, and some of the incidents involved volumes of the gas in excess of 100 ppm.

On February 6, Tony Andrade was notified by the Health Department that his house, like those of Coddington and Burge, was officially uninhabitable. Andrade was offered no help by the state. The bland notice simply arrived in the mail one day.

He was distraught. His entire life was in his home, and he had no idea what to do. His wife and daughter were constantly ill, and so was he (although he minimized it), but where could they go? He could not afford to pay for two houses. The big picture was not for Tony.

Dewitt C. Smith, director of Pennsylvania Emergency Management Agency, was cleaning out his "in" basket that week when a memo from the Health Department caught his eye. It informed PEMA that Tony Andrade of Centralia had been notified his house was unsafe owing to dangerous concentrations of mine fire gases. In the upper right-hand corner, Smith said, someone from PEMA had written that the Health Department had been trying to dump "this turkey"— meaning the mine fire problem—on PEMA for a number of years.* PEMA, the message continued, should not touch it with a ten-foot pole.

*Smith would not name the author of the message.

16
Fateful Tumble

Todd Domboski poses near the subsidence that almost claimed his life on February 14, 1981 in Centralia. The steam contains a lethal volume of carbon monoxide. (Photo: Fred Prouser, Associated Press)

CARRIE Wolfgang looked out her front window and saw a large group of men coming out of Tony Andrade's house. It was Valentine's Day, 1981, a Saturday. She decided they looked like government men and telephoned her daughter, Florence Domboski, who lived a block away on Wood Street, to tell her about it. Mrs. Domboski dispatched her twelve-year-old son, Todd, to find out who the men were. Todd took off on a run, cutting through the large yard between Eleanor Tillmont's house and Rita Kleman's. As he passed near his grandmother's house, which adjoined Mrs. Tillmont's, his sixteen-year-old cousin, Eric Wolfgang, called him over to show him a problem he had found in Todd's motorbike. Todd stopped briefly to view the work, then was off toward the Andrade's home once again.

He didn't get far before something caught his eye. It was a wisp of smoke rising from some sticks and leaves on the snowless ground a couple of feet from a big ash tree. His curiosity compelling him, he walked up to the smoke, which he could now see was coming from a small hole. Without warning, the ground gave way and he found himself up to his knees in a smoking hole. Todd tried to climb out, but the bottom dropped out once again and he sank to his waist. He yelled for help and tried to push himself out of the hole with his arms. That ground gave way, too, and Todd dropped out of sight, continuing to scream for help. A dense, foul-smelling cloud of steam and mine fire gases shot up out of the hole.

Todd's head was about three feet below the surface, but he felt himself sliding down further. He grabbed a thick root from the ash tree and hung on as the ground around and beneath him continued to collapse. Because of the steam, he could not see out of the hole. Todd could hear "wind," a strange whooshing sound caused by the mine fire far below sucking air. Whenever the "wind" blew, the ground beneath him collapsed a little more. Todd tried to pull himself closer to the surface, but his arms seemed paralyzed.

Eric, startled by Todd's frantic screams, sprinted to the edge of the hole and peered down, ignoring his own safety. There was no sign of Todd, but he could still hear his cries for help. The plume of steam was growing larger. It was hot and smelled like sulphur. Eric dropped to the ground and stuck his head and shoulders into the hole, marveling at the strange wind noise he heard. Suddenly he saw a patch of red, and remembered his cousin was wearing a red hunting cap that day.

"Grab my hand," he yelled. Gripping Todd's hand firmly, he dragged his cousin out of the hole and pulled off his jacket, thinking

Todd might actually be on fire. Eric was well aware of the mine fire problem and almost immediately surmised what had caused the hole to open. Todd's jacket was caked with warm mud, as were his jeans, but there was no fire. Eric tried to calm his hysterical young cousin, who had been in the hole about forty-five seconds, and pushed him into their grandmother's kitchen. Mrs. Wolfgang, after extracting from the pair what had happened, told Todd to run across the street and tell the men. She still did not know who they were.

It wasn't just any group of men Mrs. Wolfgang had spotted. This was the day Congressman Nelligan had picked for his meeting in Centralia to discuss the mine fire. With Nelligan were State Senator Edward Helfrick, State Representative Ted Stuban, State Representative Robert Belfanti, Andrew Bailey, acting director of OSM since the resignation of Walter Heine at the end of the Carter administration, Beasley, Biggi, Ivor Williams, and several county and borough officials. That such a stellar collection of officials was nearby when Todd dropped into the subsidence had people in Centralia shaking their heads in wonder for months.

The officials had concluded their meeting with Centralia Council and were partway through a tour of the mine fire impact zone. DER gas inspector Edward Narcavage was explaining the gas problem at Andrade's house when Nelligan noticed several persons running into the yard across the street. At that moment, Todd Domboski reached Locust Avenue and shouted to them that he had just fallen into a hole from the mine fire. He was still covered with mud and still very upset. The officials saw the steam billowing out of the hole and rushed to Mrs. Tillmont's yard. Senator Helfrick grabbed his aide, Frank Lawski, and told him to get Governor Dick Thornburgh on the car telephone.

Todd was rushed to Centralia Ambulance headquarters at the municipal building and given a dose of oxygen by a local paramedic. One of the officials urged Mrs. Domboski to take her son to Ashland State General Hospital for a blood gas test, which would determine if he had inhaled a dangerous quantity of carbon monoxide while in the hole. Fortunately, the blood gas test showed there was not a harmful amount of carbon monoxide in Todd's system, although he was hyperventilated.

Someone in the crowd that gathered in Mrs. Tillmont's yard dropped a cinder block into the subsidence hole. No one heard it strike bottom. Centralia's tiny police force finally shooed the citizens away for their own safety and stretched snow fence across the entrance to the yard. State Department of Environmental Resources gas inspectors at Centralia were ordered to mount a 24-hour watch at the site. Narcavage tested the steam with his portable carbon monoxide monitor and watched the needle zoom off the end of the dial. Todd would have died of asphyxiation had he been trapped in the hole for very many minutes.

Meanwhile, Helfrick had reached Thornburgh on the phone and had described Todd's accident to the governor, urging him to declare a state of emergency in Centralia. Thornburgh replied that he needed more information before making a decision. Helfrick, angered that matters had been allowed to deteriorate so much in Centralia, offered to meet with the governor and brief him personally. Thornburgh told Helfrick he could see him Tuesday morning. Monday was Presidents' Day, a state holiday, and the governor apparently did not want any business matters disturbing his three-day weekend.

■ ■ ■

Almost forgotten in the rush of events that day was the meeting Congressman Nelligan convened in Centralia that morning. He had called the February 14 meeting after first conferring in Washington with President Reagan's new and controversial Secretary of the Interior, James Watt, and officials of the U.S. Office of Surface Mining. Nelligan's problem was that good intentions alone would not solve the problem; only political power could do that. Unfortunately, he had only the enthusiasm and limited powers of a freshman congressman, albeit one who knew his way around Washington after a career in the General Accounting Office and on various congressional staffs. That and moral suasion just weren't enough to scare the Interior Department bureaucracy.

The new Secretary of the Interior, listening to his OSM advisers, told the new congressman that the department needed to know what the people of Centralia wanted the federal government to do about the mine fire—something that should have been blatantly obvious. For months, OSM had promised Centralia Council that it would decide the best method to fight the mine fire. Now Secretary Watt had passed the decision back to Centralia Council.

So at the meeting in Centralia that day, Nelligan pressed Centralia Council for a decision. His own opinion, he told council, was that short-term actions should include relocation of families with serious mine fire gas problems. Over the long term, Nelligan favored relocating the entire village of Centralia to a safe site a few miles away. Relocation would cost $14 million, much less than total excavation or even the intercept trench. The choice seemed majestically simple.

Council members did not want to make that decision. They remembered what had happened in 1978. They had endorsed an intercept trench proposed by the Bureau and had been criticized by some persons whose homes would have been purchased and demolished. The Bureau then had decided not to do the trench.

Mayor John Wondoloski suggested the decision be left to the Columbia County Commissioners. Nelligan, exasperated, accused him of passing the buck. Council vice president Robert Lazarski, angered by Nelligan's overbearing attitude, said he personally favored total excavation but felt it was unfair to ask councilmen who were paid only $20 per month to make such a momentous decision. After all, they were not mining engineers. The congressman said he could not take up Centralia's cause in Washington unless he had a firm idea of public sentiment in the village. He suggested a referendum on moving the village and council quickly agreed.

■ ■ ■

What caused the subsidence that almost claimed Todd Domboski's life? Mine maps of Centralia show there was once a sloping mine shaft at that location. Long ago it had been filled with dirt and rubbish. Hot steam from the mine fire gradually moistened and softened the mixture until its own weight made it collapse. In an interview with *Associated Press* a few days after the incident, OSM Region I Director Patrick Boggs said simply that the fire caused a mine chamber beneath Mrs. Tillmont's yard to collapse.

James Paone, chief of the Bureau of Mines' Division of Environment, had warned Centralia residents in 1978 that "serious subsidence problems all over town" would occur "in fifteen to twenty years" if nothing further was done to halt the spread of the mine fire. Only Paone's timetable was incorrect.

The impact on Centralia of Todd Domboski's near tragedy cannot be overestimated. For days afterward, the people spoke of little else. Todd's accident also forced Pennsylvania and the U.S. Department of the Interior to acknowledge the Centralia mine fire for what it was—a great public danger. The extensive press and television coverage now made it impossible for them to do otherwise. The real question was whether government would do the right thing—stop the mine fire once and for all—or simply appease Centralia with a showy gesture. Senator Helfrick said that day he considered *all* the state and federal Centralia projects from the past to have been mere appeasement.* He was certain, though, that his fellow Republican, Dick Thornburgh, would not equivocate.

*That apparently included his own. Helfrick's construction firm, K&H Excavating, did the second state project at Centralia in 1962. Helfrick was not an elected official at the time.

17
Watt and Thornburgh

James G. Watt, Secretary of the Interior from 1981 to 1983. (Photo: U.S. Department of the Interior)

ALL who were at Centralia on February 14, 1981 were horrified. Had Secretary Watt been there, or Governor Thornburgh, aid might have flowed to the beleaguered village within the fortnight. Nelligan had little influence with the governor, but he set out to persuade a skeptical Watt that Centralia must be helped. He thanked God, he later said, for letting Todd Domboski drop into the subsidence but sparing him, too.

James Watt had been a logical choice for Secretary of the Interior, given President Reagan's personal philosophy. Watt was an archconservative, a business sympathizer, and a proven foe of preservationists and traditional environmentalists. He had lobbied against federal clean water legislation while working for the Chamber of Commerce of the United States in the late 1960s, and most recently had been president of the Mountain States Legal Foundation, which supported conservative and pro-business causes in the courts. He had also worked in the Interior Department from 1969 to 1975. The James Watt that Centralia would come to know was a firm supporter of President Reagan's plan to greatly reduce the size and impact of the federal government and turn over as many of its functions as possible to the states.

Nelligan was an old friend of Watt's press secretary, Douglas Baldwin, who had served with Watt on the staff of Senator Milward Simpson (R–Wyoming) in the early 1960s. This friendship gave Nelligan more access to Watt than many congressmen enjoyed but did not, of course, guarantee the results he wanted.

Nelligan telephoned Baldwin early in the week after Todd's mishap and told him several Centralia families desperately needed Interior Department assistance to escape homes made dangerous by the mine fire. Watt called back the following day, Nelligan says, and they discussed Centralia at length. The Secretary was more receptive than he had been in January, but not much more. Nelligan recalls being lectured about how the Reagan administration was trying to cut federal spending, not seek new ways to increase it. Indeed, Interior Department programs were among those specially chosen by the administration for cutbacks.

Watt asked Nelligan why Pennsylvania could not help Centralia with state tax dollars. The congressman, stumped for an answer, admitted to not exploring the possibility. Parrying, Nelligan insisted the Centralia families needed immediate help. Aid would flow faster from the federal government than the state, he argued. Watt remained skeptical but told Nelligan he would take the matter under consideration.

Nelligan was pleased at the amount of press coverage Todd Domboski's accident was getting, although he did not mention this to Watt. The congressman had even been called by the Los Angeles *Times*. Nelligan believed publicity was vital to his plan to help Centralia, and like any politician, he enjoyed the attention.

■ ■ ■

State Senator Edward Helfrick was making little headway with Thornburgh, although the senator, a loyal Republican, was loath to admit it. Helfrick met with Thornburgh on Tuesday, February 17, and urged him to declare a state of emergency at Centralia. He was certain such a step, in addition to allowing the governor to use state emergency funds or take money from other parts of the budget to help Centralia, would speed emergency federal aid to relocate his endangered constituents. This the governor would not do, although to mollify Helfrick he told him his staff would study the matter.

A native of Pittsburgh, Thornburgh was both an engineer and a lawyer. He ran unsuccessfully for Congress in 1966 and became U.S. attorney for Western Pennsylvania after Richard Nixon was elected president in 1969. Thornburgh served as U.S. attorney until 1975 and won acclaim for his vigorous pursuit of political corruption cases, particularly in the Shapp administration.

He joined the Justice Department as a deputy attorney general in 1975 and stayed into the Carter administration. Thornburgh won the Republican gubernatorial nomination in 1978, defeating, among others, Philadelphia District Attorney Arlen Specter. He went on to defeat Pittsburgh Mayor Pete Flaherty in November, campaigning hard on the theme of corruption in the Shapp administration.

Only three months into his term, Thornburgh was severely tested by the Three Mile Island nuclear plant crisis of March 1979. His handling of the disaster, and his criticisms of Metropolitan Edison, which operated TMI, led some to believe him an environmentalist. That was not exactly the case, as his handling of Centralia would illustrate.

Thornburgh's political philosophy took a sharp turn to the right after Ronald Reagan was elected in 1980. As a young attorney in Pittsburgh, and even as U.S. attorney, he had been a moderate Republican in the Scranton and Rockefeller mode. Thornburgh increasingly modeled his policies on those of President Reagan and became one of Reagan's strongest supporters among the Republican governors. Although, in the case of Centralia, he insisted on a federal solution to the mine fire, something that was anathema to Secretary Watt and the philosophy of Reaganism, Thornburgh would push Watt only lightly, appearing reluctant to offend the Secretary or his conservative Republican supporters.

Helfrick departed convinced of Thornburgh's good intentions. There were further meetings that day with Lieutenant Governor William Scranton III, son of the former governor, and with Dewitt Smith of Pennsylvania Emergency Management Agency. Everyone told him how concerned they were, and Helfrick left Harrisburg believing help for Centralia was just around the corner. Events would quickly disabuse him of that notion.

Thornburgh's only response to Todd Domboski's accident was to appoint Smith to coordinate yet another study of the mine fire problem. Smith was also to head a task force of state and federal officials that would report to Thornburgh. No one from Centralia would be allowed to complicate the deliberations by attending the meetings. The only apparent purpose for this new task force was to fool the public into believing the governor was taking firm action to help Centralia. DER could have briefed the governor on the full dimensions of the Centralia problem in the course of an afternoon, had Thornburgh been interested. Membership of the new task force almost duplicated the membership of Biggi's Centralia Mine Fire Advisory Group—minus, of course, the Centralia representative.

Smith, it should be noted, is as able a public servant as was ever created, and he took his duties seriously. A retired commander of the Army War College who served with distinction in the field and at the Pentagon, Smith believed it was the duty of government to help the downtrodden. He seemed sincerely interested in finding ways for the state to help Centralia, but his first loyalty was to the governor. Sometimes the people of Centralia would forget that.

Smith's first visit to Centralia was February 19. He was accompanied by Commissioner of Deep Mine Safety Walter Vicinelly, whose office administered the gas monitoring program in Centralia, Helfrick, and about two dozen other state, federal, and local officials. When the car rounded the last curve on Route 61 before Centralia, Smith was amazed to see steam rising from the ground near the side of the highway. He turned to his companions and said it reminded him of "a poor man's Dante's Inferno."

"There's no question of the governor's concern about this," he told a reporter later that day. "My purpose here today is to listen, learn, and think about it."

Florence Domboski (left), mother of Todd Domboski, confronts DER official Walter Vicinelly (right), who came to Centralia with a delegation of state officials to inspect the mine fire situation five days after Todd's accident. Second from left is Joan Girolami. (Photo: David DeKok, News-Item)

Vicinelly was surrounded by a crowd of angry women as he and Smith walked along Locust Avenue after viewing the profusely steaming subsidence that almost claimed the life of Todd Domboski. Florence Domboski, still shaken by the accident, asked what the state was going to do to help Centralia. Vicinelly told her the state would do something, but not right away. It would most likely be a long-term project.

Councilman Robert Lazarski was alarmed to learn a few days later that DER had found methane, a potentially explosive gas, in the steam venting from the subsidence. Not until several worrisome days later, when the analysis came back from the Bureau of Mines lab in West Virginia, did Lazarski find out the steam contained only 0.05 percent methane, far below the explosive level of 5.0 percent. Still, he had to wonder what was going on in the mines below Centralia. Two residents of the impact zone, Mary Andrade and Sean Reilley, had heard thuds or rumblings beneath their respective homes. Perhaps it was methane explosions deep beneath the surface, where the concentration of the gas was no doubt greater. Perhaps it was the collapse of mine tunnels. Lazarski was spending many hours trying to organize help for Centralia and was getting nowhere.

For some families, it was the gases that caused the greatest worry. Nine-year-old Rachel Lamb, whose breathing problem temporarily improved after OSM flushed around the house in the summer of 1980, now was hooked to an oxygen machine virtually every night. Five-year-old Shannon Buckley suffered one respiratory ailment after another during the fall of 1980 and was hospitalized on several occasions. Her doctor finally ordered James and Evelyn Buckley to remove Shannon from the house for a week, and as much as possible after that, so on evenings and weekends they drove their daughter to the home of one relative or another. James Buckley grimly joked that they had become "stationary gypsies."

The gas alarm at St. Ignatius School sounded nineteen times in January and February, and parents became angered when the nuns refused to evacuate the school when an alarm occurred. After some parents threatened to pull their children out of the school, the nuns relented. Now students marched out of the building when the alarm sounded, just like during a fire drill. Narcavage, Stanchek, and Readly would hurry to the school to check the air, usually finding it safe by the time they arrived.

Thornburgh, silent as ever, was mulling over the report handed him by Smith and Vicinelly after their February 19 visit to Centralia.

The report has never been made public and is unobtainable under the state's weak Open Records Act, but after reading it Thornburgh ordered PEMA to offer the Coddington, Andrade, and Burge families the use of house trailers owned by the Department of Community Affairs (DCA). It was a minimal offer, costing the state nothing since it already owned the trailers.

Columbia County Emergency Management director Carl Sevison said state officials told him the trailer offer was the first phase of a three-phase solution to the Centralia problem. No one ever found out what the other two phases would be. Sevison said PEMA offered the trailers because Smith found a "potentially dangerous" situation in Centralia. Not *actually* dangerous, *potentially* dangerous. It was no mere slip of the tongue. Pennsylvania officials would never admit anyone in Centralia was in danger. That might lead to embarrassing questions about why the state was doing nothing to resolve the problem. Smith's statement was the first blow in the Thornburgh administration's battle to publicly minimize the danger of the Centralia mine fire. It was a battle they would ultimately lose, but the mental cruelty of the effort increased the suffering of the people.

Centralia was attracting attention from journalists around the world. Raymond Reilley of Byrnesville answered the phone at Centralia Fire Company one afternoon and found himself speaking to BBC Radio in London. NBC and ABC did stories for their evening newscasts. Most important of all, the *Associated Press* bureau in Harrisburg took a great interest in the story. The *News-Item* began relaying the best of its Centralia stories to the *Associated Press,* and many of them went out over the wire. This gave the Centralia story a much wider audience—in effect, all of North America, Western Europe, Japan, and Australia. These dispatches, in turn, prompted some of the larger newspapers, magazines, and broadcasters who subscribed to the news service to send their own reporters and photographers to Centralia. *United Press International* covered the story, too. There would prove to be an almost insatiable interest in Centralia stories, and OSM found itself answering questions from reporters almost daily.

One Centralia resident, Helen Womer, believed the mine fire was receiving entirely too much attention from the media. She had admonished Todd Domboski not to talk to reporters, a warning he steadfastly ignored. In a February 24 letter in the *News-Item,* Mrs. Womer said there was no mine fire under Centralia, although she acknowledged that a mine fire outside the village was causing dangerous levels of gas in the homes of some of her neighbors in the impact zone. This she attributed to the "incompetency and bungling" of government agencies like the Bureau. Mrs. Womer intended to stay in Centralia, and woe unto anyone who believed it was too dangerous to remain. "As long as there is a shred of hope left in me and I have the support of my family and friends, I will work tirelessly against monumental odds toward keeping as much of Centralia intact as is safely possible," she wrote. Although she acknowledged the gas danger in this letter, she would soon deny there was any danger at all.

State Representative Robert Belfanti, meanwhile, was attempting to educate key members of the state General Assembly about what was happening in Centralia. He approached House Minority Leader James Manderino and carefully suggested that perhaps the House Mines and Energy Management Committee should hold a public hearing in Centralia to explore the mine fire problem. He warned Manderino that eventually there would be a catastrophe in Centralia; not only would it look bad in the local papers, but it would make Pennsylvania look bad in the eyes of the nation. Sooner or later, Belfanti said, word would get out that the mine fire had been burning for nineteen years and neither federal nor state government was willing to accept responsibility. The hearing was scheduled for March 12.

OSM officials were increasingly concerned about the potential for more subsidence in Centralia. In a February 18 letter to Boggs, Biggi wrote: "Based on a preliminary review of mine maps by Carl Sauer, similar conditions exist along the crop line in the area of this newly-formed hole [the Domboski subsidence] which could result in further incidents of subsidence and gas venting." There was another problem, too, Biggi wrote. "The detection of possible combustion gases venting from this hole represents an additional serious threat to the public health and safety because of the potential for an underground or near-surface explosion of the gases."

OSM approved closing the hole in a briefing paper dated February 23, although the work would not commence for almost a month. It is clear from the briefing paper that doubts remained about the wisdom of this action, because it was noted that DER would monitor nearby homes to see if any change in the gas levels occurred after the hole was closed.

Smith's task force on the mine fire held its first meeting on March 6 and made no decision—at least none that was announced publicly—whether to recommend Thornburgh declare a state of emergency in Centralia. This was one of the main purposes of the meeting. John Comey, Smith's spokesman, said afterward that Smith planned to conduct a new study of the mine fire and make a report to Thornburgh within a month. Centralia residents began marking off the days. They liked Smith and were certain the report would help them.

Biggi's warning about further subsidences in Centralia was borne out on March 10. Anne Maloney, who lived across South Street from Tony Gaughan, was burning some refuse in her back yard when she saw the ground near her drop several inches. Most of the subsidence had occurred far below the surface, but poison gases detected by Narcavage and Readly a few inches above the depression left little doubt as to its cause. Coming only a month after the Domboski incident, the new subsidence served to remind people of the grave dangers they faced.

Mayor John Wondoloski was in a state of agitation, showing reporters and anyone else who happened along a letter he received that very morning from Patrick Boggs of OSM warning of subsidence danger everywhere in the impact zone. The letter likewise warned that residents could be exposed to "sudden high levels of toxic gases" if a subsidence occurred beneath a house. Mayor Wondoloski issued an on-the-spot proclamation urging people to stay out of their back yards, a wise precaution, though difficult to follow.

Eight impact zone residents told their stories to the House Mines and Energy Management Committee at the March 12 hearing. It was a day of revelations for committee members, many of whom were not from coal mining areas and had little idea what they were being dragged to Centralia to see. "We have a problem all over this part of town, of people getting sick and not holding anything in their stomach," John Coddington told them. "When you're looking at TV, next thing you know an hour and a half has gone by and the program's over."

Tony Andrade tried to explain why his family and the others were reluctant to move into the trailers offered by PEMA: "If I had the means, I'd walk out of that house. But I'm not going to walk out of there on a temporary basis when I don't know how long temporary is. You're asking me to abandon what I've worked for all my life."

Christine Oakum made an eloquent plea to the committee to consider the safety of children in the impact zone. "A Bureau of Mines representative told us a house could be checked out okay when the inspector comes in the morning," she said, "but that in the afternoon a strong surge of gas could come in and kill every living thing in the house."

Helen Womer presented her belief that there was no mine fire under Centralia, and stated that a conspiracy existed among state and federal officials to empty Centralia of people so they could grab the coal under the village. Criminal indictments should be sought, she said, against the Bureau officials who ordered the trenching stopped in 1969.

State Representative Ivan Itkin, a Democrat from the Pittsburgh area, asked General Smith if it wasn't true that Thornburgh had $5 million available for emergency projects, a sum more than adequate to relocate the endangered families. Smith said it was true.

■ ■ ■

That evening, three employees of OSM were working late at the agency's headquarters in downtown Washington, D.C., trying to make sense of the Centralia mine fire. Two of them, Andrew Bailey and Charles Beasley, had witnessed Todd Domboski's brush with death on February 14. It was clear to them OSM no longer had the luxury of doing nothing about the Centralia mine fire. Their immediate superior, Perry Pendley, agreed. There were too many stories about Centralia on television and in the press to continue studying the mine fire indefinitely. If the Bureau's recommendations for Centralia were unacceptably expensive, then perhaps they could devise some less grandiose proposals of their own. Shortly before midnight, they delivered the options to Pendley, who was waiting at his office at the Interior Department. He would deliver them to Secretary Watt in the morning.

The new options were far more modest than those proposed by the Bureau the previous fall. They ranged in cost from nothing at all, for doing nothing, to $5 million, and reflected Beasley's firm belief the mine fire problem could be solved without digging a massive trench costing tens of millions of dollars.

Option 1 would involve relocating only the four families—Coddington, Burge, Andrade, and Buckley—whose homes had been declared unsafe by the Health Department, and only for thirty days. They estimated this plan would cost about $9,000. It was viewed as a short-term response that would buy time to hold additional discussions with Pennsylvania officials.

Option 2 was an expanded version of Option 1. Under this plan, all families living in what OSM defined as the "outcrop area" would be relocated for up to thirty days at an estimated cost of $30,000 to $50,000. The outcrop area was defined as the area between the outcrop of the Buck vein and South Street, where the amount of cover above the sloping vein was believed to exceed one hundred feet. It was about sixteen acres.

Helen Womer tells members of the Mines and Energy Management Committee that she does not believe there is any mine fire under Centralia. Mrs. Womer vigorously opposed relocation of families in the mine fire impact zone, arguing that none of them were truly endangered. (Photo: David DeKok, News-Item)

Option 3 would involve OSM purchase of all houses in the sixteen-acre area, relocation of the occupants, demolition of the houses, and excavation of all overburden and coal. The pit would then be lined with clay and backfilled. The total cost was estimated at $4 million.

This excavation proposal, which was key to Beasley's plan to protect the remainder of Centralia, was based on a number of assumptions. One was that the mine fire was only in the Buck vein. If this was true, it would not matter if the fire went around the excavated area and moved beneath houses beyond South Street. The depth of the cover would make it highly unlikely the gases could reach the houses. If the mine fire had jumped to the Seven Foot or Skidmore veins, which outcropped beyond South Street, however—a distinct possibility after nineteen years—there was no telling how many families would be endangered. Beasley was also assuming the fire would not race out of control once the excavation opened new and plentiful sources of air. It was a constant source of dread for anyone planning to dig a trench to block a mine fire.

Another part of this plan became holy writ to OSM. Beasley hoped to deal with the rest of the mine fire by cutting off its oxygen supply. It seemed so simple, so logical. The fire was fed a massive volume of air by the Centralia mine drainage tunnel; close it off and other portals like it and the mine fire would eventually go out. "The fire would be effectively contained, with little possibility that the fire would create subsidence, or that gases could penetrate to the surface to endanger other parts of town," Beasley wrote.

Option 4 involved only purchase and demolition of the houses in the sixteen-acre area and fencing of the area where they once stood, at a cost of $1 million. Option 5 was a more costly version of Option 3, priced at $5 million, and Option 6 was the do-nothing option.

On March 16, Watt summoned Pendley, Bailey, and Beasley to his office to discuss the options and recommend the one they considered the best. Watt was a lawyer and knew nothing about mine fires other than that they existed. Beasley told him it was imperative to remove the families from the sixteen-acre area. "I guarantee you there will be more subsidence areas, because those gases are weathering that roof and it's going to keep falling," Beasley said. The next subsidence might well claim a life. He explained his plan for excavating the area after the families were out of the way.

It was not to be. Beasley's plan fell victim to Watt's desire to be a good member of the Reagan team and do all he could to cut federal spending. Watt, like Beasley, saw that the Interior Department had to do something to help Centralia, but he chose Option 4, the cheapest of the permanent relocation options. "Reagan was really holding federal spending down tightly," Beasley said. "I think he [Watt] got caught in that whole process of just stopping everything. Nothing was being funded. . . . The money was there, obviously. Five million dollars is not preclusive to that fund. It's a big fund."

Excavation might have eliminated the gas threat. It could also have revealed the fire to be so much larger than expected that the department would have no choice but to enlarge the trench. Watt could have had no illusions that relocation would end the danger to Centralia. The option paper for the project spells that out in detail. Interior officials believed selection of Option 4 would "place responsibility for final solution on the state and local government." There would be no further federal spending to help Centralia, as far as the Secretary of the Interior was concerned.

Since Interior planned to abdicate any further responsibility to help Centralia, there would be no need for the drilling, backfilling, and tunnel-sealing plans approved earlier. These were canceled on Beasley's orders. Likewise, it seemed silly to them to allow the Bureau to spend $750,000 to do exploratory drilling at Centralia, drilling the Bureau believed was crucial to designing an effective project to stop the mine fire. OSM decided to take the money from the Bureau to help finance the relocation. The remaining $250,000 came from a Bureau antisubsidence project in western Pennsylvania.

No one in Centralia had any inkling any of this was going on. As far as the families were concerned, OSM remained stonily insistent that no monies from the Abandoned Mine Land Fund could be spent to relocate them. Unknown to them, OSM lawyers had reversed their position, ruling that Watt's emergency powers under the Surface Mining Control and Reclamation Act allowed him to acquire property to protect the public from abandoned mine land dangers. The last remaining problem for the Interior Department would be persuading Thornburgh to sign a memorandum of understanding committing the state to paying the entire bill to put out the mine fire.

■ ■ ■

The collapse of John Coddington the night of March 19 pushed the people of the impact zone—with some exceptions, like Helen Womer—to the edge of panic. They wondered who would be next, and if they would be so lucky as Coddington to have someone nearby to rescue them. They had heard of Narcavage's statement the Coddingtons might have perished that night if John had not fallen off the bed, alerting his wife and son.

Perhaps by coincidence, Nelligan was briefed the morning of March 20 on details of OSM's plan to relocate families in the sixteen-acre area. He was told Thornburgh had not yet agreed to the plan, primarily because the governor was traveling outside the state and could not be reached. There had been discussions with the state's lobbyists in Washington, and with Robin Ross, deputy counsel to the governor.

Nelligan asked if he could release the news to the public. He was told to go ahead as soon as Arlen Specter and John Heinz, Pennsylvania's U.S. senators, had been notified. Nelligan caught a plane to Wilkes-Barre late that afternoon and was met at the airport by reporters from the three television stations in his district. His staff had alerted the stations to be present for a major announcement.

No one from the Governor's Office knew the announcement was coming, which may well have been a ploy by the Interior Department to place irresistible public pressure on Thornburgh to sign the memorandum of understanding. "The plan is definite, the agreement is not," said Nelligan press aide David Nathan that evening. "I'm not certain Governor Thornburgh knows about it." Nathan denied that Coddington's collapse had anything to do with the timing of the announcement.

Watt had Thornburgh over a barrel, and the governor knew it. The people of Centralia were crying out for relief, and the pressure on Thornburgh to help them was growing. Yet Paragraph D of the memorandum of understanding could easily be interpreted to mean Pennsylvania was accepting all further responsibility for stopping the fire. "As soon as possible thereafter the entire site will be conveyed to the Commonwealth of Pennsylvania, which will undertake any further activities which it deems appropriate," it read.

In the end, Watt won. He and Thornburgh met in Washington the morning of March 30 to sign the memorandum of understanding, soon to become known in Centralia as the memorandum of misunderstanding. It was the day John Hinckley shot President Reagan and several other persons outside the Washington Hilton.

Why did Thornburgh sign it? One suspects it was because the blame would shift to him if the relocation was canceled and someone died.

The memorandum of understanding, when its full implications became known three weeks later, proved a great embarrassment to the Thornburgh administration. In a letter to Thomas Larkin and Joan

Girolami later that year, Robin Ross explained why Thornburgh signed the agreement:

> Governor Thornburgh rejected Interior's attempt to relieve itself of its responsibilities for the fire and its consequences. The facts of the situation seemed then and still seem today to dictate approval of the plan to acquire the houses and disapproval of the attempted delegation of responsibility.
>
> The owners faced an intolerable threat and the likelihood of receiving nothing for their homes when they had to move to save their lives. Interior was offering a way to help these people, and it could not be rejected by the Governor even before the homeowners were given the opportunity to consider the offer. In light of these considerations, the reasons for the Governor's signature on the Memorandum are obvious.

18
Thornburgh in Centralia

Governor Dick Thornburgh answers questions from reporters during his visit to Centralia on March 31, 1981. State Senator Edward Helfrick (R–Mount Carmel) is second from left. Thornburgh announced agreement by the Interior Department to relocate up to thirty families in the mine fire impact zone. He took most of the credit for himself, although his own role was minimal. (Photo: David C. Haupt, *News-Item*)

GOVERNOR Thornburgh's visit to Centralia on March 31, 1981 seems in retrospect to have been little more than a political stunt. Thornburgh used the occasion to take most of the credit for OSM's plan to relocate up to thirty Centralia families. He deserved little or none of it.

After Thornburgh and Secretary Watt signed the memorandum of understanding on March 30, the governor's staff moved quickly—and quietly—to arrange for Thornburgh to visit Centralia the following day. Selected newspaper and television reporters were notified by telephone that evening. The staff took pains to keep the visit secret from local Democratic legislators like State Representatives Robert Belfanti and Ted Stuban. This was to be an event for Republicans only.

Thornburgh could have come in February, when the fear and confusion were at their peak and the visit would have boosted morale, but he was too busy, could not be bothered, or perhaps simply feared to step into a situation of political risk. The people would have asked him for something he had decided the state could not give them, an end to the fire.

Thornburgh and Congressman Nelligan flew to Centralia in a state police helicopter, arriving at 11:30 A.M. A large contingent of lesser officials, press aides, and camp followers arrived by car. His staff had succeeded in keeping the visit secret from the Democrats. Belfanti did not learn of it until late in the morning, when it was already too late to drive the sixty miles from Harrisburg.

Thornburgh's first stop was a private meeting with members of Centralia Council to brief them on "his" plan to relocate the families. When Thornburgh finally strode into the main hall with Nelligan and Helfrick, John Coddington rose and led the people in a round of applause. Few Centralians could avoid being caught up in the good feelings generated by the visit; had not the governor saved them from the mine fire? One man in the audience decided to record Thornburgh's speech on a small tape recorder he brought with him.

The governor began his speech on a political note, lauding Nelligan and Helfrick and saying nothing about Belfanti or any other Democratic officeholders who had worked to help Centralia. They would get a cursory mention later in his remarks. There was scattered applause, for neither politician was perceived to have done much to help Centralia, although Nelligan did deserve a large share of credit for the relocation and Helfrick for focusing Thornburgh's eyes on the problem when his inclination was to ignore it. Thornburgh introduced General Smith and the applause was loud and sustained.

The governor attempted to justify the long state inaction in Centralia by making the claim that no one in his administration had any information about the mine fire problem when the crisis broke in February. He spoke of his Centralia task force as if it had spent every day since February in Centralia, when in fact Smith had visited only a few times.

Thornburgh described the negotiations with Secretary Watt of the previous day: "This agreement establishes a plan to permanently relocate those families in Centralia who feel their health and safety is being jeopardized by the mine fire. An important part of this plan is that it lets the affected families decide for themselves whether or not to move," he said. "And I suggest to you this is the most sensitive and humane approach to the difficult issue of health and safety." The governor emphasized he viewed relocation as "a first step in solving the problems of the mine fire . . . which will observe its unhappy twentieth anniversary next year." Perhaps understandably, Thornburgh did not recount how a previous Republican administration in Harrisburg had allowed the fire to burn out of control, setting the stage for the present calamity.

"I pledge . . . that we will continue to do all that we can *responsibly* [his emphasis], and all within our power and jurisdiction, to assist those who desire to relocate to new homes, as well as minimize any adverse economic effects this may have on the borough," he continued. The key words here are "responsibly" and "within our power and jurisdiction." Although it appears Thornburgh is pledging the state will do all it can to extinguish the mine fire, he in fact is merely reiterating what had been his position all along, that Pennsylvania did not have enough money to deal with the problem, which was a federal responsibility anyway.

"The special task force that was established under the direction of General Smith will continue to monitor relocation efforts and economic impacts while they continue to work with other federal and state authorities toward long-term solutions to the fire," he said.

It was during the question-and-answer session with reporters that Thornburgh veered sharply into the realm of make-believe. The first question was whether his task force had looked "at the problem of extinguishing the fire."

"That problem is being studied on a continuing basis by the Department of the Interior and the task force, and particularly our Department of Environmental Resources is lending whatever expertise they have to that effort," he answered. Thornburgh had to know by now that Watt had no intention of doing anything about the mine fire. Beyond that, it was deceitful of him to suggest more study of the mine fire was needed. Most of the principals knew what had to be done. It was simply a matter of who would pay the bill, and Thornburgh didn't want to pay the bill any more than Watt did.

"No one, as of today, has come up with a magic wand that can be waved to put out this fire," he continued. "But the efforts to deal with the technology of the fire, whether it can be put out, how it can be put out, whether it is desirable to do so, those matters are all being carefully studied within the Department of the Interior, as I satisfied myself yesterday."

One of the reporters asked Thornburgh to describe what would be done after the relocation, since he had described relocation as only a first step. "Well, I don't want to indicate, I don't want to tell you more than I know," Thornburgh said. "What this action this morning represents is the most that can be done now to alleviate what we think is the concern of highest priority. And that is the health and safety of the residents of this community. The study and monitoring of the conditions here continue, with an eye toward insuring the next step, whatever it may be, will be taken in the shortest possible time."

Another reporter asked if Thornburgh had given his staff a timetable for coming up with a permanent solution to the mine fire. The governor made a brilliant escape: "My understanding is that the Department of the Interior hopes to have finished a study by July 1 that evaluates whether and how a quote, permanent solution, unquote can be achieved. I'm not sure that there *is* [his emphasis] a permanent solution. . . . General, is General Smith here? Is that date correct?"

"I think it's at that time they not only expect to have it in, but to have rendered a judgment on it," Smith said reassuringly.

This study never appeared, was never again discussed, and did not appear in the voluminous Interior Department records on Centralia that can be examined under the Freedom of Information Act. It appears to have been conjured up by the governor to cut off questions about his lack of a plan to extinguish the fire.

Thornburgh carefully avoided acknowledging during the speech or press conference that the state believed anyone in Centralia was endangered by the mine fire gases. When a reporter asked if the state would advise a family in "extreme personal danger" from the gases to join the voluntary evacuation, Thornburgh gave a disingenuous answer that waxed rhapsodic on what a "fine, decent community" Centralia was and how hard it would be to leave it. "I think that's an awfully tough decision to make, and I believe it must be made by each individual, and in discussion with their neighbors and their families, whether or not their concern is such that they want to move," he said. Nothing would be allowed to disturb the Health Department myth that Centralia residents faced no physical danger from the gases, that they had worried themselves into believing there was one.

Thornburgh has a notorious temper that is easily provoked during press conferences. He remained calm until close to the end of the Centralia press conference, when he was asked what led Secretary Watt to reverse the previous policy that no money from the Abandoned Mine Land Fund could be used to relocate Centralia.

"I think what moved him to act was a desire to help," Thornburgh snapped. "I think there are a lot of people in Washington today who are tired of being told that they are insensitive to human needs. I think Jim Watt expressed, on the part of the administration in Washington, a genuine desire to be of help in time of need for the people in this community."

"Will the state be picking up any of the tab whatsoever for the project?" another reporter asked.

"We've had our task force and PEMA people here for the last forty-five days, and we'll devote whatever resources are necessary to help solve the problem," the governor insisted.

After the press conference, Thornburgh was driven to the mine fire impact zone, where he visited the Andrade, Coddington, and Lamb homes. He had coffee with Tony and Mary Andrade, and afterward Andrade expressed heartfelt thanks.

Introduced to John Coddington, Thornburgh said, "You've got a heckuva way of getting attention, fellah," referring to the night Coddington was overcome by mine fire gases. Coddington invited the governor to feel the heat rising from a borehole next to his former service station, then impishly warned him not to get too close.

Thornburgh then visited the bedside of Rachel Lamb, who was attached to her oxygen machine for the asthma that was so aggravated by the gases in the house. She presented him with a letter. David Lamb presented Thornburgh with a petition bearing fifteen hundred signatures asking the state to take action on the mine fire problem and for the governor to visit Centralia. Lamb and some other Centralia residents had gathered the signatures before Thornburgh decided to visit Centralia.

As he walked along Locust Avenue, Thornburgh commented on the many strands of red ribbon hanging from trees, light poles, and houses. Someone told him it symbolized the people of Centralia held hostage by the mine fire. Offered a ribbon, he pinned it to his lapel. Joan Girolami and some of her friends were behind the ribbon hangings, taking a cue from the yellow ribbon hung during the recent Iranian hostage crisis. To them, it also symbolized government red tape that prevented anything from being done to stop the mine fire. No one told Thornburgh that.

The governor's final stop of the day was the steaming vent pipes, where he posed for pictures. One photograph from the session shows Thornburgh and Helfrick wincing, eyes shut tight, after a gust of wind blew the hot, sulfurous steam in their faces. That would be the closest the governor ever came to knowing the misery of the mine fire.

19
Organizing the Resistance

Edward and Kevin O'Hearn on the porch of their house on South Locust Avenue, Centralia, in 1981. Their parents, Francis and Eleanor O'Hearn, were members of Concerned Citizens Against the Centralia Mine Fire, which was organized in 1981 to fight for an end to the mine fire problem. The protest signs were a relatively permanent fixture. (Photo: David DeKok)

WHEN David Lamb handed Governor Thornburgh the petition, he told him it was circulated by Concerned Citizens Action Group Against the Centralia Mine Fire, a group neither Thornburgh nor many others had heard of. Most Centralians would come to know the group as Concerned Citizens and would quietly applaud its goal of ending the mine fire problem for all time. Others, inside and outside Centralia and probably including the governor, believed this band of activists to be a plague.

There had always been citizen activists in Centralia, but they had not been organized. Helen Womer and a few of her neighbors had tried to win help in the summer of 1969. Tony Gaughan and his wife had made an attempt in 1976. Joan Girolami had led a few of her neighbors in a letter-writing campaign in 1979 and 1980, trying to win relocation for families with gas in their houses. They annoyed the Bureau of Mines, but few outside the Bureau paid them much attention, particularly in the news media. Mrs. Girolami made little effort to expand her ad hoc group beyond the narrow confines of East Park Street.

Much had happened since then, and there were a few persons in Centralia who believed the problem had become so serious they could no longer wait for Centralia Council's well-intentioned hand-wringing to win them deliverance. Joan Girolami was one, Christine Oakum was another, and so was Eva Moran, a former member of council who had a reputation as somewhat of a troublemaker.

Mrs. Moran, who ran a tavern and candy store on Locust Avenue, recruited Thomas Larkin to their little cell of freethinkers. Larkin, who lived in an apartment across the street from Mrs. Moran, was a fifth-generation Centralian who had studied for the Catholic priesthood, then decided after four years of seminary not to accept ordination. Larkin was thoughtful, intelligent, and well-spoken, and Mrs. Moran decided he would be good for the group.

They had their first meeting March 2 around Mrs. Moran's kitchen table and talked long into the night about the mine fire and how Centralia Council seemed to be doing nothing about it. During this long conversation, Concerned Citizens was born. By the time of the next meeting on March 17, Concerned Citizens had twelve members. Most of them, with the exception of the Morans and Larkin, lived in the impact zone and had gas monitors in their homes, or worried they soon would.

Mrs. Oakum wanted Concerned Citizens to fight for accurate information about the health effects of carbon monoxide, which she still could not obtain from the Health Department. Larkin, recalling there had been a mine fire in Carbondale, suggested they find out how people there coped with it. Lamb urged they circulate a petition demanding Governor Thornburgh pay a personal visit to Centralia to see the disaster firsthand.

The petition became their first project. They canvassed Centralia in three days, working with extra fury after John Coddington was overcome by the gases the evening of March 19. They trudged through a snowstorm the following day, and rejoiced that evening when Congressman Nelligan announced that up to thirty Centralia families would be relocated by the Interior Department. That gave them pause, until they remembered the fire was still burning and many in Centralia would not be helped by the new relocation project.

Not many Centralia residents joined Concerned Citizens. Eleanor O'Hearn, who was secretary, estimates the maximum dues-paying membership at 60, of which no more than 25 were active. Out of a Centralia population of 1,018 (1980 census), that doesn't seem like a lot, but in many communities the number of people willing to work in a cause is small compared to the number who support the cause but prefer to root from the sidelines.

Concerned Citizens' next project—support of a yes vote on the mine fire referendum that Nelligan proposed at the February 14 meeting—would bolster that theory. It would also establish the group as a force to be reckoned with. Centralia Council had voted to conduct the referendum on May 19, the day of the regular state primary election. It would not be binding, but the symbolic value would be great. Council planned three public meetings to brief residents, particularly those who didn't live close to the mine fire, on the seriousness of the fire threat.

Any journalist who thought the Centralia story had ended with Thornburgh's visit was sorely mistaken. Reporters from across the nation and around the world continued to make their way to the mountain village, and the events that transpired in the six weeks leading up to the referendum were consistently newsworthy, if not downright bizarre.

Thornburgh had barely left Centralia when controversy developed over which homes would be acquired during the relocation. Joan Girolami was dismayed to learn her house had once again been excluded from the list, despite periodic gas alarms. OSM was acquiring only those houses within the sixteen-acre area it had defined. That meant Bob Gadinski's side yard could be acquired, but not his house. He protested and won an exception, but Mrs. Girolami was again left behind.

At the first informational meeting on April 20, two Bloomsburg businessmen appeared and said they represented a corporation that wanted to purchase Centralia for $30 million for the coal beneath it. Burt Wandell, who billed himself in his advertisements as a "Christian realtor," and David Linnet, who ran a woodstove factory, said the firm would pay people twice the value of their homes. The identity of the company had to remain secret because of fears other corporations would rush in if the identity became known. No one bought their story. Linnet and Wandell had good reputations in the Bloomsburg business community, but their refusal to name the firm severely damaged their credibility in Centralia, and council did not invite them back for a second visit. Though Linnet and Wandell were soon forgotten, their visit to the April 20 meeting overshadowed a far more important development. Council president Edward Polites announced that council had learned the Interior Department did not plan to participate in any further projects to stop the mine fire. It would simply be allowed to burn. Thornburgh administration officials were left sputtering four days later when an Interior Department spokesman publicly confirmed the report, saying the memorandum of understanding signed by the governor committed Pennsylvania to fund any future projects at Centralia. Robin Ross, deputy legal counsel to Thornburgh, protested that the department's interpretation of the agreement did not agree with that of the state, but his rebuttal did not ease the embarrassment for the Thornburgh administration.

Centralia residents must have felt like people on a sinking ship after the last lifeboat has departed. The Interior Department would not help them, and the state showed no inclination to help them. There were jokes about appealing to the Soviet Union for foreign aid. Larkin, who had been elected president of Concerned Citizens, sent a letter of protest to President Reagan. "You have made a commitment to help the small towns of this great country," Larkin wrote. "Centralia is one of those communities. Please, Mr. President, don't let the Department of the Interior abandon us."

Council pushed ahead bravely with its plans for the referendum, trying in vain to persuade Nelligan to attend one of the two remaining public meetings. The referendum had been his idea, and Lazarski believed Nelligan had a moral obligation to come to Centralia and answer questions. Nelligan would later say he did not have time to attend and would make it quite clear he viewed the meetings as unimportant.

One of the more important persons council did persuade to speak was Dr. Joseph Weber, the internal medicine specialist from Ashland who treated John Coddington the night he was overcome by the gases. Weber had no obligation to protect Thornburgh's flank by denying that the people of Centralia were in any danger from the gases, and he gave them straight information about the dangers of carbon monoxide, information the Health Department had withheld.*

"No one in the mine fire area is without risk," Weber said. He described the physical changes that would warn of health problems from the gases and warned that persons with heart or respiratory problems faced adverse health effects from even low levels of carbon monoxide. Most chilling of all, Weber warned women in the impact zone to avoid becoming pregnant until the gas problem was solved. Carbon monoxide could cause serious problems for a developing fetus, including premature delivery, low birth weight, and defects in the placenta. He advised women in the impact zone who were already pregnant to find somewhere else to live or to spend as much of the day as possible away from their houses. As bad as Weber's speech painted the gas danger, the people were enormously grateful to the doctor for taking the time to explain it to them.

No one in the impact zone expected the Interior Department could make their lives any more miserable, but on April 29 the department announced a new policy for Centralia that would, in effect, penalize homeowners involved in the relocation because their houses were near the mine fire. The ruling, which embarrassed Nelligan, who had publicly promised otherwise, had the effect of cutting prices paid for Centralia houses during the 1981 relocation by about 20 percent.

The ruling was based on a legal opinion by Chuck Hardy, assistant solicitor in OSM's Division of Surface Mining, written in response to an inquiry by Patrick Boggs, OSM Region I director. Hardy said the section of the Surface Mining Control and Reclamation Act requiring OSM to appraise property it planned to acquire "as adversely affected by past coal mining practices" meant just that. "To ignore the fire would be to artificially establish some value unrelated to present reali-

---

*Dr. Evan Riehl, the Health Department official charged with monitoring the Centralia situation, claimed in March 1981 that the only information on carbon monoxide he possessed was the 1963 Surgeon General report on cigarette smoking.

ties," he wrote in an April 29 memorandum to Beasley. Hardy said in an earlier memo, dated April 9, that Pennsylvania's eminent domain statute, which bars penalties of this nature, was inapplicable because Centralia was a federal project.

An April 29 memorandum by a second OSM lawyer, John Woodrum, who had ruled all acquisitions in Centralia illegal the previous fall, implied that a literal reading of federal law might leave the Centralia houses without any value at all, for who would choose to buy a house threatened by deadly gases and subsidence? "The appraiser should, however, take into account the fact that the gases are migratory in nature and that a home which is uninhabitable today could have its status changed as a result of unknown developments in the dynamics of the mine fire," Woodrum wrote.

OSM believed Centralia residents would be helped to a degree by the Uniform Relocation Act, a federal law that provides up to $15,000 to help persons displaced by federal projects purchase a comparable home. It is clear from Woodrum's memo, however, that OSM did not believe this would make up the entire difference.

Reaction in Centralia was predictably bitter. The residents of the sixteen-acre area had no hand in starting the mine fire, and now OSM insisted they pay a penalty because of the fire. OSM had not penalized families relocated in 1980—a fact widely known in Centralia—but now OSM officials claimed the 1980 policy was a mistake, and "mistakes do not set precedents."

Council pleaded with Boggs to send someone to the final informational meeting on May 12 to explain the real estate policy and why OSM planned to do nothing more to help Centralia. Boggs, with evident reluctance, agreed finally to send Biggi but announced he would not be permitted to answer any questions about OSM's abandonment of Centralia, only about the relocation. Boggs insisted the mine fire was taken into account in appraising homes purchased during the 1980 relocation.

Concerned Citizens staged a protest march down Locust Avenue just before the May 12 meeting. They had publicly appealed to their fellow citizens to join the march "to save Centralia before it is too late. Show you do care what happens to your town. Don't let the government abandon us." Between forty and fifty persons heeded the call, a surprising number in a community that viewed protest marches as something akin to Communism. They carried signs saying, "Ask Not What Your Government Can Do For You—It Doesn't Give a Damn," "Save Our Town, Put Out the Mine Fire," "Why Put Out the People,

Put Out the Fire," and "Watt Is the Problem in Centralia," to name just a few. They still believed it was possible to save the bulk of Centralia from the fire.

Biggi smoothly insisted at the meeting that OSM would conduct equitable appraisals of the thirty houses using the same method of appraisal used in the 1980 relocation, which was simply not true. He insisted OSM had made no decision regarding its future role in combatting the Centralia mine fire, which likewise was untrue. "As soon as I become aware of a decision, I'll let you know," Biggi said.

Lazarski pleaded with his fellow citizens to use the referendum to send a message to the federal government that Centralia had to be helped, saying it was Centralia's only way to let Nelligan and U.S. Senators John Heinz and Arlen Specter know that Centralia residents were united in their desire for prompt federal action to stop the mine fire.

Council had written the referendum question as follows: "Do you favor excavation or relocation of the entire borough as the solution to the mine fire, deadly gases and/or other dangers created by the mine fire?" In the last days before the May 19 election, Lazarski drew back somewhat from the all-or-nothing nature of the referendum, announcing a yes vote would simply mean the voter wanted the federal government to fund a just and workable solution to the mine fire.

Members of Concerned Citizens went from house to house in Centralia and the parts of Conyngham Township that were eligible to vote in the referendum, urging the yes vote that they and council so badly wanted. The Reverend James Brown, pastor of Centralia United Methodist Church, used his sermon on May 17 to support a yes vote. Some residents actively opposed it. Members of the Reilley family, which dominated the neighboring village of Byrnesville, posted signs stating, "Vote No If You Don't Want to Go." No one, least of all Lazarski, was certain how the voting would go.

To the surprise of even the strongest advocates of government help for Centralia, the referendum question polled an overwhelming yes vote, 434–204. The referendum had received such a build-up that *CBS Evening News* reported the results in its May 20 newscast. The vote was a stinging rebuke to Secretary Watt and OSM and, to a lesser degree, the Thornburgh administration. Federal and state spokesmen predictably dismissed the referendum as worthless.

General Smith later huffed that the referendum question on total excavation or relocation was "simplistic nonsense." "Nobody at that stage really knew what they were dealing with," he said, ignoring the wide publicity every aspect of the fire problem had received. "Everybody and his third cousin had a different idea about that fire. . . . I didn't think they were in the possession of the facts which would lead to the ability to render a decision one way or another. . . . So the fact that people say that doesn't mean you can go out and spend $50 million."

Regardless of official criticism, the mine fire referendum was an expression of pure democracy on the part of Centralians. The people had observed the serious nature of the problem, considered the consequences, and demanded action from the government. No longer could anyone say that Centralians could not make up their minds about the fire. The vote had not been unanimous, true, but it was a landslide. Even the unofficial leader of the no voters, Helen Womer, felt moved to call Larkin the day after the election and congratulate Concerned Citizens for the attention they had helped draw to the fire problem. This sudden amity would not last. Nelligan called the election results a "clear signal" that a majority of Centralians wanted "broadscale federal action to solve the long-smoldering mine fire problem." He promised to look for ways to relocate the community en masse and said he would ask Thornburgh to declare the village a disaster area. His actual goal was far less grandiose. Nelligan wanted Congress to restore the $750,000 that OSM had demanded from the Bureau for the Centralia relocation, money that was to have been used for finding the boundaries of the fire. He did not learn until May 14 that the drilling project had been canceled.

Nelligan was convinced, and said so publicly on several occasions, that he would be "laughed off the floor of the Congress" if he asked for a blank check for Centralia. He believed that without exploratory drilling there could be no project, which was probably true. But there were several priced-out proposals for mine fire projects already on the table, chief among them the Bureau study that was less than a year old. He was on shaky ground when he claimed no one had any idea what to do about the Centralia fire.

The fact remains that by 1981, most engineers who had studied the Centralia mine fire believed a trench would be needed to stop it, and they knew approximately where it would have to be excavated. Bureau engineers had a good idea which houses would have to be destroyed to make way for a trench. The 1980 study provided the number of houses in each of the trenching options.

The humane solution in 1981 would have been to begin the exploratory drilling, but at the same time begin a relocation of all families in the impact zone who wanted to leave. This would include the thirty houses in the sixteen-acre area targeted by OSM, but also all houses in the 200 block of Locust Avenue, all houses on East Park Street, where the Girolamis lived, and at least some on West Park Street. Some families outside the sixteen-acre area, like the Koguts and Girolamis, already had gases in their homes. Once the drilling and relocation was completed, the trench work could begin. No one would be forced to endure the gas and subsidence danger for the duration of the drilling project (a minimum of six months, once it got under way), knowing he would be relocated in any case.

Nelligan drew up an amendment to the Interior Appropriations Bill for the 1982 fiscal year setting aside $850,000 for the Centralia drilling—the extra money was for inflation. He says he did it with little fanfare, which was true. It was only later the Thornburgh administration seized upon the proposal and used it to block discussion of an immediate project to stop the fire or relocate more residents.

Just about everyone liked the borehole project, though. Concerned Citizens, bothered by repeated assertions by Helen Womer that there was no mine fire under Centralia, that it burned outside the village, saw it as a means of proving they were correct in seeking possibly drastic action to help Centralia. Mrs. Womer and her supporters were certain the project would vindicate their beliefs.

At the same time Nelligan was writing legislation for the borehole project, Dr. Edward Radford, a distinguished epidemiologist from the University of Pittsburgh, was hoping to begin a study in Centralia of the long-term health effects of the mine fire gases, particularly carbon monoxide. No such study had ever been done, and its usefulness would have extended beyond mine fire–stricken communities like Centralia.

Carbon monoxide from vehicle exhaust is a dangerous component of air pollution, particularly in cities like Denver and Los Angeles, and is present in any house or office where someone smokes tobacco. U.S. Environmental Protection Agency officials at the Philadelphia regional office suggested to Radford in the spring of 1981 that he might want to look into health problems in Centralia and said funding would be available. Radford addressed Centralia residents at a public meeting on June 17:

> You people in Centralia have a right to know whether there are any harmful effects from the long, slow process of exposure to the gases over many years. From studies with animals and cigarette smokers, we do suspect, however, that carbon monoxide does produce long-term effects at relatively low concentrations. If the study shows there have been definite adverse effects, perhaps we can get the attention of the authorities and

they'll act faster to alleviate all mine fires everywhere. . . . Perhaps there's no need for alarm. The tests might find that although there are problems in some households, the gases have not caused a widespread community health problem. It's better for the community to know one way or another.

Radford predicted the study would cost about $300,000, depending on the amount of work that proved necessary. He first planned to study the health, through blood tests, of about two hundred present and former residents of Centralia. If the initial findings indicated a widespread community problem, he planned to expand his study to about five hundred residents and research their long-term medical records. He believed a sample of five hundred was necessary for an accurate study.

Radford's study would have been of great value to the people of Centralia, given the attitude of the State Health Department. It would have served the interests of almost no one in the Reagan or Thornburgh administrations. The EPA officials who asked Radford to conduct the study were holdovers from a previous era at the agency— an era when EPA officials assumed it was their duty to protect the public from environmental pollution. They were not part of the new team at EPA being installed by Anne Gorsuch (later Burford), President Reagan's controversial EPA director.

EPA officials in Washington delayed a decision on funding for the Centralia project until February 1982, when the EPA Policy Review Board voted to kill the project. Dr. Roger Cortese, director of EPA's Office of Health Research, stated, "The problem itself did not seem to be an EPA problem." An EPA letter to Radford further added, "No conceivable regulatory aspect could be served by the study," an odd assertion in light of the EPA's national standards for carbon monoxide levels in ambient air.

■ ■ ■

Lazarski continued to explore every possibility of help for Centralia and became increasingly frustrated. He was particularly bothered by the strange silence and inaction of the Thornburgh administration, and of the governor in particular. It had been over a month since the referendum, and Thornburgh had yet to utter a word in support of Centralia. "The state has not taken strong action," Lazarski said. "Where did the governor's task force go to? Where did General Smith's report go to? Where did Senator Helfrick and Representative Stuban go? They were supposed to help. They've crawled into a corner."

Journalists continued to write or broadcast about the town with the bizarre underground fire and the plucky residents who were fighting to end it. A lengthy report by Pulitzer Prize winner Teresa Carpenter appeared in late May in the *Village Voice*. Stories appeared in early June in *Time, People,* and the *Detroit Free Press*. Radford's public meeting on June 17 was filmed by the Netherlands Broadcasting Corporation for Dutch television.

It was a picture in *People* that became the best-known image of Centralia up to that time. A *People* writer heard that Larkin could fry an egg over the mine fire. That wasn't entirely true—actually, he placed the frying pan over a hole in the ground that blasted hot air from the fire—but the egg did cook, albeit slowly. Larkin agreed to repeat the feat wearing a chef's hat and apron. He was criticized by some who thought he trivialized the fire problem, but the picture conveyed the idea of the fire's heat as none other had so far.

■ ■ ■

There were anguished protests on June 19 when the first seven families eligible for relocation received purchase offers on their homes from Columbia County Redevelopment Authority, which was handling the relocation for OSM. It was evident OSM *had* deducted a penalty of about 20 percent because of the mine fire. To make matters worse, OSM was allowing a family only ten days to decide whether to accept the purchase offer. After Nelligan and U.S. Senator John Heinz intervened, the time limit was extended to thirty days, then forty. Even that was not very long, considering a family had to find a relocation home in that period if it wanted to learn how much of the possible $15,000 in relocation assistance it would receive.

Although the number of families eligible for relocation was first stated as thirty, OSM had dropped the number to twenty-nine after reexamining the map of Centralia. Two of the twenty-nine eligible families, the Womers and Gaughans, refused to allow appraisers to enter their homes. They wanted no part of the relocation. For Tony and Mary Lou Gaughan, it was a matter of poor health and fear they would not be able to afford a house as nice as the one they had. Their house did not have a basement, only a crawl space, and seemed relatively immune to invasion by the gases, despite its location at the edge of the fire. There had been alarms, but not many.

The Womers were a different story. In public, Helen Womer condemned the relocation as unnecessary and cast aspersions on those who disagreed with her. In private, the Womers were less self-assured about their safety. In letters of May 21 and May 29 to Columbia County Redevelopment Authority, they stressed they were only declining to have their property appraised "AT THIS TIME" [their emphasis]. "Our civil rights are being violated insofar as we are being forced to make a decision without knowing (1) where is the exact location of the fire, and (2) what method will the agencies adopt to eliminate or contain it. The speed with which these acquisitions are being handled is both questionable and frightening. The situation here is comparable to the Gestapo era in Germany. To reiterate, BY THIS ACTION WE ARE NOT RELINQUISHING OUR RIGHT TO THE FUNDS AVAILABLE until the above facts are known," the Womers wrote.

OSM's haste to remove the families *was* in fact motivated by healthy respect for the dangers of the impact zone, although regulations also played a part. It handled the relocation poorly in terms of public relations. The OSM official on the scene, Marian Turzai, alienated many of the families with her patronizing style, referring to adults by their first names as if they were so many naughty children.

Discontent with the appraisals grew so great that OSM, at the request of Senator Heinz, agreed to send a delegation headed by Beasley to Centralia to answer questions. The meeting, held on July 20, turned into one of the more bitter the village had seen in nineteen years of the mine fire.

Mayor Wondoloski, acting at the request of OSM, attempted to evict three reporters who arrived to cover the meeting. After an angry standoff of thirty minutes, in which some residents supported the press and some did not, OSM and the mayor backed down and allowed the reporters to remain.

The meeting lasted over three hours and resolved little. Their anger and resentment boiling to the surface, the families argued with OSM officials from beginning to end. They protested it was unfair to deduct 20 percent from their property values for the mine fire when no penalty was applied during the 1980 relocation. Again OSM claimed that there *was* no difference in the two relocation programs.

"Could you go out and get a house with what we've been offered?" asked Evelyn Buckley. "Would you give up your home without a fight? You say we fight and make insults. Wouldn't you do the same thing in our place?" She received no answer.

Beasley took pains to emphasize that OSM had no further plans to help Centralia after the relocation project was finished. When questioned by a reporter after the meeting, he refused to rank the Centralia problem any higher than any other abandoned mine land problem and said OSM simply did not have the money to do anything about it.

20
Fire in the Night

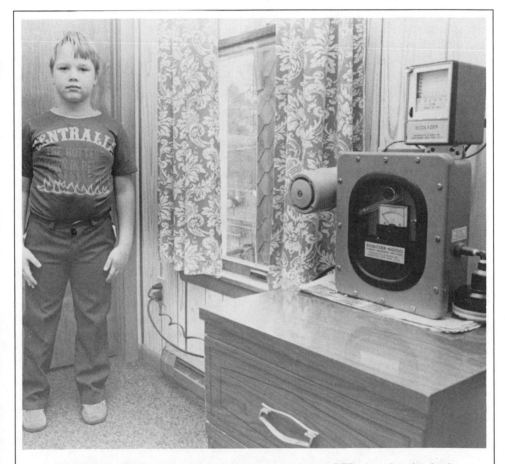

Michael Kogut, Jr., with the carbon monoxide alarm DER placed in his bed-room. Michael, who suffered from asthma, was affected more by low levels of carbon monoxide than children with healthy lungs. His T-shirt says "Centralia: The Hottest Town in Pennsylvania." (Photo: David DeKok)

NO one in Centralia had given much thought to the eastern front of the mine fire in many years. While the western front of the fire was moving toward Centralia, this section was moving away from the village into the wilderness of abandoned mine lands to the east. No one knew just when or where, but the eastern front of the fire had broken through the eastern fly ash barrier, the one completed by the Bureau in 1973. Between the barrier and Big Mine Run Road lay half a mile of forest that ended abruptly at a steep cliff a few hundred feet west of the road.

People from Centralia liked to tramp the mountains, no matter the season or harsh terrain, and council president Edward Polites and his sons discovered hot steam blowing from cracks in that cliff in late February 1981. They were startled to find steam here, so far from Centralia. It was just like the steaming pit between Byrnesville and Centralia, with one major difference—the intense heat. As they crawled up a steep rock pile that led to the face of the cliff, the heat grew almost unbearable. Polites could see yellow deposits on the cliff—later he learned they were sulfur. There seemed to be a hole in the cliff that was blowing out superheated air.

He reported their discovery to the Bureau, which after a week of considerable nagging by Polites sent Daniel Lewis to investigate. Lewis approached as close to the cliff as he dared and found the temperature there varied between 150 and 180 degrees Fahrenheit. When he came back to the site in June, he dangled a thermometer from a device like a fishing rod and was able to get much closer to the cliff. Temperatures were in excess of 1,200 degrees. The fire was near.

A Byrnesville man discovered flames at the site the night of July 23. Blue and orange tongues of fire danced amid the rocks in the rock pile, and some of the stones glowed orange. Although the flame area measured only about ten feet square, its heat was tremendous. A heavy odor of sulfur hung over the site, and DER inspectors found dangerous levels of carbon monoxide near ground level. The fire outbreak caused a sensation, and many people from Centralia came out that night and succeeding nights to gaze in wonder and fascination. Curiosity seekers who braved the heat and odor to climb the rock pile to the cliff would hear a strange sucking sound, apparently caused by the fire drawing air into the mountain. Dead leaves blew onto the burning rocks and burst into flame. Trees toppled onto the rock pile, their roots burned by the heat. It was an awesome, primeval spectacle, and it gave Centralia residents and government officials alike a hint of the terrible nature of the beast that threatened Centralia.

■ ■ ■

Concerned Citizens gained new strength during the summer of 1981 after several liberal activists arrived in Centralia and took the group's cause to heart. The first of these was David Bradley, a young toxicologist who worked for consumer activist Ralph Nader's Center for Responsive Law in Washington, D.C. Nader's organization first became interested in Centralia's plight in April, sending three representatives to the village to be briefed by Concerned Citizens. They initially thought of filing a lawsuit on behalf of Centralia but later decided it would be premature.

Bradley began working with Concerned Citizens in July. He provided tips on the best ways of organizing to fight Secretary Watt, telling them, for example, that simply writing letters of protest to Watt or Governor Thornburgh was essentially useless. Instead of taking their case directly to the federal or state government, he said, they should attempt to influence persons like congressmen and senators who could influence the decision makers in government.

Bradley worried that Centralia residents were possibly being exposed to a wide range of other toxic substances besides carbon monoxide that a mine fire could produce. Bradley persuaded DER to conduct atmospheric tests for the presence of arsenic, mercury, and benzopyrene. No harmful amounts of these poisons were found in Centralia's air, but it was a wise precaution nonetheless, and one Concerned Citizens would not have thought to request on its own. Bradley urged the group to make peace with Centralia Council, to make every effort to enlist council as an ally in its efforts to win help for Centralia. He argued it could only increase their strength. It was a fine, if impractical sentiment. Council viewed Concerned Citizens with alarm, considering the group to have usurped council's prerogative to speak for Centralia. It would have little—and more often, nothing—to do with Concerned Citizens.

The group did prevail on council to take a formal stand on the mine fire, something council had not done in the nineteen years the fire had burned. There was considerable grumbling, particularly by Polites, but council eventually passed by a unanimous vote a resolution calling on the federal or state government to relocate all of Centralia "should the perimeter of the fire, or a portion of the fire large enough to endanger people's lives and property be found within borough limits, or unsatisfactory living conditions prevail in an attempt at excavation." Copies of the resolution were sent to the governor and Secretary Watt, who took no notice of it.

Mayor Wondoloski, an implacable foe of Concerned Citizens, argued it would be foolish to relocate all of Centralia when only part of the village was affected by the fire. Council members argued that any excavation project in Centralia would so reduce the quality of life for the remaining citizens that living in the village would no longer be desirable.

Another activist who proved a great help to Concerned Citizens was Marie Cirillo, a former nun who was now a field worker for Rural American Women. The organization, which was headquartered in Washington, D.C., worked to help women in rural areas organize to win social justice, although it did not confine itself to the so-called women's issues.

At her first formal meeting with the members of Concerned Citizens, Cirillo said many of her contacts in government, private industry and the legal profession knew about Centralia and were willing to help out any way they could. Cirillo herself was willing to come to Centralia from Washington two days out of every week, but only if Concerned Citizens members would commit themselves to a wider range of activities. The group was more than willing. It was an exhilarating time for them. For once, they seemed to be making a little headway.

Cirillo recruited other persons to help Concerned Citizens. She even arranged some small contributions from Catholic Social Services and the Keep America Beautiful Fund to the group's depleted treasury. One of her early suggestions, however, proved to be a mistake. Cirillo knew of a West German corporation, Ruhr Kohl, that specialized in moving German towns intact, then strip mining the coal beneath them. The company was noted for its sensitivity, and Cirillo found out it might be interested in mining the coal under Centralia.

Like several of the outsiders who came to help Concerned Citizens, Cirillo believed the coal reserves beneath Centralia might be the village's salvation if the Interior Department and the state continued to refuse to fund a mine fire project. She suggested to Concerned Citizens that Ruhr Kohl be contacted to see what the firm could do to help them. It seemed like a good idea, and Concerned Citizens members agreed to send a letter. The next day, Larkin received several angry telephone calls, including one from Polites, accusing the group of wanting to sell Centralia to the highest bidder.

Larkin made a public statement that it was never the intention of Concerned Citizens to sell Centralia to Ruhr Kohl, which it obviously could not do anyway, but rather to find out *how* the company moved towns. The town-selling charge would stick, however, and provide ammunition to the group's enemies in Centralia in the months to come.

One good thing came out of the Ruhr Kohl fiasco. Concerned Citizens members were introduced to Thomas Trauger, a young lawyer from Tennessee who was an associate in the Washington law firm of Spiegel and McDiarmid, and George Spiegel, a name partner in the firm. Cirillo had contacted Trauger to borrow a short film he had made about Ruhr Kohl and its relocation techniques. She was later introduced to Spiegel and managed to interest both lawyers in helping Centralia.

This would lead to one of Cirillo's more beneficial suggestions to Concerned Citizens. She believed it would be helpful to Centralia'a cause if Concerned Citizens would travel to Washington to ask for help from Pennsylvania's lawmakers and hopefully Secretary Watt himself. The trip was scheduled for October.

■ ■ ■

Centralia's news value was on a rising star. Two residents were given an opportunity in August to plead the village's case on national television. ABC's *Good Morning, America* decided to do a story about the mine fire, possibly in response to news the fire had broken out of the ground, and arranged for Thomas Larkin and Todd Domboski to appear on the show.

It had been a rough six months for Todd since his brush with death, and he had become increasingly withdrawn, reluctant to leave the safety of his house. Nevertheless, he believed it was his duty to talk to reporters about Centralia, even if the interviews made it difficult for him to forget the terrors of that day. Todd was one of Centralia's best witnesses, and he and Larkin did well on *Good Morning, America*. Anyone who watched the show came away with a graphic picture of the horror of the Centralia mine fire.

■ ■ ■

General Smith delivered his long-awaited report on the mine fire to Governor Thornburgh on July 17, long after the April release date predicted when the study was announced on March 6. He would later blame this on heavy demands on his time, as well as on the difficulty of resolving diametrically opposed opinions among state officials regarding what should be done about the mine fire.

Thornburgh refused to release the report to the public, as he often did with politically sensitive public documents. Deputy Press Secretary Kirk Wilson of the governor's Press Office would describe the report only as a "sixteen-page, single-spaced . . . comprehensive" document. That, incidentally, was about as informative as the Press Office ever was.* He later said Thornburgh might release only that part of the report that directly pertained to whatever course of action he selected.

Thornburgh broke his long silence on the mine fire on August 5 with a letter to Secretary Watt that was apparently prompted by Smith's report. He called on the Interior Department to begin work immediately on the exploratory drilling. It should be done with funds already in the budget, he said, because of the "immediacy of the danger."

The letter was replete with comments about how dangerous the mine fire was to Centralia residents, but its key point was that stopping the mine fire should be a federal responsibility. It was the same state policy of years past. "We are prepared to contribute what we can," Thornburgh wrote. "But primary responsibility for solving this problem must rest with the federal government."

He said the state's only obligation was to protect the health and safety of Centralia residents, and no more, and argued the state could not do this until the Interior Department made clear its intentions for Centralia. "Therefore, I am requesting that you convene a federal, state and local government task force to actively deal with the fire in a co-ordinated fashion and to keep the citizens of Centralia informed of all developments," he wrote.

Had the governor forgotten about the Centralia Mine Fire Advisory Group, the federal-state-local task force organized by OSM that he had ignored the previous March? It seems odd that he called for keeping Centralia citizens informed, given their exclusion from all deliberations about the mine fire and the secrecy surrounding General Smith's report.

The publicly released letter seems to have been intended more to make the public believe Thornburgh was doing something for Centralia than to persuade Watt. The governor was fond of sending letters to Watt, but would not go beyond that. Phone calls or personal visits carry more weight in the world of politics.

By the summer of 1981, OSM had told the state it would be receiving between $220 and $250 million as its share of the Abandoned Mine Lands Fund during the ten-year life of the fund (by late 1983, this an-

---

*Thornburgh's dislike of the press was legendary in Harrisburg, and his attitude was reflected in the often shabby treatment reporters received from the governor's Press Office. Thornburgh rarely gave unrestricted press conferences and was known to lash out at reporters whose questions he disliked, despite the fact that he generally received very fair coverage.

ticipated share would rise to $770 million). Some $42 million would become immediately available in 1982 when the state obtained primacy. There was also the $47 million remaining from the Land and Water Conservation bond issue.

General Smith's report, which was finally released to the public on September 1, said state officials favored either of two options for stopping the mine fire among those contained in the 1980 Bureau report on Centralia.* One was total excavation, with a predicted cost of $83 million, and the other was a combination of excavation and isolation trenches, which had a predicted cost of $42 million. Neither seems prohibitive in light of the funds available to Pennsylvania.

Knowing funds were available, why did the Thornburgh administration continue to fight with the Interior Department over who would pay for Centralia? True, the state had many abandoned mine land problems, but none so serious as Centralia, none where the very existence of a community was directly threatened. DER had publicly admitted as much. The Thornburgh administration thought Centralia could safely wait for the state's victory over Interior, protected by the gas monitoring system. Interior likewise believed the electronic devices would protect Centralia until Secretary Watt's triumph over Pennsylvania.

State Centralia policy had not changed markedly in years, just as it had been Interior Department policy since 1967 that Centralia was not worth the cost of saving. Watt's obstinate refusal to contribute more than $1 million from Interior's own large share of the AML Fund was in keeping with that unwritten policy.**

Two bureaucracies were warring, and the people of Centralia were caught in a strange no man's land. John Coddington had not been protected by the gas monitoring system, and neither had Todd Domboski, not to mention the others who breathed the poison gases at home and wondered, like Dr. Radford, about the ultimate effect on their health. General Smith called for compassion for Centralia in his report, but it had no perceptible effect on either side.

■ ■ ■

Many of the twenty-seven families moved in August or September, and it was a bittersweet time. All of the sixty-eight men, women, and children leaving Centralia were happy to escape the gases in their

---

*Smith called the report an "excellent piece of data gathering and analytical work."

**The AML Fund contained $681 million on September 30, 1981, according to OSM records. Of that, half, or about $340 million, was reserved for the coal-producing states. The other half was reserved for the federal government. Of the federal share, about $136 million was reserved for the Interior Department to spend on mine fire and other AML projects at Secretary Watt's discretion.

houses and the ever-present threat of subsidence, but they would sorely miss the village where many had spent all their lives.

Rita Kleman, an elderly widow, lived next to the yard where Todd Domboski almost died. During her last summer in Centralia, the mine fire lowered the oxygen in her basement to incredibly low levels, according to DER records. Beginning in the middle of June, the oxygen level rarely climbed above 18 percent, and on August 7 it dropped to only 9.5 percent.

Mrs. Kleman did not believe that OSM treated her fairly. "No, for heaven's sake," she said. "You can see this house. It's a perfect house. There's not a thing wrong with it. I mean, to build this house today. They gave me the price of a fire-ridden home. They gave me $26,500. You couldn't build this house for $80,000."

Not all the evacuees believed OSM had treated them unfairly. Mrs. Leona McDonald, who lived down the block from Mrs. Kleman and across the street from the Coddingtons, said OSM had treated her "More than fair and square. Anybody that sold their home to OSM really got more than if they were to sell it privately. I think the people that are complaining, they expected a lot of money. An awful lot of money."

Area realtors had said the mine fire made many potential buyers skip over Centralia in preceding years. Housing values suffered as a result, but it was on those values OSM based its price offers to the twenty-seven families.

Frank Jurgill, Sr., was angered by the price OSM offered for his home on East South Street, but he knew he had to go. Jurgill lived across the street from the Gaughans and Womers, but he had little use for Helen Womer's theories on the mine fire. All he knew was that it was impossible to draw a glass of cold water in his house or his son's house next door, no matter how long the water was allowed to run. It was 90 degrees in his cellar, and it wasn't because of the August heat. Jurgill wondered if the fire had broken through the western fly ash barrier, which was close to his house. He would always be angry at Charles Kuebler of the Bureau for closing the old pit that once vented the gases.

A few days before her move to Mount Carmel, Anne Maloney discovered the normally cool walls of her cellar had turned warm, even hot to the touch. She called Jurgill and his wife to come see her discovery, fearing no one would believe her otherwise. He would later estimate the wall temperature to have been 100 degrees. It was no wonder it was so hard to get a cold drink of water.

■ ■ ■

The *News-Item* decided in August to sample community opinion in Centralia and adjacent neighborhoods of Conyngham Township via an unscientific coupon poll. Assistant Editor Jake Betz received 176 responses from between 120 and 140 different households, out of about 470 households that were eligible. The responses were fairly evenly divided between the safe and unsafe sections of Centralia, and many respondents added comments elaborating on their answers.

An overwhelming majority—130 to 41—said they believed the mine fire was under Centralia. Some 144 respondents were in favor of relocating the entire community if evidence proved the fire was under the town; 27 were opposed, and 5 had no opinion.

Concerned Citizens fared far better than Centralia Council in the survey. On the question "Do you think Concerned Citizens Against the Mine Fire is acting in the best interests of Centralia?" 107 said yes, 59 said no, and 10 had no opinion. On a question of whether council was exerting sufficient leadership and doing all it could to solve the mine fire problem, 67 said yes and 106 said no.

Centralia residents backed the conspiracy theory by a 124–40–12 vote. On a question whether the respondent believed the Bureau and OSM had made the public aware of all relevant information on the mine fire, 10 said yes, 164 said no, and 2 had no opinion.

Governor Thornburgh took a drubbing in the survey. Respondents were asked whether Thornburgh had done enough to help Centralia, and 9 said yes, 166 said no, and 1 had no opinion. Centralia traditionally votes Democratic by a steady 2–1 margin, so the governor's unpopularity appears to have cut across party lines.

The final question asked whether Centralia should sell the mineral rights to the coal under Centralia and use the money to relocate the community. This one was close, with 83 voting yes, 89 voting no, and 4 having no opinion.

■ ■ ■

No matter what OSM might say, living outside the sixteen-acre area did not necessarily prevent the mine fire gases from entering one's home. Michael and Dorothy Kogut, who lived at 239 South Locust Avenue, were particularly worried about their seven-year-old son, Michael Jr. Young Michael suffered from asthma and other upper respiratory ailments, and even very low volumes of carbon monoxide would aggravate his breathing problem. Like Shannon Buckley and Rachel Lamb, he was what carbon monoxide researchers called a "susceptible individual."

Mr. and Mrs. Kogut had DER place the gas monitor in their son's small, second-floor bedroom. Several times they moved him to their own bedroom when the carbon monoxide made it hard for Michael to breathe. No one could explain why one room in a Centralia house could be affected, and another one be relatively safe. There would be suspicion that heating ducts and even sewer pipes played a role, but DER never did any kind of study.

Philip and Clara Gaughan, who lived at 39 South Locust, had both carbon monoxide in the main part of their house and low oxygen in the basement. They complained of dozing off during the day, the most common symptom in Centralia of exposure to carbon monoxide. Gaughan said the oxygen level in his basement had fallen as low as 14 percent. It was not as low as the deadly levels in Mrs. Kleman's basement, but extraordinary nonetheless. One window in the basement was kept open year around.

Charles and Theresa Gasperetti lived near the Koguts on South Locust Avenue and had two preschool children, Jennifer and Charlie. They were not able to get a gas monitor until the summer of 1981, when the departure of the Coddingtons and other families in the impact zone made several of the devices available. "That year my little girl was sick constantly. She had upper respiratory infections thirteen times, but we had no idea if we had gas or not," Mrs. Gasperetti said. She refused to take seriously a threat she could neither see nor smell until one day that summer when the gas alarm sounded for the first time, alerting them to a carbon monoxide level of 60 ppm. "That was the first time it really hit me hard," she said. "I knew it was there."

None of the families who were beginning to have problems with the gases expressed any desire to relocate, although they conceded it might become necessary. They had observed how the twenty-seven families had been treated by OSM. OSM did not rule out further relocations but said none would be considered unless the Pennsylvania Department of Health ruled a house was unsafe.

■ ■ ■

Centralia Council was in turmoil during the summer and fall of 1981 as the pressures of the mine fire crisis continued to grow. Councilman James Reilley resigned for health reasons in July and was replaced by Frank Duffy, a member of Concerned Citizens. Councilmen Lazarski and Polites resigned in September and were replaced by Edward Gusick and John Koschoff. Twenty-three-year-old Koschoff was the son of the man who was borough secretary when the mine fire ignited in 1962.

Lazarski and Polites had worked hard and done their best to find help for Centralia. They had consulted with lawyers on the possibility of legal action against Secretary Watt and on how Centralia might go about relocating itself if the federal or state governments refused to help.* They had organized meetings, heard out anyone who thought he might be able to help—and there were some zany ones—and kept the *News-Item* fully informed of all developments.

Given their independence of thought and action, perhaps it is not surprising state officials were happy to see them go. General Smith, while professing to like Polites and Lazarski personally, believed they provided poor leadership for Centralia. "My overall impression of Centralia is it posed one of the principal problems to the solution itself," Smith said. "It lacked from the beginning on any real, sustained leadership. It never did have the kind of unifying, inspiring, integrating leadership which a town . . . needs."

What the Thornburgh administration wanted, it seemed, was a borough council that would follow instructions and not publicly criticize the governor for failing to do anything to help Centralia, particularly with Thornburgh facing re-election in 1982. They would, by chance, get the council they wanted, but the moral cost to the people of Centralia would be immense.

■ ■ ■

Of all the comments on the Centralia problem made by state or federal officials, the one that angered Centralia residents the most was made by Dr. James Fox of the Pennsylvania Department of Health. Fox had succeeded Dr. Evan Riehl at the Division of Environmental Health after Riehl resigned to take a job in private industry, and he was now the official who would decide if a family was endangered by mine fire gases and thus deserving of relocation.

"There's no public health problem in Centralia," said Fox, during an interview with the *News-Item* in late September. The reporter conducting the interview, startled as much by the remark itself as by the sarcastic tone in the doctor's voice, asked Fox to explain why he believed this to be true. Fox replied that no Centralia home currently had a dangerous level of mine fire gases. "No Centralia home has *ever* had a dangerous level of gases," the doctor added.

The reporter asked Fox about studies by carbon monoxide re-

*Franklin Kury, a Harrisburg lawyer and respected environmentalist, advised Polites a lawsuit was impossible because the law left fighting mine fires to Watt's discretion. "I regret we cannot give you better news, because I would love to be able to bring the kind of lawsuit that you contemplated," he wrote in a May 11 letter to Polites. Kury, a Democrat from Sunbury, was state senator for the 27th District, which includes Centralia, until 1980.

searchers over the years that showed susceptible individuals, meaning those with heart or lung problems, would be harmed by even low levels of carbon monoxide. Fox scoffed at the idea that anyone in Centralia was in danger and said susceptible individuals would not be harmed by the levels of carbon monoxide in Centralia homes. Only a carbon monoxide reading of 35 ppm that lasted for eight hours, or an instantaneous surge of 200 ppm would concern him. He did not seem to know that gas monitors in Centralia were set to go no higher than 100 ppm.

Fox's comments set off a firestorm of protest among Centralia families who lived with the gas problem, and he later denied he had made them. After all the impact zone families had endured, Fox's comments were incredibly callous. They were also a perfect statement of state policy toward the Centralia carbon monoxide problem—that there was no problem. It strains belief that Fox and his superior, Dr. Donald Reid, could consider the carbon monoxide breathed daily in Centralia to be harmless, given the abundant research to the contrary.*

Fox's comments also angered General Smith. He fully agreed with what the doctor said, but felt it was indiscreet of him to blurt it out to a newspaper reporter. "I felt a spokesman up there who really ought to remain unnamed sounded insensitive, said some things that were poorly said, to put it mildly, and stupid, to put it accurately," Smith said, leaving little doubt he was referring to Fox. "Because they were too blunt, and not necessarily right. They may have seemed right at the moment, but they weren't always going to be right."

Smith argued there was no hard evidence that carbon monoxide at low levels had harmful effects on susceptible persons. He said he wrote to some of the nation's leading carbon monoxide researchers, posed that question to them, and received "wishy-washy" answers. "There isn't an ounce of evidence," Smith said. "I understand the fear, and I understand the concern, but I don't believe the evidence is there. I don't think it's fair to say that . . . the Health Department didn't look at that seriously. I think they did."

The Health Department was so intent on keeping the lid on the carbon monoxide problem in Centralia that it kept secret its own stan-

---

*The Health Department would not provide *any* information about carbon monoxide to Centralia residents, despite pleas by General Smith. The doctors did have this information, as is evidenced by a December 1984 press release headlined "Carbon Monoxide—Kills!" by Dr. Fox about the dangers of carbon monoxide produced by a home heating system. The release describes, among other things, the symptoms of carbon monoxide exposure as "yawning, headache, nausea, dizziness, ringing in the ears, and abdominal pain. Gaspy breathing and unconsciousness quickly follow." Apparently home heating was politically safe.

dards of danger for the gas, all the while insisting to Centralia residents that it had none. The standards came to light in an August 20, 1981 letter from acting Assistant Secretary of the Interior Perry Pendley to Congressman Nelligan. Nelligan was trying to find out why Joan Girolami's house had not been included in the relocation, despite its periodic gas alarms.

"The Pennsylvania Department of Health has set lower and upper limits of carbon monoxide as follows: 20 parts per million or below is considered safe; 20 to 50 parts per million is considered to be a grey area; and 50 parts per million, with exposure of four hours or more, is unsafe," Pendley wrote.

Pendley's letter surfaced in a *News-Item* Freedom of Information request almost a year later. Dr. Donald Reid confirmed the standards were, indeed, those of the Health Department. He did not say why Centralians had never been informed of them, as they had of the departmental standards for exposure to carbon dioxide and low levels of oxygen.

The Health Department standards allowed considerably more human exposure to carbon monoxide than standards set by the EPA or several other organizations, and made no allowance for susceptible individuals. They were never discussed in Centralia, even after their existence became public knowledge. The Health Department continued the pretense that there was no problem.

■ ■ ■

The gas problem at the house trailer of Terry and Millie Burge near the Coddingtons' home was among the worst in the impact zone. Their gas alarm rang periodically, and there was so much carbon monoxide in the trailer's water meter pit that Roaring Creek Water Company did not allow its meter readers to go inside.

The Burges were one of the twenty-nine families eligible for relocation. They had found a new home in the village of Fountain Springs near Ashland and by mid-October had transferred most of their belongings to their new home. There were just a few items left in the trailer, and Mrs. Burge and her father, George Dyszel, went back to gather them on Friday, October 16.

Mrs. Burge stepped inside the trailer while Dyszel backed the car over the lawn to the front door to make loading easier. As the car crossed the grass, Dyszel felt a sharp jolt. The car stopped, refusing to go any farther. Dyszel got out and saw that one wheel was mired in a steaming hole. Horrified, they called DER. Wayne Readly, a DER gas inspector, attached a chain to his pickup truck and pulled the car out of the hole. It was none too soon. As the car jerked free, the hole widened to about four feet square. Later that day, a contractor hired by Centralia Council to backfill the hole tapped the edge of the steaming pit with the shovel of a back hoe. It collapsed immediately, creating a ten-by-ten-foot opening about eight feet deep that could easily have swallowed a car.

This subsidence had been caused by the heat of the fire weathering the roof of the mine. The weight of the car made it collapse, but given a few more months, it might have taken only the weight of a human. Mrs. Burge and her father were lucky.

21
On the Road

Undersecretary of the Interior Donald Hodel (left) and Interior Press Secretary Douglas Baldwin listen to a delegation from Concerned Citizens Against the Centralia Mine Fire on October 20, 1981, during the group's two-day trip to Washington, D.C. Hodel became Secretary of the Interior early in 1985. (Photo: David DeKok, News-Item)

THE aura of power and majesty in Washington, D.C., is so immediately palpable to an angry citizen arriving from a small town that he tends to forget, at least for a while, the grievance that caused him to travel there. Washington is intimidating to a newcomer, who feels dwarfed by the wide avenues and stately buildings, by the tall columns and mammoth doors leading to hallways that seem never to end. The angry voice becomes subdued; the grievance that was so important at home seems distant, even trivial here.

It is an illusion, of course. Power comes from people, not from buildings, and people in Washington are like people anywhere. They can be influenced to help if you can reach them and make them believe your cause is just or that helping you is in their best interest. It was why Marie Cirillo wanted Concerned Citizens to go there. People in Washington would make the ultimate decision on Centralia's fate, it appeared, and she wanted Congress and the Interior Department to hear what it was like to live with a mine fire, before they reached their final verdict. "There's always that critical moment when people's minds start changing," Cirillo said later. "I guess I was hoping it could be one of those events. Where they would have enough of a scene in Washington that some people would start taking them seriously."

Much to the surprise of Concerned Citizens, Secretary Watt did not immediately reject the idea of a meeting. Planning for the trip began weeks in advance, and meetings had been arranged with Congressman Nelligan, Senator Specter, and an aide to Senator Alfonse D'Amato of New York.* Telegrams urging Watt to meet with Concerned Citizens were sent by Centralia Council president Frank Duffy, State Senator Edward Helfrick, and State Representative Robert Belfanti. Cirillo worked on it through her contacts in the Interior Department, and Specter tried from his end. By the time the delegation left Centralia early in the morning of October 19 for the four-hour drive to Washington, there was a glimmer of hope the meeting would take place. No one, at least, had said no.

Only five members of Concerned Citizens—Thomas Larkin, Joan Girolami, David Lamb, and Joe and Eva Moran—made the trip. There were supposed to be more, but Larkin had angered some members by ruling that children could not go along. Three reporters caught up with

---

*D'Amato was an acquaintance of a man who was married to a cousin of Francis O'Hearn, a member of Concerned Citizens.

the five in Washington, as did Margaret Danner of Catholic Social Services of Harrisburg, Bernard Shire of Pennsylvania Catholic Conference, and Cirillo.

Their first stop of the day was Spiegel and McDiarmid, the law firm where Thomas Trauger was an associate.* The offices were in the luxurious and infamous Watergate apartment and office complex, an amusingly ironic location for a law firm that did more than its share of *pro bono* work for "under-represented people" who were victims of the federal government or large corporations, as Trauger put it. Trauger had interested the firm in helping the Centralians, and this was the first opportunity for any of the partners to meet the group. George Spiegel treated them to lunch at one of the Watergate's elegant restaurants and told them Spiegel and McDiarmid would begin looking for ways to sue the Interior Department to force relief for Centralia.

Their feeling of elation as they left the restaurant did not last long. The next meeting was supposed to be with Senator Heinz, but Heinz had decided not to see them. A secretary told them the senator had returned to Pennsylvania the previous day on pressing business. Two aides who knew little about the Centralia problem and appeared to care even less had been delegated to find out what Concerned Citizens wanted. Later they would learn Heinz had been in Washington during their entire visit.

Cirillo had arranged a reception that night at the Appalachian Regional Commission headquarters, and it appeared to do much to restore their bruised morale. About thirty guests attended, including several lawyers from Spiegel and McDiarmid, Congressman Nelligan, and various friends of Marie Cirillo. Stories and photographs about the mine fire were hung on the wall for the guests to peruse. A folk trio sang a song they had written about the mine fire. Larkin, Lamb, and Girolami pleaded for support. "We'd like your help," Mrs. Girolami said. "Help us with fund raising. Help us with letter writing. We don't just want the boreholes. We want a project."

Nelligan was displeased at having been asked to attend a reception where only thirty persons were present, and he made his feelings known to Mrs. Girolami. He received them in his office the next morning, although with mixed feelings. Centralia was becoming a millstone around his neck, taking up more of his staff's time than any other problem in the Eleventh District. He had to deal on one hand with an Interior Department bureaucracy that was actively hostile to the idea of

---

*He is now a partner.

providing any more money for Centralia, and on the other with Centralia citizens who accused him of not doing enough to help them.

Even so, he would not allow himself to give up the fight. Nelligan seemed to thirst to be the public official who saved Centralia from the mine fire. Whenever he ran into Secretary Watt at a social function in Washington, usually at the Republican Club, Nelligan would remind him Centralia needed more than just a $1-million relocation project. "Every time I'd see Jim, I'd sing a little song [to the tune of *Rule, Brittania*], 'Oh, Centralia, I need that money now,'" Nelligan said later. "And Jim would say, 'Oh, I've gotten in more trouble, more grief because of Centralia.' And of course, he did. He came up with the bucks, and bang! He gets it in the snoot."

After the cordialities and group photographs were over, Nelligan proceeded to lecture the Centralians about what a difficult time he was having and how they were making his job harder. He told them to forget about moving Centralia, that it would be too expensive. "I'd be laughed off the floor of the Congress," Nelligan said. "You won't get anything that big." He told them not to be too greedy or too emotional, and that did not sit well with his angry guests. They perceived he was telling them to stop making such a big issue out of the Centralia problem, although Nelligan vehemently denies that.

Their spirits once again deflated, the Centralians made their way to the office of Senator D'Amato, a Republican of New York. After the shabby treatment from Heinz and the lecture from Nelligan, none of them knew what to expect from D'Amato's aide. To their surprise and delight, the senator chose to meet with them personally. D'Amato urged the group to apply pressure "to everybody. Go after all of us." He promised to support the borehole bill when it came up for a Senate vote.

There were no fears in meeting with Specter. Specter's actions and statements that year had convinced the Centralians that this was a politician who was sincerely concerned about their plight. He had visited Centralia in June to be briefed on the mine fire, and again in August when he happened to be traveling through central Pennsylvania with his family. During the summer, he took emergency action to save the borehole money when it appeared on the verge of elimination from the Interior Appropriations Bill. Specter had urged Watt to meet with the Centralia delegation and remained hopeful they would see the secretary that day.

"There's nothing like a delegation from Centralia to put a fire under this matter," he quipped after the group, its advisers, as well as reporters and television camera operators and sound people crowded into his office. "I'm glad you're here. I'm optimistic we can accomplish something."

Specter asked about the present state of the mine fire, and Larkin told him about the breakthrough at Big Mine Run and the more recent subsidence at the Burge trailer. Lamb asked Specter to use his influence to help the families who were threatened by the gases but did not live in the sixteen-acre area. Larkin repeated what was fast becoming Concerned Citizens' credo, that he feared Interior would do nothing to help Centralia until some unlucky soul died from the gases. "No, it turns on more than that," Specter said, without elaborating.

Bill Wilcox, who was Secretary of Community Affairs for Governor Milton Shapp, Thornburgh's predecessor, and was now a top aide to Specter, urged Concerned Citizens to lobby for the Senate version of the part of the Interior Appropriations Bill authorizing the drilling of boreholes in Centralia. Specter, Wilcox said, had amended the wording of the bill to require the Interior Department to submit to Congress within thirty days of the bill's final passage a report explaining how the exploratory drilling plan would be implemented. Nelligan's wording had not provided for congressional oversight.

"I don't minimize the difficulty of putting out this fire," Specter said. "It may be necessary in the final analysis to move large numbers of people."

Specter thought he had persuaded Watt to meet with Concerned Citizens, but at the last minute Watt told Undersecretary of the Interior Donald Hodel, his chief deputy, to go instead.* Nelligan later said Watt backed out because he feared it would turn into "a shouting match." Watt need not have worried. Larkin, Mrs. Girolami, and the others, all of whom could hold their own in an argument, had been unusually subdued since arriving in Washington. Perhaps it was their treatment by Heinz and Nelligan, perhaps they were simply overawed by some of the people they were meeting. The meeting with Hodel appeared to fall in the latter category.

Hodel, who came to the meeting with press secretary Douglas Baldwin and several lesser officials, spoke in short, measured, emotionless phrases that betrayed no hint of where he or the department stood on the various Centralia issues.

"We can't strongly emphasize enough how important the borehole

---

*Hodel became Interior Secretary in 1985 after the resignation of William Clark at the end of Reagan's first term.

project is," said Larkin. "Before we attack the fire, we need to know where it is." He urged Hodel to direct the Bureau to begin work on the drilling as soon as Congress appropriated the money. The Centralians feared the Bureau would wait for spring to begin drilling, as it usually did.

"Is it feasible to drill in the winter?" Hodel asked.

"Joe here worked on a drill," said Eva Moran, gesturing at her husband. "He drilled in the winter."

"Do you have a plan to put into effect when the drilling is over?" asked Baldwin, with the faintest hint of sarcasm in his voice.

"Do we have a plan?" responded Larkin, puzzled and a little intimidated. "The Department of the Interior has the expertise to draw up the plan. All we can do is give advice."

Hodel promised to look into why the Bureau planned to wait until spring to begin the drilling, perhaps not knowing at this point how strongly OSM opposed the project. As the group was leaving, he promised to check into having the sixteen-acre area expanded. An inquiry was made on both matters, but nothing ever came of it.

That evening, Nelligan and several Centralia citizens appeared on the ABC late night news show *Nightline.* Anchorman Ted Koppel did the broadcast from the studios of ABC affiliate WNEP-TV in Avoca, located about midway between Scranton and Wilkes-Barre. Larkin and Nelligan were interviewed in Washington, Joan Girolami was flown to Avoca, and the others were interviewed in Centralia. The broadcast was, overall, an excellent examination of the mine fire problem.

It had been an educational two days for Concerned Citizens. Despite the fact that not all of their experiences were pleasant, the group was happy it had gone to Washington. At least they had done something for Centralia, instead of sitting on their hands and bemoaning their fate. "We went to Washington last week," Larkin said at a Concerned Citizens meeting a week later. "We enjoyed what we did. It was tiring—and enlightening as well." Marie Cirillo later called the trip "a morale booster." She believed it might even have changed a few minds at the Interior Department, "although it's so hard to know what goes on behind those doors," she said.

■ ■ ■

Behind the doors of OSM, opposition to the Centralia exploratory drilling project was crystallizing. Most of the Carter administration holdovers like Beasley were gone. Director James R. Harris, a former Indiana state legislator, was busy implementing a new credo at OSM—let the states do it. Dean Hunt was assistant director for programs, operations, and enforcement. His responsibilities included federal reclamation projects, and he would lead OSM's opposition to the Centralia project, aided by his deputy J. Steven Griles.

A memorandum written on September 20 by OSM engineer Inhi Hong and a draft position paper written on October 29 stated four reasons why OSM believed the drilling project should be stopped: (1) the information obtained through the project would not be useful for the design of a project to extinguish the fire; (2) a "little improvement" of information about the size of the fire would not generate any "new, fresh ideas" for stopping the fire, and would not justify the $850,000 cost of the project; (3) the boreholes would increase the mine fire's intensity by acting as chimneys; and (4) Centralia residents and state officials would expect additional federal involvement to extinguish the fire.

The first three arguments were easily rebutted. The fourth was true. State and Bureau engineers, who had experience fighting mine fires, believed it foolhardy to begin digging a trench to stop an advancing fire without first finding the fire's outer perimeter. There was some information, true, but not for the entire fire. Information was particularly needed for the area near Byrnesville, south of Centralia. The Bureau planned to case and cap the boreholes as soon as they were drilled to reduce air intake to an absolute minimum. New technology made it possible to check the heat and gas content of a borehole without removing the cap.

Given Secretary Watt's attitude toward the Centralia problem, the fourth reason was probably the most important. A rising chorus of voices from Centralia, Harrisburg, and Congress was demanding the project begin quickly. There was every likelihood Congress would appropriate the $850,000 for the exploratory drilling. How could OSM stop the project now? If Congress would not be persuaded to reject the project, then OSM would take steps to make it useless for the hated Bureau's purposes. An ugly chapter in the history of the mine fire was about to begin.

One of the first things OSM did was attempt to persuade Specter to amend the wording of the bill so OSM rather than the Bureau would administer the project. OSM officials met with the senator the afternoon of November 4, and afterward a perplexed Bill Wilcox wondered aloud to a reporter why OSM was asking for this change so late in the game. "The conference committee was already meeting," Wilcox said. "It was too late at that point to do anything about it."

■ ■ ■

Helen Womer, perhaps worried that her theories about the mine fire were about to be swept away in the wake of the Concerned Citizens trip to Washington and the airing of the poison gas problem on *Nightline,* came to the November 3 meeting of Centralia Council with a proposal for a "unity meeting" of all Centralia residents. Such a meeting would allow everyone to exchange views and adopt a united stand to help Centralia. To encourage participation and candor, she said, the press would be excluded. Later she amended this to say local reporters could attend, so long as they did not bring with them tape recorders or anything to write with.

"There's too much divisiveness in Centralia," she said. "We all started off on the wrong foot, and we've been pulling further apart. Unless we are unified, we'll never get anything accomplished." It was a fine sentiment, and members of council and Concerned Citizens applauded her suggestion, though they disagreed about the press. The problem was that Helen Womer's beliefs on the mine fire were so radically different from those of Concerned Citizens that unity could be achieved only if one side unconditionally surrendered.

"I am not going to rest until that meeting is held and our town is united," Mrs. Womer said in an interview with the *News-Item* later that month. "We must get together and I will sacrifice anything. Well, not anything. No principles, of course, or the way I feel. But everybody should have courtesy toward other people and their opinions."

It became apparent during the interview that Mrs. Womer believed the people of Centralia would flock to her point of view if only she was given an opportunity to present her theories about the mine fire. She denied that her unity meeting might leave Centralia more divided than ever. "I don't think so," Mrs. Womer said. "Because I know from my vantage point, if it gets into a debate we will just adjourn the meeting and say this is not what we intended at all. Because many people don't know . . . well, I don't know all the facts, but I know a lot of facts the other ones don't seem to want to know."

The difficulty in dealing with Helen Womer was that, although she lacked evidence for many of her theories, she sounded as if she knew what she was talking about. After the mine fire surfaced near Big Mine Run Road in July, for example, she began telling people it meant the entire mine fire had moved away from Centralia. "Not one shred of evidence has ever been presented to show the fire is under Centralia," she said at the November council meeting. "I'll stand by my views until I'm proven otherwise."

Another of her theories was that other substances than carbon monoxide were causing most of the carbon monoxide readings recorded by the gas detectors. Mrs. Womer suggested that cigarette smoke, hair spray, cooking odors from sauerkraut or brussel sprouts, kerosene heaters, and stove gas jets left on caused many of the readings. She even suggested skunks were responsible for the gas readings in one home. "I can see that some of the most vocal people who are screaming gas and about their fright for their children think nothing of smoking and filling the house with carbon monoxide," Mrs. Womer said.

Her statements mixed fact with gossip and distortion, and they hurt. People in the impact zone who feared the fire came to fear Mrs. Womer and her supporters almost as much.

■ ■ ■

Cardinal John Krol and the twenty-two Roman Catholic bishops of Pennsylvania adopted a strongly worded resolution on November 19 calling on the federal government to help and protect the people of Centralia. The action, urged by Bishop Joseph T. Daley of Harrisburg, came at a meeting in Washington of the National Conference of Catholic Bishops. The resolution stated:

> We are urging that responsible officials at all levels of government take action before a tragedy occurs. As you know, the mine fire has been burning under Centralia for almost twenty years.
>
> While there have been attempts made during that time to try to extinguish the fire, these attempts have been half-hearted and not successful. We believe a coordinated effort on the part of the federal, state and local officials, as well as interested and concerned citizens and private organizations, is needed in order to solve this problem that has dragged on too long.

Copies of the bishops' call to action were mailed to Secretary Watt and the Pennsylvania congressional delegation, and although it appeared to cause no ripple in the situation, it greatly cheered Concerned Citizens members, most of whom were Catholic, and many other Centralians as well. At last their church was coming to their defense.

■ ■ ■

Any doubts the people of Centralia may have had about Secretary Watt and his opinion of their mine fire problem vanished after an incident on November 24 at the Republican Governors Conference in New Orleans. John Scotzin, a veteran reporter for the Harrisburg *Evening News,* had been sent by his newspaper to cover Governor Dick Thornburgh at the conference. He was waiting for Thornburgh to convene a panel discussion when he spotted Secretary Watt across the room. Watt was wearing his trademark cowboy hat, leaning against a door frame and chatting with a young woman, Scotzin recalls. It had not been a good day for news, and Scotzin tried to think quickly of something to ask Watt that would be of interest back in Pennsylvania. Bill Green, a press aide to Thornburgh, suggested he ask Watt about the Centralia mine fire.

"I introduced myself, and told him the Centralia mine fire is quite a burning issue in our territory," Scotzin said. "He grinned and said, 'Do you mean that as a pun, John?' He was very affable."

Watt proceeded to give the reporter a statement of his views about the Centralia mine fire problem, a statement few in Centralia would soon forget. "It's really a state responsibility," Watt said. "The governor and I met several months ago. There is not a threat to health and safety. It goes down deep; the deeper it burns, the less risk there is to safety. Eventually it will burn out."

"When will that be?" inquired Scotzin, who couldn't quite believe what he was hearing.

"I don't know," Watt said. "I'm advised that the action we took in purchasing the first sixteen to twenty threatened homes is a land-planning problem. It's a state responsibility, not federal. Governor Thornburgh is on top of it, I'm sure, with local officials." Watt made it very clear, Scotzin would write, that the Interior Department had no plans to fund any more projects to stop the Centralia mine fire.

"I went back and told Thornburgh," Scotzin said. "He was dismayed. I filed the story from my room. Then it hit the fan." Reaction was angry and came quickly, both from Centralia residents and state officials. Larkin called on Watt to provide proof that what he said about the mine fire was true. Thornburgh, who probably saw his worst nightmares about being stuck for the bill at Centralia coming true, sent Watt a letter of protest.

Interior press aide Ed Essertier found himself swamped with calls from reporters seeking an explanation of Watt's remarks. He could tell them little, because Watt had traveled to Oklahoma after leaving New Orleans and was unaware of the tempest he had raised. Essertier finally reached Douglas Baldwin, who provided him with a story to get the boss off the hook.

Essertier told reporters the next day that Baldwin had witnessed the entire incident and, well, it was being viewed in entirely the wrong light. To begin with, Essertier insisted, the interview had been an "over the shoulder" encounter while Watt was walking down a hallway. The secretary's remark that the mine fire posed no threat to health and safety in Centralia meant it no longer posed a threat to the health or safety of the families relocated from Centralia, he said. Watt's assertion that the mine fire would eventually burn out anyway should be interpreted to mean that the state and federal governments are attempting to establish a way to block the fire. "If so, we're hopeful it will burn itself out," Essertier said.

A letter from OSM director James R. Harris to Joan Girolami proclaimed the incident simply "an unfortunate misunderstanding." Congressman Nelligan later defended it as "a Watt attempt at humor" taken out of context.

Scotzin, the dean of the Capitol press corps in Harrisburg, now retired, remains miffed at accusations he quoted Watt out of context or ambushed him to get the interview. He stoutly defended the accuracy and truth of his exclusive and the method he used to get it. "Hell no, he didn't talk to me as he was leaving," he said. "The meeting hadn't started! It was *not* as he was leaving the room. He knew who I was. I identified myself as a reporter."

Watt seems to have been hurt and perplexed by the continuing criticism from the people of Centralia. Had he not relocated twenty-seven families at a cost of $1 million? "Yeah, he was put out," Nelligan said. "He used to say to me, 'Boy, you've got a tough district.' I said, well, I'm taking it on the chin, too, but these people need help. He said, 'Boy oh boy, you talk about getting a kick in the teeth.' I said, that's politics, kid. He said, 'Yeah, I know it.'"

It may have been the protest signs that irritated him more than anything. Members of Concerned Citizens had erected protest signs at various locations around the village. Larkin's said, "The U.S. Dept. of Interior Plays Nero While Centralia Burns." Mrs. Girolami's put it more bluntly—"Watt Is the Problem in Centralia."

Closeted in his Washington office, it must have been easy for the secretary to imagine Centralians would be grateful for his small gesture, which came amid the budget slashing he was doing with such enthusiasm for President Reagan. Specter had urged him to visit Centralia and see for himself how the people were suffering, but he had not gone and so could not understand the anger and hatred engendered by nineteen years of contempt and neglect. "When I see Watt walking down Locust Avenue, I'll know you can go ice skating in hell," Larkin said. "He doesn't have the courage to face the people of Centralia."

■ ■ ■

Buoyed by their trip to Washington and angered by Dr. Fox's remarks about the gas problem, the members of Concerned Citizens made plans to travel to Harrisburg to demand greater state involvement in fighting the mine fire. They hoped to meet with Thornburgh and the doctor, but were told that both, by coincidence, would be out of town on December 7, the day of the trip. Meetings were promised with representatives of the governor, with the House Mines and Energy Management Committee, the Northeast Caucus, made up of legislators from northeastern Pennsylvania, and with U.S. Representative Allen E. Ertel (D–17) of Montoursville, who unbeknown to them was planning to run for governor against Thornburgh in 1982.

This time nineteen members of Concerned Citizens made the trip, but Larkin and Mrs. Girolami had hoped to fill the bus they had chartered. Larkin was becoming discouraged by Centralians who would cheer from the sidelines but wouldn't take the field. "I just can't understand these people," he said during a conversation on the way to Harrisburg. "Are they so frustrated?"

At meetings and workshops, Concerned Citizens had compiled a list of ten demands to submit to Thornburgh. It was a provocative list, but as citizens—and the governor's employer, to risk a timeworn cliché—they were well within their rights.

They demanded more mechanically reliable gas monitoring equipment, and backup equipment in case it failed. Somebody's gas monitor was always broken down, it seemed, leaving that family with no early warning of danger. Sometimes the Ecolyzer used by DER in its daily inspections would be broken for weeks.

They demanded to know how Dr. Fox justified his assertion that there was no gas problem in Centralia. How could he say that after John Coddington had collapsed and numerous other persons had become ill? Then there were the low-level readings in many other houses. They also demanded to know when Dr. Edward Radford's study of the long-term health effects of the mine fire gases would begin, unaware that this demand was beyond the governor's power to grant.

Several of their demands centered around the memorandum of understanding signed by Thornburgh and Watt in March. They demanded to know how the governor viewed the agreement, and why he

Members of Concerned Citizens Against the Centralia Mine Fire on the steps of the state capitol in Harrisburg on December 7, 1981, heading for meetings with state officials on the mine fire. Right to left: David Lamb, Louis Girolami, Philip Gaughan, Thomas Larkin. Their happy, confident demeanor masked feelings of anger at the way Centralia was being treated by the Thornburgh administration. (Photo: David DeKok, News-Item)

General Dewitt Smith (left rear), director of Pennsylvania Emergency Management Agency, glares at Joan Girolami (front right) during a meeting on December 7, 1981, at the state capitol in Harrisburg. Right rear is Robin Ross, deputy counsel to the governor, and front left is Thomas Larkin. This was Concerned Citizens' last meaningful discussion with the Thornburgh administration. (Photo: David DeKok, News-Item)

had signed it. They demanded he either rescind it or have it amended so families outside the sixteen-acre area could be relocated.

"After the perimeter of the fire has been determined, we demand total excavation of the mine fire—it is being done at Larksville, it can be done in Centralia.* To this end, greater COOPERATION must be achieved among the federal, state, county and local governments," they wrote. "We demand that the residents of Centralia have direct involvement in any task force meetings or any other meetings concerning Centralia, including PEMA meetings."

It appeared to members of Concerned Citizens that Thornburgh had done little to help them. The memorandum of understanding was being used by OSM as support for its claim it had no further obligation to help Centralia. They had asked the questions before, but all that came out of Harrisburg was flackery—or silence. The governor's minions were always telling them how concerned Dick Thornburgh was about their plight, but then lesser officials like Dr. Fox would treat them with contempt. Their smiles for a *News-Item* photographer as they climbed the steps to the Capitol masked their deep anger, anger that would be much in evidence that day.

The press conference they held that morning beneath the Capitol rotunda was one of the few emotional highs they would have. It was a chance to be proud and defiant in front of the reporters and photographers before the meetings with state officials began. Larkin spoke for them all. Eleanor O'Hearn displayed a bumper sticker bearing the inscription, "Centralia, Pa. Mine Fire: HELL ON EARTH." Her angry face and the bumper sticker became the *Associated Press* photograph of the event.

State Representatives Robert Belfanti and Ivan Itkin, both Democrats, a Catholic priest who was representing Bishop Daley, and several other public officials also spoke at the press conference. Itkin, who is from the Pittsburgh area, had directed his staff to search the state budget for any potential sources of funding to help Centralia. They struck gold. "The state is not without its resources," Itkin said. "Some of the internal documents we've seen show the state has funds available. There's $47 million left in the Land and Water Conservation bond

---

*The Larksville mine fire ignited around 1977. Like the Centralia fire, it originated in a landfill, this one made up of furniture, clothing, and other combustible debris from the terrible Hurricane Agnes flood that ravaged Wilkes-Barre and many other communities along the Susquehanna River in 1972. The Bureau began a project to extinguish the Larksville fire in 1981.

issue." Someone must have known that money was there, but members of the General Assembly apparently had not been among them. Itkin suggested $10 million be set aside from the special fund by the General Assembly as the 25-percent state share of a project to stop the fire. "I'm not out to bankrupt the state, but I think the state can handle $10 million," Itkin said.

The key meeting of the day came that afternoon with officials of the Thornburgh administration. If Concerned Citizens had any doubts where Centralia stood with the state, they were resolved at this meeting. "The governor is totally committed to *trying* [emphasis added] to find a solution to the mine fire," said Robin Ross, deputy counsel to the governor. "The governor was particularly shocked last summer when the burn-through occurred. He immediately sent a letter to Secretary Watt." Why Thornburgh was shocked by the relatively harmless surfacing of the fire at Big Mine Run and not by the continuing presence of deadly gases in Centralia homes was anyone's guess.

"Do we have to have a tragedy in Centralia before we get any help?" Joan Girolami demanded.

"I think you've already had a tragedy," Ross snapped. "It's an ongoing tragedy."

"Why won't the state give us any help?" she pressed. General Smith, who was sitting next to Ross, was glaring at her.

"State government is not set up to deal with mine fires," Ross said. "It's an unprecedented disaster, similar to TMI [Three Mile Island]. There are fourteen to fifteen other mine fires in Pennsylvania. Their representatives want immediate help. That's the competition."

That was a specious argument. State government had extinguished several huge mine fires, including ones at Mount Carmel and Shenandoah. Both those projects were entirely funded by the state from the Land and Water Conservation bond issue. No other mine fires in Pennsylvania threatened the existence of an entire community.

General Smith questioned whether a majority of Centralia citizens wanted to relocate to escape the mine fire. As noted earlier, he dismissed the May referendum as worthless, despite the fact it basically confirmed the findings of OSM's socioeconomic study in 1980 and was itself reinforced by the *News-Item*'s coupon poll in August. The same numbers kept appearing—two to one in favor of relocation.

"I want to know how Dr. Fox could say there's no threat from the gases in Centralia when six homes have been condemned," Joan Girolami said.

"There's no question in our mind that gas is still a potential problem," Smith said. It was still only a *potential* problem in the minds of Smith and other Thornburgh administration officials.

"I'd like to see the families who have sick children given trailers," Mrs. Girolami said, referring to the four evacuation trailers that had stood empty since the end of the summer relocation.

"If anyone wants a trailer, all they have to do is ask," Smith replied.

"People have asked for trailers and been refused," countered David Lamb, mentioning his sister-in-law, Sheila Klementovich.

"Well, we can't just move anyone in," Smith said. "She may have thought she had a problem, while the Department of Community Affairs and the Health Department thought it didn't exist."

The trailers had become a cruel hoax. The state could claim they were available in case the potential gas problem ever became a reality, but families with high gas levels in their homes and frequent gas alarms were denied permission to move in because they did not meet the standards of the Health Department. It was not easy to live in one of the trailers, and no one made the request lightly.

"Some people have an actual problem with the gases," Smith said. "Others have a psychological problem with it."

"It's easy for you to sit there and say there is no problem," Lamb said angrily.

At this point, a Health Department spokesman entered the discussion to claim that Dr. Fox had been "misinterpreted and misquoted" in the *News-Item* story in October, a claim the department had not made until that moment.

"We're asking for the truth, not half-truths and half-falsehoods," Larkin said as the meeting broke up. "That's all we want."

■ ■ ■

Two days after Concerned Citizens returned home in frustration, there was another warning that the mine fire was a force of nature that could not be ordered to behave while elected officials and bureaucrats pondered what to do about it. Larkin was in his living room reading a book at 2:30 A.M. on December 9 when the lights went out. He walked out the front door to Locust Avenue and saw that all of Centralia was blacked out. He went back inside and called Pennsylvania Power and Light.

Power company workers had no trouble finding the problem—a tree had fallen in the wind and pulled down the power line, but this was no ordinary incident. The tree had stood in the triangular-shaped forest between Route 61 and the road that led to Byrnesville, south of Centralia. Steam from the mine fire was beginning to rise from cracks in the ground, and the workers were careful where they stepped. When morning came, they saw the roots and bottom of the tree were charred. Steam gushed from where the tree had stood. The mine fire had weakened the roots and the wind had done the rest.

22

The Year of the Scream

John Koschoff, Jr. (right), became president of Centralia Council in January 1982. His older sister, Helen M. Koschoff (left), a Centralia lawyer, acted as adviser to her brother and later became Centralia solicitor after her husband, Wayne Rapkin, resigned the position. (Photos: David DeKok, News-Item; © Stephen Perloff, 1983)

THOMAS Larkin and David Lamb were nervous as they stepped out of the elevator, which had taken them to the ninth floor of the Fulton Bank Building in Harrisburg. They were about to challenge the right of the agencies of government to exclude them from a meeting at which the fate of Centralia would be discussed, possibly decided. It seemed only right that someone from Centralia be there.

OSM had asked for the January 5, 1982 meeting with DER ostensibly to decide how to spend the $850,000 appropriated by Congress for the Centralia exploratory drilling project. President Reagan had signed the bill on December 11, and the legislation gave the agency thirty days to report back to Congress with a plan for the drilling and a plan to protect lives and property in Centralia from the mine fire.

There had been disquieting hints, however, that OSM might simply ignore the mandate of Congress. Thomas P. Flynn of the Bureau told the *News-Item* that OSM might use the money to finance a "positive ventilation project" to draw the harmful gases away from Centralia. Flynn's remarks triggered angry protest from OSM, and Bureau director Robert Horton responded by imposing a gag order on all Bureau employees. Henceforth, no one was to answer questions from the press about Centralia. All questions, no matter how trivial, were to be referred to him without comment.*

OSM and the Thornburgh administration had announced that the January 5 meeting would be closed to the public. A spokesman for PEMA said the meeting would be closed because "technical matters" were to be discussed. It was the latest administration excuse for conducting public business outside the public eye.

Concerned Citizens viewed the closed meeting as an affront to Centralia, and so did Centralia Council. The difference was that Larkin and Lamb decided to attend the meeting, invitation or no invitation. Concerned Citizens had worked hard for the borehole project, and now OSM seemed ready to wipe it out with the stroke of a pen. No one from Centralia Council went, despite Councilman John Koschoff's initial indignation that no one from council was invited. Koschoff became

---

*Horton wrote in his November 30 memorandum, "As I have tried to emphasize— the Centralia mine fire, and particularly BOM vs. OSM, is a very sensitive issue. Discussions with reporters, indications we will not do as Congress directs, views counter to OSM's—are not helpful."

president when council reorganized January 4, and a phone call from Harrisburg quieted his protests. He now claimed he did not want to antagonize the Thornburgh administration and jeopardize council's sudden "smooth working relationship" with the state.

Administration officials had advance warning that members of Concerned Citizens and the press might demand to be admitted to the meeting, and twice changed its location. It was only through a chance encounter with State Representative Robert Belfanti, who made some phone calls for them, that Larkin and Lamb were able to learn that the meeting would be held in DER Secretary Peter Duncan's suite on the ninth floor of the Fulton Bank Building.*

The meeting had already begun when they arrived. Belfanti asked the receptionist to summon Duncan from the meeting. She did, and the secretary emerged to tell the legislator that OSM did not want him there, and Larkin and Lamb that they could not attend because technical information being discussed "might be misinterpreted."

Belfanti apologized to the Centralians, saying he could do no more. Larkin and Lamb stared at the closed door, hearing muffled voices from the other room. After fifteen minutes the affront became intolerable; with considerable trepidation, they opened the door and walked inside, accompanied by a *News-Item* reporter who was with them that day.

Everything stopped. The reporter stated his belief that the Federal Open Meeting Act gave the public the right to attend and listen. Steven Griles, who was Dean Hunt's deputy at OSM, said the meeting was to discuss a contract and working relationship between two governmental bodies and thus did not have to be open. The reporter insisted the law did apply. Griles invited the trio to call the Office of the Solicitor at OSM for what surely would have been a predictable opinion. He denied that anyone at the meeting had anything to hide and demanded the intruders leave. No one else at the table spoke, and Griles refused further comment. The Centralians and the reporter turned and left, each deciding further argument with Griles would be useless.

Eleven days later, the *News-Item* found out why OSM was so insistent the meeting be closed. A damning memorandum written by

---

*Belfanti had persuaded state reapportionment officials to place Centralia in his realigned 107th Legislative District. His first opportunity to face the electorate would be in November 1982. Centralia remained in State Representative Ted Stuban's 109th District until the end of 1982.

David Simpson of the Bureau, who had been at the January 5 meeting, arrived in the mail at the newspaper January 16.* Simpson was not the sender—it arrived in a plain white envelope with a Washington postmark and no return address—but he admitted writing it. The leaker's identity was never discovered, although one suspects OSM expended a great deal of effort to find out.

Simpson wrote that Griles threatened Pennsylvania officials with a cutoff of funds for the home gas monitoring in Centralia unless the state agreed to (1) accept the $850,000 from OSM, (2) carry out the exploratory drilling itself, and (3) accept responsibility for paying for any further attempts to attack the mine fire. Simpson did not record the reaction of state officials to this vile attempt at bureaucratic blackmail.

Griles, through OSM spokesman Frank Kelly, denied making any threat, and state spokesman Kirk Wilson said none of the state officials at the meeting interpreted what Griles said as a threat. General Smith, however, told a different story. Asked whether Griles threatened the state, he said, "I would have said there was a hint of that in the air. I can't remember if it was direct or oblique. But there was a hint of that in the air." Smith said he was "aghast" when he came out of the meeting.

Centralians and Thornburgh administration officials alike were aghast when they read the January 28 report by OSM to Congress that stated how it planned to carry out the Centralia drilling and protect the lives and property of the people there. Instead of finding the boundaries of the now twenty-year-old fire, OSM proposed to use part of the $850,000 to drill ten to fifteen boreholes to gather data for a study of whether the mine fire could be extinguished by cutting off its air supply. Any remaining money from the grant would be used to implement the air cutoff plan—there seemed to be no way for the Bureau to convince OSM this idea would not work at Centralia—or would be turned over to the state for "additional drilling."

OSM believed the full-scale drilling project of 85–109 boreholes favored by the Bureau and DER was necessary only for an excavation project, which it vehemently opposed. The report to Congress strongly implied Pennsylvania would not get that remaining money unless it accepted responsibility for paying the cost of that excavation.

OSM's proposal for study of an air cutoff plan seems particularly odious in light of Congress's mandate to the agency to protect the lives and property of the people of Centralia. An option paper dated January

---

*Simpson was chief of the Bureau's office in Wilkes-Barre.

4 made it quite clear that such a plan would do nothing to make Centralia safer and would actually increase the danger. OSM officials believed, according to the option paper, that cutting off the major sources of air would "let carbon dioxide, an inert gas, fill the entire chamber of the underground gob area and extinguish the fire."* The problem was that closing the air portals would also close natural chimneys that vented part of the huge volume of carbon monoxide generated by the mine fire. There would be a "potential for build-up of carbon monoxide content in the mine atmosphere into the explosive range." The deadly gas would seek new avenues to the surface "through undiscovered fissures and cracks in the overburden above the fire zone." Some of those led to Centralia homes.

Not surprisingly, OSM did not report the more perilous part of its Centralia plan to Congress. One suspects that Hunt and Griles never expected to implement the plan, that they expected to bludgeon Pennsylvania into doing their bidding. If so, they were wrong.

There was quick and almost universal censure of the OSM plan. Both Centralia Council and Concerned Citizens condemned it, and Concerned Citizens staged a protest rally on the first anniversary of Todd Domboski's fall into the subsidence to petition Secretary Watt for a better plan. Over sixty persons attended.

"We ask you to support our council," Larkin told the rally. "We ask you to unite behind council and show the powers that be that we will no longer remain silent, but shout loudly that we demand the right to have a voice in the decisions that will so affect our future."

"A commitment was made, a commitment was broken," State Representative Belfanti said. "The Secretary of the Interior must be made to realize something must be done in Centralia."

Nelligan and Specter publicly criticized the OSM plan, and Specter sent a letter to Watt asking why the plan was approved without consulting the citizens of Centralia, particularly those in Concerned Citizens. Only Thornburgh remained silent, failing to send even his customary finger-wagging letter to Secretary Watt.**

"I think we sell Centralia down the drain if we don't fight for the borehole project," said Joan Girolami during an argument one evening in February with Helen Womer, who had pleaded with Concerned Citi-

---

*The low probability of success of an air cutoff plan is described in Chapter 14.

**DER Secretary Duncan sent a letter condemning the plan to, of all people, state Senator Edward Helfrick. One of the senator's aides released the letter to the press. Helfrick insisted that Duncan's letter should be viewed the same as if it came from Thornburgh, which of course it wasn't.

zens to stop criticizing the OSM proposal for fear the agency would simply abandon Centralia. "It's either slowly die or fight for what we feel is right."

On March 3, Mrs. Girolami's daughter, Denise Pasipanko, received an extraordinary letter from OSM in response to a letter she had sent protesting the agency's decision against a full-scale drilling plan. The letter, signed February 25 by acting director Thomas Butler, said OSM would present a full-scale drilling plan at a public meeting in Centralia prior to the awarding of a contract. Mrs. Girolami, jubilant, telephoned the *News-Item* with the news.

Soon after the newspaper began making calls to confirm the story, OSM director James R. Harris (Harris was away from his office the day the letter went out) issued a statement claiming the letter was erroneous. It was not erroneous, however, only premature. Thornburgh made a splashy announcement on March 4 that OSM had agreed to revise its plan and find the boundaries of the fire, although the agency still planned to study an air cutoff plan. The pressure from Congress and the citizenry had forced OSM to back down.

One clause in the agreement between OSM and the state received little attention at the time, probably because it appeared so harmless. "A major concern throughout the project will be keeping citizens and local government officials informed," Thornburgh said in his March 4 statement. "As part of this cooperative agreement, the state will provide primary liaison." This would mean that any discoveries of public interest during the borehole project—such as how far the fire had penetrated into Centralia—could only be released, and more importantly, interpreted, by the Thornburgh administration, not OSM. In an administration obsessed with secrecy and news management, whose own Health Department showed more interest in covering up the seriousness of the gas problem than protecting the public health in Centralia, the potential for mischief this presented was great, particularly in a year when Thornburgh had to face the voters.

■ ■ ■

One worry the Thornburgh administration did not have in 1982 was that Centralia Council might, during the heat of the governor's re-election campaign, speak out against the governor's mishandling of the Centralia problem. The election of John Koschoff as council president gave the administration a Centralia Council that would be subordinate to Harrisburg and remain silent about the governor, unlike when Polites and Lazarski were in charge.

General Smith says the state wanted to shape a Centralia Council that would be the voice of all Centralia. Smith says he envisioned council and Concerned Citizens working together in a common front, although with a clear understanding that council would represent Centralia to the outside world. "I was anxious to get a new council in there and I was anxious to make them function," he said later.

It is difficult to believe unity was the Thornburgh administration's main concern when it made Centralia Council a junior partner in 1982, and it is hard to think of anyone less likely than Koschoff to unify Centralia. Koschoff had little tolerance for anyone who disagreed with him. Only twenty-five years old, immature, and inexperienced in the ways of governing, he brought the brutal politics of the schoolyard to Centralia Council. He often claimed his first goal was to protect the health and safety of Centralia residents, but he never did a thing for families with gas problems. His second goal, he would say, was to preserve as much of Centralia intact as possible. That meant anyone who supported relocation was an enemy. Indeed, Koschoff appeared to have strong feelings about only one thing—smashing Concerned Citizens. He made no secret of his feelings, which were aggravated by the group's support of relocation and, says an insider, by jealousy of the favorable publicity the group received and its access to top-ranking public officials.

Koschoff enjoyed loyal support from Councilmen Edward Gusick and Kenneth Wagner, and acquiescence from the rest, at least at first. He persuaded council to hire Wayne Rapkin, a Centralia lawyer, as solicitor.* Rapkin was married to Koschoff's sister Helen, also a lawyer and an aggressive defender of her younger brother's interests.

Concerned Citizens made every effort to cooperate with council, sharing documents and inviting members of council to attend their meetings. Their efforts met with failure. Koschoff and his associates, along with Mayor Wondoloski—none of whom lived in the impact zone or had any apparent appreciation for the problems faced by those who did—treated Concerned Citizens with increasingly open hostility.

The Thornburgh administration, far from trying to end the persecution of Concerned Citizens, aided and abetted it. Council demanded that the state stop providing information to Concerned Citizens, says

---

*The *News-Item* checked to see if this violated the state ethics code for public officials. It did not. Miss Koschoff served as counsel for the Pennsylvania Commission for Women from 1980 to 1982. Thornburgh appointed her a member of the commission on June 20, 1983.

former Councilman Roy Kroh. The state willingly complied, resenting and fearing the group's aggressive and independent pursuit of an end to the mine fire and perhaps, the innocent meeting in December with U.S. Representative Allen E. Ertel, who had since announced his intention to oppose Thornburgh for re-election in 1982.

Kroh says he, Koschoff, and Rapkin attended a meeting in Harrisburg about the mine fire early in 1982. He knew none of the Thornburgh administration officials at the meeting, Kroh says, but Koschoff and Rapkin greeted them like old friends. It struck him as odd that they obviously knew everybody in the room.

■ ■ ■

The leaders of Concerned Citizens were facing up to the bleak realization that fighting for a just solution to Centralia's plight had won them powerful enemies in their hometown. Instead of support from the community, which they expected, they were attacked inside and outside council chambers. Concerned Citizens was accused of dividing the community, of wanting to sell the town.

"Do you know of any town that's not divided over a problem?" Joan Girolami said in an interview that spring. "I'd bet a lot of the division wouldn't be here if officials had taken the proper action. Council plays with it. They tell the citizens they shouldn't be here, that they [council members] run the town. Concerned Citizens has only been together a year. The town's been divided a lot longer than that."

"John Koschoff says he has to do what is best for the whole town, but some people need help now," she continued. "The rest of the town won't let the south side go. They say we make up our gases, that it's okay to live on top of six-hundred-degree temperatures. It's not their home and it's not their families."

No longer was it only a matter of Concerned Citizens battling the federal and state governments for help for Centralia. It was increasingly a battle with Helen Womer and her supporters, which included the Koschoff faction on Centralia Council as well as people like Mary Lou Gaughan and Leon and Elaine Jurgill. In between was an uncommitted bloc that probably included about 70 percent of Centralia's residents.

In political terms, the members of Concerned Citizens were revolutionaries who had organized a political front after watching their lives and property, or those of friends and relatives, become endangered because of incompetence and shameful neglect by the federal, state, and local governments. To them, Centralia was Babylon, a place from which to escape if, as seemed likely, the fire and gases could not be stopped.

Helen Womer and her supporters were attempting to launch a counterrevolution. They were dedicated to preserving Centralia intact and often seemed oblivious to the advancing mine fire. In their minds, Centralia was still the wonderful village they remembered from their childhood, a Brigadoon of the Anthracite Region.* The fire was outside the village, possibly now moving in the opposite direction. The gas problem was an exaggeration by people who wanted only to profit on the sale of their homes to the government. Unknown forces from the outside were preventing a simple solution to the fire and gas problem and would move in and grab Centralia's coal wealth after the village was destroyed. That was how they thought, and they searched out and clung to shreds of evidence that seemed to prove their case.

Concerned Citizens was at the beginning of a crisis. Its cause was just and would survive, but its leaders would find themselves unable to cope with the personal abuse and intimidation that were the only weapons available to their enemies. The war with OSM and the state was a civil sort of thing; the Centralia civil war was not.

■ ■ ■

It was May, and DER inspectors Dennis Wolfe and Wayne Readly discovered carbon monoxide was entering impact zone homes through the sewer system. Their monitoring device found high readings in kitchen sinks, shower stalls, and bathtub drains. The problem was worst along the 200 block of Locust Avenue, although Joan Girolami's house on East Park Street was also affected.

Most families kept their gas alarms in the basement, where the gas entered through cracks in the foundation. There was speculation that was why the sink and drain readings had not been discovered until now. No one could rule out the possibility, though, that some recent change in the mine fire had caused the gases to infiltrate the Centralia sewer system.

The readings continued into the summer, bad on some days, nonexistent on others. Boreholes were opened and closed as needed in an attempt to draw away the gases. The readings ranged from a few ppm to 65 ppm. The regular alarms did not stop, either.

---

*Mrs. Womer, for example, told the *Washington Post* in 1982, "This was once a model community, it was so close-knit, and we had so much fun, we'd have town picnics and everybody would show up."

Fire officials in Conyngham Township worried about the mine fire outbreak site along Big Mine Run Road. A forest fire started at the site on April 25 and burned about an acre before firefighters brought it under control. It was surmised that dead leaves had blown onto the hot rocks and ignited.

Flames from the mine fire were no longer visible at night, although the heat was still there, causing huge pieces of the cliff to split off and fall into the forest below. Trees were dying on the hill above the cliff, and some had sprawled forward like dead men, bleached boney white by the heat and burned off at the roots.

People waited for the beginning of the exploratory drilling with a mixture of eagerness and dread.

■ ■ ■

Robert Brennan, one of OSM's best engineers, faced a difficult task in finding the boundaries of the mine fire, much like that of the blind men trying to describe an elephant. Each of the 85 to 109 boreholes would tell him a little about the nature of the fire, but none would tell the entire story. One borehole could tell him the fire had reached the mines beneath his feet, but it could not tell him how large an area the fire covered in that sector of Centralia. It was up to him to assemble the puzzle.*

The temperature in the borehole, of course, was of prime importance. Brennan planned to begin drilling at the outer limits of the conceivable fire area to find out "where the fire isn't." One drill rig would work on the Centralia side of the mountain, another on the Byrnesville side. Once the cold perimeter was discovered—normal mine temperature being about 55 degrees—the drillers would move toward the fire's known hot areas.

Next in importance among the borehole data was air pressure—was air being forced up and out of the borehole or pulled down into the mine? Brennan knew if air was being forced out of a borehole, the fire was near. If there was a downdraft, it meant air was flowing through the mine on its way to a fire elsewhere.

Then there were the gases found in a borehole. If Brennan found an oxygen volume of below 19 percent (normal was 20.95 percent), it would mean a large fire close by was generating other gases. If a high

---

*Brennan, who received his engineering training at Pennsylvania State University, worked for the Bureau for most of his career and did not join OSM until February 1, 1982, the day most Bureau personnel who worked in abandoned mine land reclamation were transferred to OSM. Secretary Watt ordered the transfer in the name of efficiency.

volume of carbon monoxide was found, it would indicate a smoulder-ing fire. A low volume of the deadly gas, on the other hand, meant the fire was very hot—in excess of 1,000 degrees—and liberating hydro-gen from the anthracite coal. It was the reason mining engineers did not like to pour water on a mine fire. The intense heat could break down the water into hydrogen and oxygen and cause powerful explosions.

Brennan worked through the spring and summer of 1982 on the plans for the drilling at Centralia. Once the drilling began, he would have six months to complete the work. That had been agreed to by OSM and DER. He would turn over the drilling data to a private con-sulting firm that would have four months to analyze his work and rec-ommend how best to stop the mine fire. OSM did not want former Bureau engineers deciding that.

Brennan lived in Mount Carmel and knew many of the Centralia people. He was an engineer who resisted attempts to make him any-thing else. If you asked him a question, he would give you an honest answer, even if it got him into trouble. The Thornburgh administration would learn that to its sorrow.

■ ■ ■

The House Mines and Energy Management Committee, at the request of State Representative Belfanti, was holding another hearing in Cen-tralia. It was a hot July day, much different from the committee's last visit, in March 1981. That was not the only difference. No Republican members of the committee had come to Centralia. After the com-mittee's initial visit of the day to Shamokin, to see a successful ex-periment in using anthracite culm to generate cheap steam energy, the Republican members of the committee mumbled excuses and re-turned to Harrisburg. Even committee chairman James Wright made a hasty exit.

"I didn't know until the day before the Republicans weren't going to come," Belfanti said. "Now it seemed to me, and to other members who were Democrats, that it was a boycott. Somebody from the ad-ministration put the word out, let this thing stay low-key—we don't want to make a big deal out of Centralia. Because I don't think the Governor's Office had made any decision whatsoever about what they were going to do about this problem, other than continually blame the federal government for not taking action. And that was a cop-out."

■ ■ ■

Spiegel and McDiarmid's lawyers had continued to study the Centralia problem for Concerned Citizens, and had found a promising angle for a lawsuit on behalf of the people of the impact zone based on OSM's own regulations. As lawyer Dan Guttman explained it at a July 19 public meeting in Centralia, OSM violated those regulations by relocating sixty-eight residents of the impact zone and then taking no action to reclaim the land, that is, to extinguish the mine fire. It was an angle Franklin Kury, the lawyer approached by Polites and Lazarski the previous year, had missed. Unfortunately, it seemed that Concerned Citizens could do or propose nothing that would not be denounced by Centralia Council.

Almost before Guttman finished speaking, council members condemned the proposal. Koschoff insisted it would be "premature" to file a lawsuit before the borehole project was completed, that it would risk losing the project entirely. Although Concerned Citizens members agreed with Koschoff that it would be better to wait until they knew the full threat posed by the fire, Centralia Council and Mayor Wondoloski issued a public statement on July 23 denouncing the proposed lawsuit and Concerned Citizens in strong terms. It mattered not at all that Concerned Citizens had made no decision about a lawsuit and had invited council members to hear the lawyers' presentation. Matters were beginning to turn ugly.

If the proposed lawsuit provoked hot anger from council, however, the $30,000 grant to Concerned Citizens from the Campaign for Human Development (CHD) pushed the Koschoff faction over the edge. Concerned Citizens intended to use the grant to mobilize Centralia citizens to fight for an end to the mine fire threat. They also planned to hire a project coordinator, open an office, and find a medical researcher willing to study the effects of the gases. Larkin believes the subsequent campaign against the group was led by Mayor Wondoloski, Koschoff, his sister Helen, and Helen Womer. Calling it a campaign does not fully suggest the hate that was in the air.

At the September 8 council meeting, Koschoff and his sister raged against Concerned Citizens, questioning their motives for obtaining the $30,000 and accusing the group of attempting to usurp the functions of council. Koschoff demanded a copy of the application, which Joan Girolami refused to give him. "I'm appalled the people in the Catholic Church who approve such grants would give this money to Concerned Citizens," Koschoff said. "This money should go to needy causes, like buying food and clothing for poor people."

Koschoff accused Concerned Citizens of not representing the majority of Centralia residents, and of making no effort to get along with council. "Borough council runs the town and represents the majority of the townspeople," he said. "Concerned Citizens represents only themselves. The name of your organization is appropriate. All residents of this town have a right to be concerned about your organization."

Helen Koschoff attacked Joan Girolami for her support for relocation of families endangered by the gases, asserting there was no evidence to show that any Centralia resident was endangered by the mine fire. "Are borehole temperatures showing there is a mine fire in our town?" she demanded, referring to early results from the drilling project. "Did the Department of Health declare any health hazards exist?" Helen Koschoff and her husband taunted the citizens to report any "mine fire hazards" to borough officials.

Koschoff's harassment of Concerned Citizens finally became too much for officials in Harrisburg. They secretly contacted Koschoff in September and asked him to stop his attacks, but it did little good.

All this might have passed as the foolishness of small minds but for the harassing telephone calls and death threats made to the officers of Concerned Citizens. No one ever found out who made them. The calls began at the time of the $30,000 grant controversy and continued for months. Thomas Larkin's death threat came at 4 A.M. one morning in September. The caller said Larkin would die if Concerned Citizens accepted the CHD grant. He was shaken, very shaken. The calls continued on succeeding nights. More often than not he heard only heavy breathing on the other end of the line.

Theresa Gasperetti, angered by Helen Koschoff's statement that no one in Centralia was endangered by the mine fire, appeared at the September 14 council meeting and made a tearful defense of her own family and others who struggled with the gas danger. All it got her was a place on the call list. The calls came at all hours of the day and night, and at night the phone would ring and ring and ring until she or her husband answered it.

David Lamb would pick up the phone and hear a torrent of obscenities, the breather, or a voice warning him he would not leave Centralia alive. Lamb, who was separated from his wife, lived alone in an apartment he made for himself above his motorcycle shop.

No matter what the members of Concerned Citizens said in their own defense, the criticism from Wondoloski, Helen Womer, and the Koschoffs was unrelenting. They accused Concerned Citizens of wanting only to destroy Centralia. "The overwhelming mistrust that the people have of the Concerned Citizens is to me the reason for our division in the community," Helen Womer said at a Concerned Citizens meeting on September 23. "Talk of relocation is premature and destructive. This is our position."

Concerned Citizens tried to carry on, but the abuse was taking a toll. Larkin developed a duodenal ulcer that his doctor blamed on severe stress. Some of his own relatives in Centralia would avoid him when they saw him coming down the sidewalk. His weight ballooned. Joan Girolami, too, developed an ulcer, and like several of her women friends in the impact zone had begun taking a few tranquilizers to get through the day. Unlike them, she refused to use Valium and was privately horrified at the extent of its use in the impact zone. Her two daughters resented the amount of time she spent on the mine fire.

■ ■ ■

On the morning of Friday, October 1 a Centralia woman who refused to identify herself called the *News-Item*. One of the drill rigs had just been moved from behind the Smollocks house, which was near SS. Peter and Paul Russian Orthodox Church on East Park Street, and she had seen tar melting off the drill, it was that hot. The reporter telephoned Robert Brennan at his field trailer, and by luck he was there. Brennan said the crew had just finished drilling borehole N-21. Its temperature was 220 degrees, hotter than any borehole drilled to date. Then he hesitated.

"I guess you know we have a 500-degree hole up there," Brennan said in his typically deadpan voice. M-2 was located about midway between Tony Gaughan's house and the Russian church, Brennan continued. It was one of the boreholes drilled many years ago to give warning if the fly ash barrier failed and the fire was coming through. OSM inspectors discovered in late May that M-2 had jumped 308 degrees, from 194 to 502 degrees, in a little over five weeks. Since May it ranged between 470 and 502 degrees, which could only mean fire, Brennan said. This fire breakthrough might well account for the upsurge of gas incidents—the sink and drain readings—that began in May in houses two blocks west of M-2 along the 200 block of South Locust Avenue.

The reporter knew nothing of any of this, and neither, he suspected, did anyone in Centralia. It was a major news story, the biggest since the collapse of John Coddington. This is what the people of Centralia had longed to know, whether the barrier was intact. No one with access to this information could have been ignorant of its importance—or political danger. Someone had buried it, he thought.

There had, in fact, been a cover-up, but he was wrong—someone in Centralia did know about M-2 and participated in what has to be one of the more unsavory actions by government during the long history of the Centralia problem. After the OSM inspectors told their

OSM engineer Robert Brennan (fourth from left) speaks to reporters while flanked by angry Thornburgh administration officials on October 5, 1982, after he was almost fired for revealing that the mine fire had broken through the fly ash barrier near Tony Gaughan's house the previous May. (Photo: David De-Kok, News-Item)

superiors about M-2, a decision was made to make no public announcement and to simply follow longstanding policy regarding the temperature reports. That, said David Simpson of OSM, was to mail copies to Koschoff and DER. Centralia Council or DER could break the bad news, if so inclined. Neither chose to release the information.

The *News-Item* story on October 1 had an electric effect on the people of Centralia, no matter where they stood on the fire issue. A follow-up story in the newspaper the next day revealed the extent of the cover-up, and public outrage at Koschoff and DER—but particularly at the council president—began to swell.

Brennan revealed on Monday, October 4, that new boreholes drilled in the neighborhood of M-2 showed the fire advancing into Centralia along a two-hundred-foot front. A borehole drilled only fifty feet south of the Russian church found a 580-degree temperature. Brennan recommended that DER place a gas alarm in the church basement.

Associated Press in Harrisburg picked up on the story that afternoon from the *News-Item*. Brennan told the wire service what he had told the newspaper that morning and added that drilling results showed the fire advancing on Byrnesville along an eight-hundred-foot front. He said if the fire continued on its present course it would pass directly under Byrnesville. Not only that, he told the *News-Item* later, the fire near Byrnesville was also headed straight for Route 61. A two-hundred-foot section of the highway was only fifty feet above the Buck vein and at one point less than twenty feet of cover separated the highway from the old mines. Large clouds of steam already rose from both sides of Route 61. "PennDOT* has been alerted," Brennan said. "They're very concerned about this."

The *News-Item* reached DER press secretary Bill Pennewill to ask why the M-2 discovery had been withheld from the public.** Pennewill avoided the question. ("You're saying we withheld the information? Is that your opinion, that we withheld the information?") before finally answering that DER did not make the finding public because "one borehole is not significant enough to answer any questions." Reelection politics was probably the reason the Thornburgh administration suppressed the M-2 discovery. At the time OSM sent out its report

---

*PennDOT stands for Pennsylvania Department of Transportation.

**One of the strictest Thornburgh administration information control policies was that reporters were not allowed to talk to state employees—except perhaps agency heads—unless a public relations person cleared it, which often they did not. If they did, they often listened in on the interview. It was the governor's belief that his administration should speak "with one voice."

to DER on the borehole, the administration was smarting from recent attacks on the Centralia issue by Congressman Allen E. Ertel, the Democratic nominee for governor.

It was Koschoff's bad luck to have to chair a Centralia Council meeting the evening of October 5, before public anger had a chance to subside. He had not told the other members of council about M-2, and in a closed-door session before the meeting they demanded to know why.

Councilman Kroh says Koschoff told them he was preoccupied with the impending death of his father at the time the report arrived and failed to realize its significance. Kroh urged Koschoff to confess to the public and apologize. That Koschoff would not do. He went into the meeting room and told Concerned Citizens that no one ever informed him the borehole had shot up 306 degrees. No one believed him. Theresa Gasperetti and Catherene Jurgill had obtained copies of the report OSM had sent him.

"You wouldn't even have to go over the whole paper, John," Mrs. Gasperetti said. "We're telling you here. This one paper, right here. Right here! M-2. In the borough! Five hundred and two degrees!"

"I'm telling you I wasn't aware of it," Koschoff said.

They demanded his resignation, but he did not oblige them.

■ ■ ■

Brennan believes his troubles began when Thornburgh picked up the Harrisburg *Patriot* the morning of October 5 and read the *Associated Press* story about the fire breakthrough. It was the newspaper's top story, running six columns across the top of page one. It is his understanding the governor then telephoned DER to find out what had happened.

DER and PEMA were furious with Brennan about his disclosures to the press. Thornburgh was in an unexpectedly tight election race with Ertel, and this sort of news leak was not supposed to happen. Under the agreement signed with OSM, the state had sole control of information from the Centralia project. Now Brennan had divulged what a clear and present threat the mine fire was to the people of Centralia and Byrnesville. The cover-up of M-2 had been exposed, and the state had egg on its face. Someone in the upper reaches of the Thornburgh administration called OSM director James R. Harris and complained bitterly about Brennan's disclosures. Harris dispatched Dean Hunt to Centralia with orders to fire Brennan on the spot, the intended victim said later.

Hunt arrived in Centralia Tuesday afternoon, as did a contingent of DER and PEMA officials. Brennan survived the showdown, convincing Hunt that all he did was answer questions from a news reporter. He did not go to the newspaper with the information. The officials tried to persuade him to shade the truth when he talked to the press, but Brennan refused. "It only comes out one way," he said.

DER and PEMA then demanded he be gagged, and Hunt agreed. Brennan would refer any press inquiries to John Comey, the PEMA press secretary. OSM would send Art Anderson, another engineer, to supervise Brennan.

When the *News-Item* reporter on the story heard about the gag order from Brennan, he called Comey to find out why. Comey told him that there *was* no gag order. "It's an effort to coordinate our statements. We want to make suré the state and the borough get the information before the press does." A day later, after a furor erupted over the gag order, he added, "As far as the state is concerned, we have no gag order. OSM is free to say what it likes. But Bob Brennan will not interpret the borehole data."

■ ■ ■

Sixty-seven-year-old Agnes Owens had a ticklish problem. She lived alone on East Park Street next to the Russian church, and the drillers had found a 580 degree temperature ten feet from her back door. When they pulled the drill bit from the hole, a geyser of steam shot out.

There had been a carbon monoxide alarm in her house since 1979, and in recent months it had sounded with ever-greater frequency. Once it sounded while an elderly lady friend was visiting, and the woman fainted dead away. Mrs. Owens revived her with smelling salts. Although the house had been her home since birth and she did not want to leave, Mrs. Owens realized how bad the situation was getting and decided it would be best to move to an evacuation trailer. The problem was the state Health Department, whose doctors would not certify any Centralia homes were dangerous. By their own admission they did not take carbon monoxide into account in making that decision.

It had reached the point where her alarm was sounding several times each week, then several times each day. DER technicians replaced her alarm, believing it defective, but the new alarm behaved no differently. "She was getting all those gases and her alarm was going off and they were saying the poor lady's nuts, she just hears bells ring," Brennan said later. "Like hell, she was. We had 700 degrees under her house!"

Councilman Kroh was walking past Mrs. Owens's house the morn-ing of October 7 when he heard her alarm go off. He investigated the matter, speaking to both Mrs. Owens and Brennan, and then called General Smith to ask if Mrs. Owens could move to a trailer. Her gas alarm sounded twenty times that day.

General Smith approved a trailer for her that afternoon. Comey stressed the move was approved only because of her age, because she lived alone, and because of *her concern* about her close proximity to the mine fire. It was not because of the carbon monoxide, twenty alarms apparently not being enough to warrant state concern.

Kroh incurred the wrath of the Koschoff faction for helping Mrs. Owens. They already despised him for talking to the press.

■ ■ ■

It was, by all accounts, the most chaotic council meeting in Centralia's history. The warfare between the Koschoff faction and Concerned Citi-zens reached its peak on November 1 at some point during a three-and-a-half-hour meeting punctuated by screaming, name-calling on both sides, and demands for Koschoff's resignation.

Koschoff, mocking the complaint by Concerned Citizens that he withheld the report on M-2, ordered that every piece of correspon-dence be read aloud, including the entire text of a story about Cen-tralia in the Philadelphia *Inquirer*. Councilman Michael Lupatsky protested finally that the meeting was becoming a farce. "I thought they wanted everything read," Koschoff said.

Concerned Citizens members stalked out of the meeting near the end to express their displeasure with the council president. It seemed there was nothing else they could do. Koschoff held the upper hand, and state officials backed him to the hilt.

■ ■ ■

David Lamb awoke with a start. There was a frantic pounding on his apartment door. It was 4:14 A.M., November 3, and Lamb wondered if this was another attempt at harassment. He opened the door and a young man screamed at him to get out. His motorcycle shop was on fire.

Lamb ran back inside and dragged his ten-year-old son out of bed and to safety outside. He unlocked the door and ran inside his store. Waist-high flames were rising off the carpeted floor between two motorcycles. Lamb grabbed a fire extinguisher and managed to beat down the flames. Lying on the floor was a crude Molotov cocktail that had been hurled through a window. Gasoline spilled out and ignited when the bottle hit the floor, but the bomb did not explode. An explosion might well have started a conflagration that Lamb and his son would not have escaped.

The man who warned him was a passing motorist. State police investigators never solved the crime, and Lamb was never certain if the bomber was someone who opposed Concerned Citizens or who disliked him for some other reason. In any case, the bombing terrified Concerned Citizens. Larkin and Mrs. Girolami resigned shortly thereafter, and so did Lamb, Clara Gaughan, Eleanor O'Hearn, and Alice Rooney. Concerned Citizens was not dead—a few members remained—but it was in shambles.

"We gave what we could," Larkin said. "Joan's health was in jeopardy, my health was on the verge of being in jeopardy. I guess because of these factors and some others we felt it was time for somebody else to pick up the ball. We carried the ball a long way."

Asked if he thought Concerned Citizens failed to define its goals well enough to the community, Larkin answered in the affirmative. "Apparently we must have [failed]," he said. "And apparently, those who were violently opposed to us were able to spread their animosity and their hatred far better than we were able to spread our purpose. Even though over, and over, and over again we said we're not out to sell, we want to save the town. If we can save it, let's save it."

■ ■ ■

Thornburgh eked out a victory over Allen Ertel, who did better than many expected against an incumbent governor who outspent him considerably and who refused to debate. Centralia did not become an issue. Congressman Nelligan lost his bid for a second term to Frank Harrison, a Wilkes-Barre lawyer who had promised to make helping Centralia a top priority. Nelligan lost Centralia, as most Republicans do, but had the satisfaction of knowing he did much better there than Thornburgh.

23

Unity Day

U.S. Representative Frank Harrison (D–Wilkes-Barre) and State Representative Robert Belfanti (D–Mount Carmel; right) examine the area where the mine fire passed beneath Route 61 south of Centralia. The date of their visit was January 10, 1983. (Photo: David DeKok, News-Item)

CHRISTMAS of 1982 was a particularly bleak one for those families in the impact zone for whom the clanging of the gas alarm was as familiar as the crunch of boots in the snow on Locust Avenue. The worst of the Koschoff faction's campaign against Concerned Citizens was over, but there was no end in sight to the mine fire. State and federal officials said repeatedly that nothing could or would be done until the final report based on the borehole project was released that summer.

The mine fire was racing toward Route 61 and the Penn Fuels natural gas pipeline that paralleled the highway. It appeared to Robert Brennan that the fire would be under both in a matter of days, as he predicted in October it would. Moving along the Buck vein on the Byrnesville side of the mountain, the fire was advancing several feet per day—the speed of light in mine fire terms. Here on the south side, where the mine support pillars were intact and the way mostly clear, the fire could move much faster than on the Centralia side, where the fire had to pick its way through much collapsed roof rock.

Once it reached the highway, then what? State transportation officials, among them Secretary Thomas Larson, worried the fire would cause subsidences. They were told by OSM and DER that the fire was burning near the Buck outcrop and that dangerous subsidences were far more likely here than further down the mountain. At one point near the Centralia borough line, less than six feet of cover lay between the highway and an eleven-foot deep mine chamber. The fire would heat the roof rock, causing it to expand and tighten. When the fire moved on, the rock would cool and contract. "That's when the subsidence problems start," PennDOT engineer James Kendter warned. If a car, school bus, or other vehicle plunged into a subsidence, though the drop would be relatively short, the driver and passengers might well be injured, even killed by the impact. Poison gases from the mine fire might kill any survivors before help arrived, particularly if the accident occurred in the middle of the night.

Larson began discussions with General Smith about the impending crisis. In a letter of December 30, he proposed asking OSM officials to declare the highway threat an emergency and proceed with a federal project to make the road safe for the motoring public. It was none too soon. Temperatures had risen steadily during December in the boreholes near Route 61. Proof the mine fire was under the highway came January 5, 1983, when OSM inspectors discovered the temperature in borehole DT-3, located on the west berm of Route 61, had risen to 770 degrees. Three weeks earlier it had been 149 degrees.

DER, OSM, PennDOT, Columbia County, and Penn Fuels representatives held an emergency meeting on January 6 in Centralia. DER decided safety would not allow a wait for OSM to approve emergency funding, and announced that the state would pay for the work itself. "We have a pretty nasty situation for a short stretch along Route 61," said Michael Bielo, who worked in DER's Office of Resources Management. "There's not a lot of cover, there's a big void and high temperatures. We want to get it filled up quickly."

DER planned to pour crushed rock and water into the mine voids beneath the highway to shore up the surface. This would be done not only south of Centralia, where the fire had crossed Route 61, but also under a four-hundred-foot section of Locust Avenue, chiefly in the 100 and 200 blocks. Many families lived along the 200 block, and there was concern the drilling and flushing might force greater volumes of gas into adjoining homes. "I really doubt that," Bielo said. "It's such a small, isolated area. It's a possibility, but it's remote."

Penn Fuels officials insisted the natural gas pipeline was not presently endangered by the mine fire. During the coming days and weeks, they would resist well-meaning pressure from Centralia's new congressman, Frank Harrison, Representative Belfanti, and others to move the pipeline away from the mine fire. Although the situation appeared dangerous to the casual observer and was the subject of much morbid speculation in Centralia, and although one can question the wisdom of Penn Fuels' decision in 1964 to build a pipeline across the ultimate path of the mine fire, in 1983 the company had good arguments to support its contention the pipeline was unlikely to rupture or explode.

The pipeline is only three feet below the surface along the east berm of the highway. Because the Buck vein slopes downward, the only point of vulnerability for the pipeline was that section of the highway where thin cover separated the road from a mine void. Even this minimal cover insulated the pipeline from the full fury of the fire below. On the day DT-3 was measured at 770 degrees, the warmest temperature around the pipeline was 64 degrees. That was unusual for a cold January day, but it posed no danger. According to information provided by Penn Fuels, the pipeline valves could withstand up to 900 degrees at 400 pounds of pressure. The pipeline welds could withstand up to 1,000 degrees.

Damage to the pipeline by subsidence worried people as much as the heat, however. DER officials, noting the pipeline was made up of twenty-five-foot sections of pipe welded together, said it was unlikely any subsidence would be large enough to cause the pipeline to rupture. If it did, Penn Fuels argued, there would be a fire but no explosion at the site of the break. Service to three thousand customers in Mount Carmel and Shamokin would be cut off if that happened, which could be quite unpleasant in the dead of winter.

Penn Fuels had a contingency plan to move the pipeline, which officials estimated it would take forty-eight hours to implement, working around the clock, or four days if normal hours were followed. Later, they said the plan would be implemented if the temperature around the pipeline reached 300 degrees, hot enough to melt the coating on the pipe. The company would shut off the gas at Ashland, then bring tankers of liquified natural gas from Reading to Mount Carmel and feed it into the system there. The state Public Utilities Commission examined the evidence, sent its own inspector to the scene, and found the company's logic acceptable.

All the same, it was difficult not to feel apprehensive, particularly after Penn Fuels workers unearthed the pipeline one day to pack insulating material around its most vulnerable points, and steam curled lazily from the walls of the trench. One wonders how communities along Route 61 would react to tankers of liquified natural gas—which is highly explosive—passing through.

■ ■ ■

Representative Belfanti telephoned Congressman Harrison in Washington the afternoon of Friday, January 7, to tell him serious problems had developed along Route 61 south of Centralia. He said the mine fire might cause the highway to collapse. Harrison had been in office only three days, although he was familiar with the general facts of the Centralia problem. He telephoned Louis McNay, chief of federal reclamation projects at OSM, and found out rather quickly how little clout a newly sworn congressman really has.

Harrison asked McNay for a briefing in Centralia on Sunday afternoon. McNay consulted his superiors and told the congressman they were not certain there was any need for such a briefing, and certainly not on so short a notice. Harrison became angry and threatened to go public with OSM's refusal. McNay agreed to discuss the matter further with his superiors, and Harrison spoke later that day with OSM director James R. Harris, who agreed to a meeting on Monday.

Over the weekend, the situation worsened. A crack opened across the southbound lanes of Route 61. Safety dictated the highway be

closed immediately, but the Thornburgh administration stubbornly refused to do so. An unexpected development on the morning of Monday, January 10, forced its hand, however. Steadily falling rain caused
huge clouds of steam to rise from the burning areas adjacent to the
highway. The steam mixed with natural fog to create a cloud so dense
that headlights were useless, and drivers who entered the cloud became disoriented. Thankfully, only one collision occurred, and neither
driver was injured.

Shortly after Harrison and Belfanti arrived in Centralia at 2 P.M. for
their briefing, PennDOT closed the affected section of Route 61. The
temperature beneath the highway had reached 853 degrees and the
crack had widened perceptibly. The highway would remain closed for
five months. "It was pretty much that [day] that confirmed my decision that if there was one thing I was going to do in my term in the
House, it was going to be to try and solve this problem," Harrison said.

■ ■ ■

The drama of January did not affect only Harrison. It had a profound
effect on the people who had actively opposed Concerned Citizens.
Mayor Wondoloski, John Koschoff, Mary Lou Gaughan, and Helen
Womer, among others awoke to the realization their village was on the
verge of being destroyed by the mine fire, and they were certain there
must be something simple that government could do to save it. They
did not believe Concerned Citizens had been right to push for relocation; that was still a taboo subject, although the mayor did believe ten
to fifteen houses might have to be "sacrificed," as he put it, to excavate a small trench to stop the progress of the fire. The difference was
that now they were willing to work with Concerned Citizens toward
some kind of Centralia project, certain that their view of what should
be done would prevail. Helen Womer wanted some kind of flushing
project, preferably a sand and clay barrier.

Concerned Citizens had been so damaged by the persecution of
the previous year that it never recovered. A subgroup, Centralia Committee for Human Development (CCHD), organized by Concerned Citizens to administer the $30,000 grant, absorbed much of the energy of
the remaining members. Father Samuel Garula, the Russian Orthodox
priest in Centralia, took over CCHD after the departure of Larkin and
Girolami. He kept the group alive, but at the price of its energy and
spunk. Garula believed Concerned Citizens had moved too fast for
Centralia. He endeavored mightily to get along with the Koschoff faction and played down past associations with Concerned Citizens.

Representatives of all organizations in Centralia were invited to a

Steam rises from a crack across Route 61 south of Centralia and from a grating (right). Heat of the mine fire beneath the highway melted snow from a section of the road during the winter of 1983. (Photo: David DeKok, News-Item)

January 20 meeting to organize a common front. Concerned Citizens–CCHD sent a representative, as did such diverse groups as the American Legion and Centralia Teen Club. Other persons came simply because it seemed like a good idea. Rose Marquardt, who lived in the safe section of Centralia, was inspired to attend by Father Anthony McGinley, a retired Catholic priest who had recently moved back to Centralia after a career of teaching psychology at the college level. McGinley, who occasionally said Mass at St. Ignatius, urged the parishioners not to allow "a little group" to decide Centralia's fate. He encouraged them all to attend the meeting.

They became the United Centralia Area Mine Fire Task Force, and the first event they planned was Unity Day, intended to be a demonstration to the world that Centralia wanted and needed help. It was scheduled for Sunday, March 6, and was the brainchild of Helen Womer. She worked hard to make Unity Day a success, and not only because it was a logical extension of the community unity meeting she had proposed in 1981. Mrs. Womer was more frightened of the mine fire than she would ever admit.

She had been stunned in October when Brennan announced the fire had broken through the fly ash barrier near her house and was moving into Centralia, and she sent a telegram to Thornburgh October 20 to "urgently request immediate installation of [an] extensive clay and sand barrier to protect lives and property of residents of Centralia and Byrnesville, as mandated by Congress." In November Mrs. Womer telephoned DER to find out if her family was still eligible for relocation under the 1981 project, a project she had loudly and publicly condemned as unnecessary. DER referred her inquiry to OSM, which said the Womers and Gaughans were still eligible.*

As the weeks passed and it became clear the mine fire would bypass her house, Mrs. Womer resumed her ridicule of the idea that anyone in Centralia was threatened by the gases. She was harshly critical of DER's decision early in 1983 to purchase a new carbon monoxide monitoring system for Centralia at a cost of $253,000, suggesting the money should have been used to fight the fire. Rose Marquardt says Mrs. Womer remarked at one of the Unity Task Force meetings how wonderful it would be if everyone in Centralia who had a gas alarm unplugged it and gave it back to the government with the comment,

---

*The Womer telegram, along with a series of DER and OSM letters, turned up in response to a general Freedom of Information request filed by the *News-Item* in 1983. The documents were used in a story published June 1.

"We don't want them. We want you to monitor the fire, we don't want you to monitor our lives."

Mrs. Marquardt says no one on the Unity Task Force, including herself, believed anything drastic or overly harsh would need to be done to end the mine fire's threat to Centralia. They were certain there must be some palatable solution to it all.

■ ■ ■

Centralia never looked better than it did on Unity Day. The streets had been cleaned, and red, white, and blue ribbons were everywhere. Although the day was cold and overcast, with a threat of rain, this ensured that plenty of steam would gush out along the highway for reporters to see. News helicopters circled overhead, and reporters prowled the streets looking for quotes. Most residents were happy to oblige; the whole purpose of Unity Day, after all, was to influence the news media to help Centralia.

Walking through the crowd outside the church, one could see a host of politicians. Congressman Harrison was there, smiling, and so was Representative Belfanti. State Senator Helfrick carried a tepid message from Thornburgh in his pocket, and State Treasurer R. Budd Dwyer looked through the crowd for some of the Centralia residents, like Mrs. Marquardt, who worked in his office.

General Smith was there with his wife and daughter, fresh from his brief tenure as DER Secretary. Thornburgh had appointed him to the post on January 16. Smith resigned on February 4 after finding out how little authority the Governor's Office would give him over hiring and firing. Belfanti invited him to be the principal speaker at Unity Day, and Smith was delighted to oblige. His popularity remained high in Centralia, if not in the governor's mansion.

Over five hundred persons attended an interfaith service at St. Ignatius Church; then they poured onto the street, where Unity Day workers handed out helium balloons and small American flags. The parade moved down Locust Avenue, balloons bobbing, signs waving, and the band playing. When the marchers reached the municipal building, they set the balloons free and crowded inside the main hall. Mayor John Wondoloski was the first speaker and one of the better ones.

> Thank you for coming here today. By your presence here, you have shown to our nation that you join in our struggle to preserve the community we hold so dear.
>
> For many of us, our roots go back three or four generations. And some of us were born in the same houses in which we live. We have always been a hard-working people, and our sons and daughters have read-

ily responded when our country called. We have our differences, yet in many ways we are like a family. We share our joys, we share our sorrows. And we help each other when the need arises.

We believe the people of Centralia and Byrnesville are important. As important as any city of a million people. And we believe our communities are worth saving. Therefore, we ask all of you to continue to help us as you have today, to set Centralia and Byrnesville free in '83. Help us in our determined struggle to preserve our communities, so that we can return here together in future years to celebrate two towns that refused to die.

Many more speakers followed, each lauding the people of Centralia and calling for action to stop the mine fire. Justine Grabowski, a thirteen-year-old who lived in the impact zone, read her letter to President Reagan that won first prize in a contest sponsored by Centralia Teen Club. Councilwoman Molly Darrah displayed some of the 18,636 signatures gathered on petitions the Unity Task Force promised would be delivered to the White House.

Unity Day was like an old-time political rally or Fourth of July picnic. With such spirit, such enthusiasm, how could they lose? They would save Centralia and Byrnesville! If anyone in the hall wondered if the fire could still be stopped without destroying much of Centralia, they kept those thoughts to themselves.

■ ■ ■

Congressman Harrison faced a special dilemma in his efforts to solve the Centralia problem. He did not know what sort of project to propose, and neither OSM nor DER officials were willing to discuss the matter. Wait until the study comes out this summer he was told time and again. By then it might be too late. Hearings on the Interior Department's fiscal 1984 budget would be in early May. Once the budget bill left the House Interior Appropriations Subcommittee, it would be difficult to amend. Ron Ungvarsky, who did much of Harrison's staff work on Centralia, suspected the study was timed by OSM with that in mind.

There *were* other ways to get the money. Harrison could introduce a bill directing OSM to extinguish the mine fire, and if it passed, OSM would have to find the money in its budget or ask Congress for more. This method would be extremely difficult, especially for a freshman congressman. A second alternative would be to attach funding for Centralia to some other bill, but it had to be done while the bill was in the Appropriations Committee. Standing up on the floor of the House to introduce an amendment might work in the movies, Harrison said, but in real life it was well-nigh impossible.

There was another problem, potentially the most difficult of all. Harrison had no clout in Congress, no chits he could call in from years back. If he was not careful, other congressmen might see Centralia as simply another pork barrel project. He would need to persuade them this was a special case, a moral issue.

In his maiden speech to the Congress, delivered on February 28, Harrison reviewed the history of the mine fire and the failed attempts by the Pennsylvania and federal governments to bring it under control. He spoke late in the afternoon, during a period called "special orders." Only two other congressmen were in the chamber, the one who was presiding and the one waiting to speak. Attendance made little difference, however; the speech was broadcast on closed-circuit television into every congressional office. Harrison recalls the effect of his speech:

> I was surprised over the next week or so how many guys caught me in the cloakroom or as we were mobbing in together to vote. One guy from Oklahoma said, that's a blankety-blank problem you've got up there, isn't it? I remember one older representative, I think he was a Republican. He caught me one day going in and said, are you that guy with the fire burning under a town? Then the Los Angeles *Times* ran that cartoon. The devil looking at people, and they thought it was Centralia. That made an impression. A couple of California people said to me they had seen it in the *Times,* and was I the guy who had that?

■ ■ ■

Nicholson Construction Company, headquartered in the western Pennsylvania community of Bridgeville, was selected to do the flushing work DER hoped would prevent subsidences under Route 61. Nicholson was directed to flush under the section of highway where the fire had crossed, and under a two-block section of Locust Avenue in Centralia that was directly in the path of the northern arm of the mine fire.

The company spent most of February pouring crushed rock mixed with water into the voids under the highway south of Centralia. Drilling of boreholes in the 100 and 200 blocks of Locust Avenue began the week after Unity Day in preparation for the second part of the project.

Company officials thought little of it when the boreholes gushed steam. They covered them with steel plates, but each plate had a hole in the center so it could be lifted with a grappling hook. The steam— with its sickening odor of sulfur—began drifting into houses along the 200 block. When some of the people complained, they were told they would just have to put up with it until the end of March, when flushing would begin. After an angry meeting between Centralia officials and

Nicholson personnel, the company agreed to provide better covers for the boreholes, but that was not the end of problems caused by the drilling.

The boreholes had somehow altered the flow of mine fire gases, and two houses in the 200 block that never had high carbon monoxide levels now had a serious problem. Two elderly sisters, Elizabeth Gillespie and Kate Kane, lived at 210 South Locust, and David and Alice Glowatski, a young couple, lived next door.

Dr. Donald Reid of the state Health Department pronounced the gas readings from the homes "unacceptable" and said the residents should be evacuated if DER could not keep the fire gases out of the houses. Reid now claimed to accept the more stringent Environmental Protection Agency standards for human carbon monoxide exposure, as well as research findings that persons with chronic heart and lung conditions, or pregnant women, could be harmed by low concentrations of the poison gas. It was a surprising and welcome change of heart on the doctor's part, considering the Health Department's previous attitude toward the carbon monoxide problem. Asked why his opinion had changed, Reid insisted that earlier carbon monoxide incidents were not as long-lasting as those in the two houses.

DER canceled the Locust Avenue flushing at the end of March after conceding the drilling "may or may not" have been responsible for the upsurge in gas levels in the two houses. DER gas inspectors Dennis Wolfe and Wayne Readly reopened a nearby vent pipe and the levels dropped off to normal. No one wanted to find out if the flushing would create a dam effect, forcing huge volumes of carbon monoxide to back up into basements.

It was a humiliating spring for DER. Earlier in March, its engineers were forced to admit that one of the Nicholson drills ignited a small, new mine fire south of where the main fire crossed the highway. Then there was the conflict over liability releases DER lawyers demanded Centralia residents sign before they could receive one of the department's new, improved gas monitors. The monitors would be connected to a central computer at DER's office in Centralia Municipal Building, allowing instant readouts of the amount of carbon monoxide in a monitored home, in addition to sounding an alarm when the level exceeded 35 ppm.

The releases would bar Centralia residents from suing DER or the Thornburgh administration for damages if the machines malfunctioned. No release had been required to receive one of the old gas alarms, and Theresa Gasperetti wondered if DER knew some terrible worsening of the gas problem lay ahead. Most residents refused to sign. Vincent Flannery, a seventy-two-year-old Byrnesville resident, gathered signatures in his village against the releases, then walked up the hill to Centralia and gathered some more. DER Secretary Nicholas DeBenedictis, who took over after General Smith withdrew, decided finally the releases were not worth the trouble they were causing.

DER's troubles were far from over. A series of subsidences on or adjacent to Route 61 during April and May called into question whether the $333,000 flushing project had accomplished anything at all. One of the subsidences, on April 19, cut off Byrnesville's water supply.

DeBenedictis hoped he could soon turn matters around. He was young, energetic, an engineer, and had the complete confidence of Thornburgh, those who knew him said. One of the first things he did was seize upon a chance encounter with Secretary Watt to press the state's case for federal help for Centralia. DeBenedictis and Watt were guest speakers at the Pennsylvania State Association of Township Supervisors convention in Philadelphia on April 20, the day after the subsidence cut off water to Byrnesville. The DER secretary was introduced to Watt and asked him for a meeting to discuss Centralia. Watt consented to see him for fifteen minutes.

"He was straight up," DeBenedictis said. "He said, do you think you are ready to go in and fight with us on this, do you think we can get the town to address the issue and be reasonable, and so on. I said, I think if we present the options, Pennsylvanians are reasonable people."

DeBenedictis told Watt the state was not interested in total excavation of the mine fire, which everyone knew would be the most expensive, although also the most effective method for extinguishing the fire. He also told Watt he believed digging out the entire mountain would be, in any case, a difficult feat of engineering. "At that point," the DER secretary said later, "I saw a decided shift."

Watt would never abandon his deep conviction that projects like Centralia were the responsibility of the states, not the Interior Department, but he could not ignore the politics of the situation. Public opinion favored federal help for Centralia, and so did increasing numbers of Congressmen.

■ ■ ■

That spring the mine fire erupted above ground for the first time since 1981, creating a spectacular nighttime display. Flames had long since disappeared from the 1981 outbreak site, although the ground remained very hot. This new outbreak was perhaps two hundred yards south of the old one and at least three times as large.

Frances McKeefery, a member of Centralia Committee for Human Development (CCHD) who lived in the impact zone near St. Ignatius Church, telephoned the *News-Item* on April 6 to report rumors in Centralia about a new surface outbreak. A reporter was dispatched to find it, and after a thirty-minute search through rugged terrain, he located it in a ravine at the base of a three-hundred-foot cliff. During the day, one could look into a hole in the face of the cliff and see rock glowing orange. At night, tongues of orange and blue flame flickered eerily among the rocks at the bottom of the ravine. A lone blue flame burned like a beacon fifty feet up the cliff. The scene was Hell itself.

■ ■ ■

OSM had to go before the House Interior Appropriations Subcommittee on May 4 to justify its budget for the next fiscal year and to answer questions congressmen had about OSM policies and performance. The agency was not popular on Capitol Hill, chiefly because in many cases it had neglected to collect fines against coal operators who violated federal strip mine regulations. Its delegation could expect a thorough grilling.

Harrison had seen the interim report on the drilling project prepared by Robert Brennan and Art Anderson, but this report, while confirming the severity of the fire problem, did not provide any cost estimates or, for that matter, recommend any methods for stopping the fire.* That was reserved for a study being prepared for OSM by GAI, Incorporated, a Pittsburgh-area geotechnical engineering firm, using information gathered during the drilling. It would not be released until July, and by that time the Interior Appropriations Bill would be out of committee and onto the House floor. Harrison decided to ask for an appointment with the subcommittee to explain why no money for Centralia could be requested at this time. He suspected the members would not second-guess the report's conclusions and hand him a blank check.

By good fortune, two veteran congressmen from the Pennsylvania coal regions sat on the subcommittee. One was Joseph McDade, a Republican from Scranton who had obtained over $100 million in Interior Department money for his district during his many years in Congress.

*Brennan and Anderson were ordered not to include "recommendations or interpretations" in their interim and final reports, according to an OSM memorandum dated January 14.

He was the ranking Republican on the subcommittee. The other was John Murtha, a conservative Democrat from Johnstown. They would be key to Harrison's quest to win help for Centralia.

Harrison was not convinced members of the subcommittee really knew how bad the Centralia problem had become. That was all too common in Washington: one crisis blended into another, and anything could be viewed in the abstract. He believed if McDade or Murtha could be persuaded to visit Centralia it would be impossible for them and by extension, the subcommittee, to view Centralia as anything but a special problem requiring federal help. Murtha, who had seen mine fires before, was at first doubtful but agreed finally to go. McDade begged off, citing a prior commitment, but promised Harrison he would do all he could to help Centralia.

Harrison and Murtha flew to Centralia the morning of April 22, two days after DeBenedictis's secret meeting with Secretary Watt. It was a bright, sunny day, but there was plenty of steam—and anxious residents—for Murtha to see. He admitted the fire was much worse than he ever imagined and promised Centralians he would attempt to put money in the federal budget for Centralia.

McDade kept his promise to help Harrison. Late in the afternoon of May 4, he walked into the subcommittee hearing and told the OSM delegation, led by Dean Hunt, that OSM was to help Centralia. Period. OSM feared few congressmen as much as McDade.

Harrison was granted five minutes before the subcommittee on May 5, the day set aside by the chairman, Sidney Yates (D–Illinois), to hear special funding requests from members. Yates was sympathetic when Harrison asked for a rain check, explaining he would be back for Centralia funding after the GAI report came out on July 12. Murtha's report had made an impact. "We made money available last year, and I'm sure we'll do it again this year," *Associated Press* quoted Yates as telling Harrison. "We do recognize it as being a very serious, disastrous kind of thing. We are very much in accord with what you want to do. Nobody knows quite how to do it yet."

■ ■ ■

The engineers of GAI did not fully realize at first how large a project they had agreed to undertake. Soon after beginning work on December 13, 1982, they discovered how much data had been collected by the Bureau, OSM, and the state during twenty-one years of studying the Centralia mine fire. Stan Michalski, one of the leaders of the project, described what was involved:

We literally hauled all the office files out of Wilkes-Barre. We scoured the countryside. We got maps off of private citizens in Pottsville, maps that were held by people who retired. . . . We had a tremendous amount of data. It was literally a truckful.

We worked through all of the data in the first month or so that we were involved, part of January and part of February, and got a good feel on what was known about the fire up to that time. Based on that information, we began designing a monitoring program that would yield data that would be of use to determine where the fire was, and other questions OSM had with regard to putting it out or getting it under control. They also made available to us a huge data base that was put together by Compuserv out of Columbus, Ohio.* It had all the thousands of boreholes that were drilled over the years, the fly ash holes and all that stuff that went back twenty years. They had all that information.

Throughout this whole project, particularly in the latter half, there were very frequent meetings with OSM. We had people coming in from Washington, literally from all over the country. There were things we were coming up with that people from OSM didn't necessarily agree with, and there were some very lively discussions at some of these meetings.

We insisted on having it our way, and we were not about to bend to anything OSM thought. We kept hammering at them that we wanted to dispel all preconceived notions regarding this fire. This was a fresh look. We didn't want to have anybody's opinion who was involved in this for twenty years. Eventually, we did have our way.

One thing they did tell us to do, they said that this fire, if we aimed to put it out or control it, that we must use technologies that are known to work. They didn't want us recommending any kind of esoteric experimental technology. So we had to use technologies that were known to work in the past, in the Anthracite coal fields.

Many of the "lively discussions" referred to by Michalski were with Robert Brennan, who found himself increasingly out in the cold when it came to deciding what was true about the mine fire and what was not.

■ ■ ■

One of the greatest fears of people in the impact zone, apart from the gases, was that OSM and DER would decide not to relocate them, possibly because the Koschoff faction on Centralia Council might claim relocation was opposed by a majority of Centralia residents. Unity Day, it now appeared, had been a temporary phenomenon at best. The

*It was commissioned by the Bureau and used to prepare the 1980 study.

18,636 signatures gathered for Unity Day collected dust in a display window of a shop along Locust Avenue. They quite obviously had not been delivered to President Reagan and never would be, probably because the Unity Task Force leadership feared the petition might lend support to relocation or some other unacceptable solution.

Charles Gasperetti, his wife Theresa, and Mary Ellen Lokitis were tired of being told to wait for the GAI report and were worried relocation might not come even then. They decided in May that they wanted to be relocated as soon as possible. Suspecting that many other impact zone residents did, too, the two women went door-to-door in the impact zone the week of May 16, gathering signatures on a petition for immediate relocation. They obtained signatures from seventy of about one hundred adults who lived in the zone. Six refused to sign and the rest were not home, although some of these added their names later. It was a powerful statement.

Charles Gasperetti presented the petition to Centralia Council on May 26. After Gasperetti finished his speech, Koschoff attempted to adjourn the meeting, but shouted protests from the audience and objections from council members Michael Lupatsky and Molly Darrah forced him to back down. Council voted unanimously to accept and endorse the petition.

Koschoff then qualified his vote, saying no one should be relocated from the impact zone until the federal and state governments approved a plan to fight the fire. This prospect must have sent chills through those in the audience who recalled the history of government indecision on the mine fire. They might wait for years. "No way!" Theresa Gasperetti said.

DER's response to the petition was even more disturbing. Spokesman David Mashek said it would be "more appropriate" to wait for the release of the GAI report in July "and then hold hearings to get the response of all the citizens. . . . Our department takes the same position and is in agreement with President Koschoff." Dr. Allen Perry, OSM's official spokesman on Centralia matters, simply repeated the party line—that relocation was a state, not federal, responsibility.

DER's statement may well have been mere lip service to the myth that Centralia Council was the only legitimate voice of the people of Centralia. After all, DeBenedictis had met with Watt to discuss funding of a major Centralia project. DER geologist Robert Oberman had raised the possibility of a trench to Centralia residents as early as January. Surely the Koschoff faction's opinion would not determine what would be done to stop the mine fire.

But what if Watt turned around and opposed a federal project, as his personal philosophy told him he should? What if Congress refused to provide funds or delayed them interminably? The state had its own share of the AML Fund, but that money was already committed to other projects. The political damage would be severe if they were canceled to fund a Centralia relocation. It would be much easier to defer to the "will of the people"—as determined by the Koschoff faction—and do nothing, or just a token project.

■ ■ ■

Centralia Committee for Human Development spent much of June trying to work with Centralia Council to set up a procedure for determining public opinion on what should be done about the fire. The Koschoff faction wanted to know how people felt, but wanted as little to do with CCHD as possible. Helen Koschoff, who had become borough solicitor in March, was particularly adamant about this, says Rose Marquardt.

Council, to cite one example, wanted to hire an independent engineer to evaluate the options in the upcoming GAI report, apparently out of distrust of OSM. CCHD offered to contribute $2,500 toward the cost of the work, which amounted to half the cost. Council accepted the offer, then announced at its June 21 meeting that CCHD would not be allowed an equal voice with council in deciding how the analysis would be conducted. "The condition under which we gave the $2,500 is that we have input," said an angry Sister Honor Murphy, an energetic, sixty-nine-year-old Dominican nun from Tennessee who became project manager of CCHD in June.

"You will, just like any other citizens of Centralia," John Koschoff said. "I don't think the amount of money makes any difference. As far as I'm concerned, someone who gives five dollars is the same as you. All we can do is assure you that when the final report is released, you'll get a copy at the same time as everybody else."

Sister Murphy announced the next day that CCHD's grant to council had been canceled. The two sides did manage to agree to organize an Input Task Force to replace the Unity Task Force. The new group was directed to organize and supervise community forums at which all citizens of Centralia and Byrnesville could offer their opinions after the GAI report was released on July 12.

OSM maintained tight control over the report's contents, vowing to let no one see it before the day of release. Harrison telephoned Watt the afternoon of July 11, hoping a congressman could find out at least a few key details of the report. He also hoped to arrange a meeting with Watt the next morning to discuss Centralia after the report was released. Watt returned the call at 7 P.M. Harrison decribed the ensuing conversation as "very unpleasant."

Watt refused to tell him anything about the report. He insisted that Pennsylvania "has the lead" on Centralia, but that the Interior Department would provide money for a project through the AML Fund. He complained, according to Harrison's memorandum on the conversation, that Pennsylvania was already receiving a great deal of AML Fund monies. Several times during the conversation, Watt said he had served in the Interior Department 15 years earlier and had been briefed on the Centralia mine fire by engineers who told him it would burn out in six months. Later, according to Harrison, Watt said he was not sure he had been briefed on Centralia, but that "those Pennsylvania mine fires keep coming at us."

Watt said the people of Centralia had not decided what they wanted done about the mine fire. Some wanted it extinguished, regardless of the cost, and others wanted to relocate the town "and let the fire take care of itself." He asked Harrison where he stood on the question. Harrison told Watt he agreed the people were divided about the fire, and that he had not taken a position beyond wanting something done about the fire. Harrison asked the secretary how soon significant action could be expected at Centralia, and says Watt told him, "It will not be soon. I don't want to make promises to the people I can't keep." Watt noted the fire had been burning for more than twenty years and would take a long time to put out, but "the political reality is that we will have to do something."

Mayor John Wondoloski of Centralia meets the press outside Centralia Municipal Building the night of August 11, 1983 to announce that Centralians had
voted in favor of relocating the community to get away from the mine fire.
(Photo: David DeKok, News-Item)

AS Congressman Harrison and his aides sat in a darkened room of the Interior Department the morning of July 12, 1983 and watched the GAI report flash on a screen, they were stunned, then depressed by the findings, which foretold the death of Centralia. There would be no escape from the fire for anyone who remained in Centralia, no matter whether they lived in the impact zone or on the north, or safe, side of town. If the fire did not directly threaten their lives and property, the project GAI suggested to save as much of Centralia as possible would turn their lives into a nightmare.

For years, people who lived on the north side of Centralia believed they were protected by an underground pool of mine water that lay beneath part of the village. The fire was assumed to be only in the Buck vein, and the Buck dipped into the water. GAI had shattered that assumption. There was evidence of the fire in the Skidmore, Seven Foot, and Buck Leader veins, from which it could reach the Mammoth, Four Foot, Holmes, and Primrose veins. This meant the fire could vault the mine pool.

This was the most controversial finding in the GAI report and had been the subject of fierce debate between Robert Brennan of OSM and Stan Michalski and the other GAI scientists. Laboratory tests and visual examination of core samples proved the fire was in the upper veins, the company insisted. Brennan believed that what GAI considered evidence of burning was simply natural discoloration of the coal.

Admittedly, it would take many years for the fire to reach the north side of Centralia, and natural obstacles might prevent the fire from vaulting the mine pool. But in the worst case, GAI said, the fire could expand from its present 195 acres to about 3,700 acres, enveloping Centralia, Byrnesville, and the eight-house hamlet of Germantown between Centralia and Ashland. Ashland, Big Mine Run, Girardville, Connerton, Lost Creek, and Raven Run were just beyond the prospective reach of the fire. Perhaps with a turn of bad luck they would go too.

The report made clear that saving even part of Centralia would be, at this late date, an expensive and difficult task. Eight possible methods for extinguishing or containing the fire were examined in the report. Many of these had been explored in the 1980 Bureau report on Centralia, but there were a few new ones, like use of inert gases or various chemical agents to smother the flames. In keeping with OSM's order, GAI treated seriously only methods already known to work in the Anthracite Region.

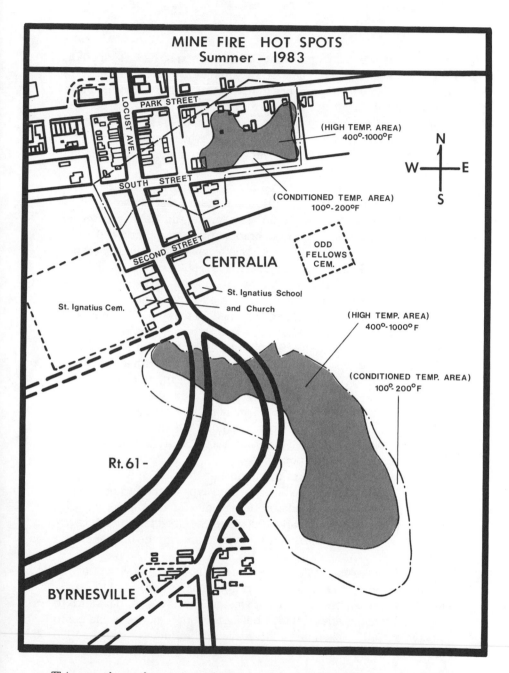

MINE FIRE HOT SPOTS
Summer – 1983

PARK STREET

LOCUST AVE.

(HIGH TEMP. AREA)
400°-1000°F

N
W — E
S

SOUTH STREET

(CONDITIONED TEMP. AREA)
100°- 200°F

SECOND STREET

CENTRALIA

ODD
FELLOWS
CEM.

St. Ignatius School
and Church

St. Ignatius Cem.

(HIGH TEMP. AREA)
400°-1000° F

(CONDITIONED TEMP. AREA)
100°- 200° F

Rt. 61 –

BYRNESVILLE

This map shows the portions of the mine fire closest to Centralia and Byrnesville in the summer of 1983. More of the fire lies to the east. The hot spot in
Centralia has been generally static since 1983, but the one near Byrnesville
has been moving steadily west. (Map credit: Thomas Koch)

Just as in the 1980 report that OSM had tried so hard to discredit, excavation was the recommended method—but what an excavation! GAI said a trench to stop the fire from moving further west under all of Centralia would need to be 3,700 feet long and 450 feet deep—the height of a forty-five-story building—at its deepest point.* Worse, if placed at its optimum location, the trench would snake through the middle of Centralia and destroy over half the community it was meant to save.

GAI said the trench could possibly be moved two hundred or three hundred feet further east, to within a hundred feet of the fire. This would save more homes but would risk allowing the fire to race beyond a half-completed trench. A noncombustible gas might need to be sprayed at the fire to hold it back while excavation of the trench progressed, but GAI offered no guarantee this would work.

As much as anything, the GAI report showed the fiscal folly of the Scranton administration's refusal to take effective action against the fire in 1963 and the Bureau's decision in 1967 to replace a planned intercept trench with a fly ash barrier that it had strong reason to believe would fail. H. B. Charmbury, Secretary of Mines in the Scranton administration, had rejected a plan to encircle the fire with a trench that would have cost $277,490. The cost estimate for the Bureau trench in 1965 was $2,225,000. The project was canceled when further study pushed the estimated cost to $4.5 million. The penny-wise, pound-foolish Bureau could not justify spending that amount to save a village with an assessed valuation of less than $500,000, as Columbia County officials were so helpful to point out.

GAI projected the cost of the main trench at $62 million, a figure arrived at by calculating the amount and type of rock to be moved, then turning to standard construction guides for 1984. High inflation during the late 1970s and early 1980s and the need for a much larger trench to contain the mine fire in 1983 accounted for the huge increase in the cost.

This trench alone, unfortunately, could not contain all sections of the fire. GAI recommended a second trench one mile east of Centralia near the outbreak sites, a third one west of Byrnesville, and a fourth to the south of that village. The total bill for the four trenches would come to between $105 million and $115 million. The Bureau report in 1980 estimated the cost of a similar project at $41 million. OSM had be-

---

*This trench and all others mentioned in the GAI report would be backfilled with incombustible material upon completion.

lieved that project and most others in the report would be extravagant wastes of the AML Fund and had pushed surface sealing as a low-cost, effective alternative.

GAI dismissed surface sealing so thoroughly that one must question whether OSM engineers like Charles Beasley truly believed in the method or recommended it only to avoid dealing with the harsh reality of the Centralia problem. GAI wrote:

> Surface sealing is not considered a viable option at Centralia because of: 1) the large surface area that would be involved, 2) the complexity of sealing a large number of strip pits and mine entries through which air could enter the mine workings, 3) the probability that all the structures in Byrnesville and a large portion of Centralia would require removal if a thorough job was to be done, and 4) the probable large-scale continuing maintenance effort required over an indefinite time period to preserve the integrity of the fire seal.

Total excavation of the fire—an option already rejected by DER—would cost a heart-stopping $660 million, GAI said, up from $107 million in the 1980 report. It had the greatest likelihood of success, but that did not outweigh the tremendous cost. A flushing project would cost an estimated $32 million, the report said, but as in the 1980 report, flushing was dismissed as unfeasible because of tortuous subsurface conditions and the method's record of failure.

If the federal or state government wanted to save Centralia and Byrnesville at the least possible cost, GAI recommended excavating the $62-million main trench through Centralia and flushing the mines under Byrnesville, where such work was believed to have a better chance of success than under Centralia, at a cost of $2.5 million. Byrnesville would become a safe island in a sea of fire.

GAI warned that the cost of preserving Centralia and Byrnesville would be great, both in dollars and in disruption of the quality of life caused by years of excavation. Those whose homes would not be destroyed by the trench might suffer in vain, because there was no guarantee the trench would be successful. Isolated pockets of fire might already be west of the main trench site, the report cautioned, or might ignite in the future by spontaneous combustion. "In view of these factors, the relocation of households and businesses in response to local conditions brought about by the fire would appear to be a course of action worthy of consideration," GAI concluded.

Harrison had been reluctant to go to Centralia that day, fearing someone would accuse him of seeking political gain, but the report had changed his mind. "The situation was far more serious and far more expensive than anybody had ever dreamed," said Ron Ungvarsky, Harrison's aide. Harrison suspected now that Centralia and Byrnesville residents would want to hear how he would try to help them.

Their mood on the flight to Centralia was somber; it had been a bad day all around. Congressman McDade had been given the advance look at the GAI report that Watt denied the Democrat Harrison, and McDade's staff had leaked the major findings to the *News-Item*. It made Harrison look like a nobody in the Congress, but in a brutal sense he was.

They arrived just in time for the 3 P.M. briefing for the press, which would be followed by a 6 P.M. briefing for local residents. DER secretary Nicholas DeBenedictis and Dr. Allen Perry of OSM were in charge. The bad news of the day was obvious. The good news was that Secretary Watt made it known through Perry that he was, indeed, willing to consider paying the lion's share of a Centralia project. But what kind of project? That was up to the people to decide, according to Perry and DeBenedictis. Few doubted, however, that whatever the residents chose would have to meet certain guidelines. "The immediate issue is the protection of the health of the residents most directly affected," DeBenedictis said. "We are also looking for a long-term solution, which is to find the best way to put out the fire."

Robert Lazarski, the former vice-president of Centralia Council, asked the DER secretary whether the people would, in reality, be allowed to have the final say on what was done. "These people think they'll be deciding their own fate," he said.

"It may or may not be so, depending on which option they pick," DeBenedictis said. "No one person will make that decision."

Charles Gasperetti raised the issue of mass relocation. He asked whether relocation of impact zone families could take place before winter, and whether families whose homes were not needed for a trench could be relocated anyway. The fear of being left behind was very great.

Harrison promised to discuss the question with the Interior Department. DeBenedictis refused to state whether there would be any relocation beyond that forced by a trench. The community, he said, would have to decide if relocation was necessary. Perry came the closest to endorsing relocation. He said the residents might well decide none of the options for containing or extinguishing the mine fire were worth the terrible environmental disruption they would carry in their wake.

They would have between two and four weeks to decide, De-Benedictis said. Koschoff urged everyone to read the report, consider the options, and offer their opinions at the proper time and place. He would not answer a question from former council president Edward Polites as to what would constitute a consensus. "We're going to take a tally of what the people want after they have an opportunity to review the options," Koschoff said.

If there was any single theme that ran through the briefings July 12, it was that life would be unbearable during the five years it would take to excavate the main trench.

Only a handful of residents ventured to ask questions at the evening briefing. Most seemed overwhelmed by the magnitude of the problem. Even Helen Womer seemed subdued when she appeared with Father Garula of CCHD the next morning on the NBC *Today* show. "I think every one of us had the opinion we would get the government's attention, and they would do something about the fire," said Rose Marquardt. "Not the ultimatum that was given to us at the end. That was the farthest thing from our minds. We had thought, well maybe they'll do the sand and clay [barrier]. Never once were the trenches [or anything of that] magnitude ever mentioned. It was a shock. That was a shock to everyone."

As the meaning of the report sank in, the community became more bitterly divided than ever. The fragile consensus achieved for Unity Day disappeared completely amid old fears and new uncertainties.

Byrnesville, always distrustful of Centralia, decided to conclude a separate peace with the government. Twenty-seven of twenty-eight property owners in the village signed a petition in support of the flushing project proposed in the GAI report, even though it would leave Byrnesville isolated in a burning wasteland.

Those few in Centralia who bitterly opposed any relocation, and who did not believe a trench was necessary, clustered around Father Anthony McGinley. They included Helen Womer, Leon and Elaine Jurgill, Mary Lou Gaughan, and Anne Marie Devine. They called themselves Residents to Save the Borough of Centralia.

Joan Girolami came out of retirement, as it were, to resume her role as advocate. She insisted she was acting only for herself this time, but much of what she did influenced others, and many of the younger women in the impact zone looked to her for leadership. One question she raised was whether fair market value would be paid for houses acquired for a trench project or a general relocation, unlike in 1981, when the appraised value of a home was lowered because of the mine fire. No one would make any promises, but Belfanti said he and Harrison would try to make certain there was no penalty this time.

Relocation was discussed repeatedly in the weeks that followed the July 12 meeting. Perry said relocation "must be considered" to protect the health and safety of the people. DER geologist Robert Oberman said if relocation was chosen, the trench would be moved west, outside Centralia.

The Input Task Force held neighborhood meetings to allow all residents a chance to say how they wanted the fire fought, whether they wanted it fought at all, or whether they simply wanted to leave Centralia. A majority of persons who attended—about half the households were represented—chose relocation. Even persons who lived on the north side of Centralia favored relocation.

Centralia Council, perhaps sensing defeat and fearing that a majority vote for relocation would mean all would have to leave, announced on July 25 that it favored a "stay or leave" plan, whereby anyone who wanted to relocate could do so at government expense. The government would attempt to implement a "mutually acceptable" plan to protect anyone who wanted to stay from the fire.

After strong criticism from State Senator Helfrick and DER, Centralia Council backed away from the proposal and decided to hold a simple referendum on August 8, in which property owners could vote whether to endorse relocation. Since it was a nonbinding referendum that did not fall under Pennsylvania's election laws, council could draw up whatever rules it wanted.

Another controversy erupted in the meantime. Helen Womer announced August 4 that United Centralia Area Mine Fire Task Force— the old Unity Task Force—had gathered 333 signatures (this would eventually rise to 412) on a petition calling on the government to do nothing about the fire that would not leave Centralia intact.

> We the undersigned request our community be kept intact and that an option be selected with the least disruption, if any, to our community to effectively contain the mine fire, thereby preventing its spread to our own and nearby communities.
>
> We also request that anyone in the mine fire-affected area whose health and welfare are *legitimately* [emphasis added] threatened be given an opportunity to relocate with fair market value and relocation funds.

People who signed this petition agreed, in effect, that the mine fire was still outside Centralia and questioned whether anyone's health was truly threatened by the fire. One wonders, in light of events before and after the petition was announced, how many people understood what they were signing.

Rose Marquardt questioned the wording of the petition at a meeting held at Helen Womer's house before the petition was circulated. She said it would be deceptive not to mention the proposed trench. People had a right to know what would happen if they chose not to relocate, and the statement created the impression there was still an easy solution to the fire. She said the others, who included Koschoff and Councilwoman Molly Darrah, refused to change the wording.

The tide was running toward relocation, but few were willing to bet on the outcome of the referendum. The antirelocation forces played on the real affection Centralians felt for their community and raised fears about the outside world and how threatening it would be, never mentioning how threatening Centralia itself had become for many. When Mrs. Marquardt refused to help circulate the petition, Elaine Jurgill accused her of not believing Centralia was worth saving. That is not the point, she retorted. The people have to be told what the future holds.

There can be little doubt the Thornburgh administration wanted Centralians to vote for relocation. In the days leading up to the August 11 referendum, state officials spared no effort to portray how horrible and uncertain life would be for those who did not choose to leave. The Health Department described the dangers of living near a trench project. DER's Oberman assured them flushing would not stop the fire. DER press secretary Bruce Dallas told *Associated Press* the morning of August 11 (the story appeared in the *News-Item* in time for some voters to read it) that a trench would be dug regardless of how the vote went. The only question was where—in Centralia or west of the village.

Television crews and print reporters were waiting when the first voters arrived at Centralia Municipal Building, which itself was closed to the press, shortly after the polls opened at 8 A.M. Between nine hundred and a thousand property owners in Centralia were eligible to vote, Byrnesville having been excluded because of its petition in favor of flushing. Only persons who were listed on the Centralia property tax rolls, or who could prove they paid the taxes for someone else, like an aged parent, were allowed to vote. Inevitably there were problems. Beverly Gusick, one of two judges of election, said some people threw pencil stubs at election workers after being told they could not vote.

Mayor John Wondoloski came out of the municipal building at 8:45 P.M. to announce the results. Relocation won, he said as television lights snapped on and cameras flashed. The margin was 345 votes to 200, or 63 percent to 37 percent. Although Wondoloski did not say this, it was almost a two-to-one margin, the same as in the 1981 referendum when the vote had been 434–204. Wondoloski said that Centralia Council would work to implement relocation and that he would like to see a New Centralia arise somewhere but doubted it would ever happen.

Wondoloski, Helen Womer, and Joan Girolami appeared that night on ABC *Nightline,* along with OSM director James R. Harris. Mrs. Womer charged that relocation was approved only because a majority of Centralia property owners were scared into voting for it. Her petition had been signed by 412 persons "who want to stay in the community." Asked why only 200 persons then voted against relocation, Mrs. Womer insisted the others became frightened by what state officials said at the August 8 Centralia Council meeting, after the petition was circulated.

Mrs. Girolami told interviewer Lynn Sherr she was pleased by the vote but hoped the government would pay her fair market value for her home. She commended state officials for "laying the cards on the table" about the danger of remaining in Centralia and for telling people there would be no more appeasement projects.

Harris called the vote for relocation "probably the wise option" and predicted all Centralia residents would eventually have to move. He did not believe extensive trenching could be justified if only part of Centralia relocated, and he questioned whether Congress or the state would ever be willing to pay the tremendous cost of a trench.

Governor Thornburgh released a statement the following morning calling on Pennsylvania's congressional delegation to cosponsor legislation providing $50 million for the relocation of Centralia, a figure taken from the GAI report. In a separate statement, he took personal credit for initiating the exploratory drilling project and commended himself for allowing Centralia residents to hold the referendum. "I did not feel it was the government's place to dictate to our citizens a choice in a matter like this that so directly affected their family and community lives. We therefore asked the citizens of Centralia to meet and discuss and advise us what they wanted to do so that we might, in the best tradition of government, assist them to meet their desires and needs," the governor said.

■ ■ ■

In truth, OSM had decided before the referendum that relocation was the only acceptable means of dealing with the Centralia fire. Harris later explained that decision:

So then we arrived at the conclusion that, based on the economics of the situation, you could hardly justify spending some $64 million or $68 million to go in and excavate the fire . . . when we didn't have any assurance that would clear it up. So then we arrived at the conclusion that the best thing for everybody involved was to offer the people the option of our purchasing their property and their moving to another location, which then of course was the policy we adopted, but didn't move on until such time as they had their referendum and the majority of the people in the town did vote for such a thing.

Harris perhaps overstates the situation in hindsight. The record shows that OSM was willing to give Centralia a relocation plan or a trench, but not both. There is no doubt that Harris, and presumably Secretary Watt, was greatly opposed to spending money on a trench. It was political reality, as Watt had put it, that required them to do something at Centralia. If the people of Centralia had asked for a trench, they would most likely have gotten it.

The real question was whether OSM would give Pennsylvania any money to fight the fire once the relocation was completed, and whether Pennsylvania would even ask for any—at least for a trench. State officials had convinced Centralia residents that there would be a trench project, but that may well have been a scare tactic to encourage less-costly relocation.

Dean Hunt, who was Harris's deputy, met with George Grode and Gwen King of Thornburgh's staff on August 4 in Washington at a meeting convened by the Federal Emergency Management Agency (FEMA) at Thornburgh's request. Hunt told them Pennsylvania could not expect OSM or the Congress to approve simultaneous funding for both relocation and a trench. "OSM does not consider the expenditure of federal funds for both options to be in the best interests of the government or the taxpayers," wrote Joseph D. Winkle of FEMA in a long memorandum on the meeting. Once the people were moved out, then a trench would be considered, although the money would have to come from the state's $770-million share of the AML Fund. There would be no special appropriation from Congress if OSM had anything to say about it. "He [Grode] said that he was in agreement with all the facts as presented by Dean Hunt and stressed the good working relationship that existed between the state and OSM," Winkle wrote.

With the people, or most of the people out of Centralia, pressure for a project to stop the fire would drop precipitously. GAI said the fire could not reach Mount Carmel, the closest town west of Centralia, because of barrier pillars in the mines and other geological factors. All that was left to save were minor reserves of anthracite coal that had little value in the market. Given these facts, it seems doubtful the state would spend $64 million to excavate the main trench, or that Congress would allow OSM to approve the project.

U.S. Senator Arlen Specter, who worked closely with Hunt and Thornburgh on the relocation funding, questioned as much in comments he made on October 14 at a public meeting in Centralia. "The issue of putting out the fire is not resolved," he said. "The cost figures are very, very high. In excess of $100 million. It's not even certain if that figure will be sufficient . . . so I do not think it is realistic to expect the federal government to both pay for . . . more than half the town moving out, and pay for putting out the fire."

And if the federal government would not pay for it, who then? Thornburgh had shown no inclination to spend any state funds at Centralia. Even the salaries of the DER gas inspectors were reimbursed by OSM. State officials, however, continued to act as if a trench was a sure thing. Thornburgh had declared this would be a voluntary relocation, and they knew this was a crucial question for Centralians, one that would determine for many whether they stayed or relocated. One must raise the hard question: was this a deliberate deception?

■ ■ ■

A small army of workers from the state Department of Community Affairs (DCA), Columbia County Redevelopment Authority, and OSM came to Centralia on August 19 to begin work on a crash survey of which families were inclined to leave Centralia and how much it might cost to acquire their homes. They were led by Jack Carling, disaster programs director for DCA, who from the sidelines had observed the Centralia drama for several years. He was friendly, compassionate, good-humored, and slow to anger, qualities in short supply among many of the public officials Centralia had known in twenty-one years.

Carling would need these virtues to defuse the anger and fear remaining from OSM's administration of the 1981 relocation. OSM was involved in the acquisition of homes this time only in that their appraisers studied the housing in Centralia and made up a table the other workers could use to make rough estimates of the value of property owned by people who wanted to relocate. Byrnesville was included in the survey despite the professed sentiment there for flushing. DER had decided flushing had little chance to protect the small village.

When the survey was completed, 391 property owners had declared an interest in having their property appraised for the relocation, and just 76 refused appraisals, a number that would steadily drop. DCA estimated the cost of the relocation at $41,831,000, a sum that included acquisition of four churches, a parochial school, and several businesses, including a complete garment factory.

For some families in the impact zone, like the Gasperettis and Koguts, choosing relocation was anything but voluntary. The continuing threat of poison gas and subsidence made their departure mandatory. Many families outside the impact zone chose relocation because they feared living near a trench project for as long as five years. DeBenedictis said this surprised him, but there was little doubt among the silent majority of Centralians—those who were not part of Mrs. Girolami's circle or Mrs. Womer's group, who tended to be more skeptical—that DER intended to dig that trench. Whether it ran through the middle of Centralia or west of the village made little difference. The blasting and truck traffic and dust would make their lives miserable.

One couple who eventually chose relocation for that reason were William and Janet Birster, who had fled their home on Wood Street in 1969 after the mine fire gases inside rose to dangerous levels. The Birsters had relocated to a house on West Park Street. It was in the ultimate path of the fire, but far enough away, they believed, so the fire would never again disrupt their lives. They were wrong. "The trench was proposed for this end of town," Birster said. "We don't know just where. . . . When they start ripping it up, it's just as good to go as to be choked when they're digging. Going along with the tide, really."

Even after the referendum, DER left little doubt that trenching was a sure thing. Press Secretary Bruce Dallas was quoted by *Associated Press* on August 13 as saying there would be no use of eminent domain in Centralia "except possibly in a few, isolated instances, for example, in the immediate trenching area." The story, which was carried in the *News-Item*, made other references to the certainty of a trench as well.

The Thornburgh administration had painted itself into a corner. It would be so much easier and cheaper to let the fire burn, or to substitute some form of fire control that was less expensive than trenching. DER had built up the certainty of a trench so much, though, that if the state backed out, it could rightfully be accused of deception and fraud. The administration had been guilty of little lies to Centralia. A big one would not be out of the question.

■ ■ ■

It was barely light the morning of November 18 when a bus carrying about three dozen present and former Centralia residents pulled away from the run-down storefront on North Locust Avenue that was the office of Centralia Homeowners Association. They rode through the steam at the south end of town and were off to Washington, D.C.

Today would mark the beginning of the end. The House of Representatives was scheduled to take a final vote on a supplemental appropriations bill containing $42 million for the relocation of Centralia and Byrnesville. Congressman Harrison would be sitting in the Speaker's chair, presiding over it all.

Centralia Homeowners Association (CHA) was organized in the wake of the referendum and included former members of Concerned Citizens, Centralia Council, CCHD, and people who had no previous affiliation. About ninety families belonged to this new group, which hoped through organized effort to obtain the best deal possible from the government if relocation did occur. Sister Honor Murphy was executive director, and Robert Burge was president.

The selection of Burge was indeed ironic. This was the same Robert Burge who, twenty-one years earlier, had been president of Centralia Council when the dump was set on fire, subsequently igniting the mine fire. His actions or omissions and those of other members of that council, like Joseph Tighe, had played a part in getting Centralia into this tragic mess. Burge would now help lead his fellow citizens out of their fire-stricken community to better lives elsewhere.

Tighe, by contrast, had become increasingly bitter and defensive. He denied any wrongdoing, though not in a very convincing way, and vowed never to relocate, even though his house was in the 200 block of Locust Avenue, the heart of the impact zone. At the October 14 meeting with Specter, Tighe argued that only persons who had ''legitimate'' reasons should be allowed to relocate—a category he clearly did not think was very large. He said persons with high levels of mine fire gases in their houses should be relocated, but added there were ''no reports'' of anyone in that predicament. It must have been a comforting delusion that council's fire was really no problem at all.

The vote in Congress would, if favorable, almost conclude a legislative process that had begun at the previously mentioned FEMA meeting of August 4. Thornburgh had asked FEMA officials to convene a meeting of all federal agencies that might be able to fund all or part of the Centralia relocation. He did not want the relocation charged against Pennsylvania's $770-million share of the AML Fund. George Grode, Thornburgh's representative, explained why. According to Winkle's memorandum, Grode said it ''would amount to a reprogramming of available funds, and thereby place the state in a position where it could not satisfy other established priorities."

This would explain why Thornburgh had put Centralia through such agonizing uncertainty over whether anything would be done to help the village. He had the money, or knew he would have it, but did not want to spend it at Centralia. It was true that Pennsylvania had $15 billion worth of abandoned mine land cleanup work ahead of it, by DER's estimate, but administration officials had described Centralia since 1981 as the worst abandoned mine land problem in the state, if not in the nation. Being number one apparently counted for nothing if one had no political clout.

Unfortunately for the governor, FEMA could see no reason why all the relocation money should not come out of the AML Fund, particularly since OSM had indicated a willingness to cooperate. None of the representatives of the other federal agencies at the meeting were optimistic they could help. It was a setback for Thornburgh, but he tried another tack. In his August 12 letter to the Pennsylvania congressional delegation, he asked them to seek a special appropriation for the relocation in the fiscal 1984 budget, which was then being prepared. This was soon given up as impractical. Few bills introduced in any given session of Congress become law: of 12,201 introduced in the Ninety-eighth Congress (1983–84), only 2,670 would survive. Thornburgh reluctantly agreed to seek the money from the AML Fund.

Thornburgh and DeBenedictis met at the White House on September 13 with Secretary Watt and two Reagan aides, Craig Fuller and Lee Verstandig. The president himself did not attend, nor did any of his senior aides. Watt reaffirmed his willingness to provide money from the AML Fund for the relocation. Fuller and Verstandig are believed to have agreed that the Office of Management and Budget would not oppose the expenditure. They also agreed to a Thornburgh request to appoint a federal task force on Centralia. The task force met only once, for forty-five minutes on September 22, and one suspects it may have been a face-saving gesture to a Republican governor who had been denied what he wanted but who needed something to announce to the press when he came out of the meeting.

Congressman McDade, after consulting with Harrison, Murtha, Specter, Heinz, and members of the governor's staff, introduced a $42-million amendment to a supplemental appropriations bill on September 22. The bill had recently arrived at the Appropriations Committee and was adjudged the quickest vehicle to get the relocation money through Congress. The bill specified that the residents be paid fair market for their homes with no penalty deducted for the mine fire. More important to the state, it specified that the $42 million would be taken off the top of the AML Fund and not charged to Pennsylvania's $770 million share, although the state would be responsible for a 10-percent matching share.

The amended bill was approved by the committee and the House and was not visibly affected by the resignation of Secretary Watt, but it ran into unexpected trouble in the Senate Appropriations Committee, of which Senator Specter was a member. Senator Walter Huddleston of Kentucky did not believe it was fair for the $42 million to be taken from the AML Fund but not charged to Pennsylvania's share. He feared, rightly, that it would mean less money for Kentucky. The bill was debated in committee on October 19. Specter left the hearing to vote on a bill making a federal holiday of Dr. Martin Luther King's birthday and did not return immediately. After the voting recess, Huddleston amended the bill. Now not only would the state have to pay 10 percent of the $42 million from its own funds, but the remainder would come out of the state's $770 million share of the AML Fund.

Huddleston's amendment may have increased the cost of the project to Pennsylvania taxpayers, but its simple justice cannot be denied. Taking the funds off the top would mean that other states besides Pennsylvania would pay for a majority of the relocation. Pennsylvania bore a major share of the responsibility for allowing the fire to grow to almost uncontrollable size. It was only right that the state be made to pay.

■ ■ ■

The bus rolled through Harrisburg, past Baltimore, and then was in Washington. "On the way we where told they had added more [to the bill] and it had to go back again," Theresa Gasperetti said. "When we got there, we were really down in the dumps."

During the legislative process, other amendments had been hung on the bill, eventually making the $42 million for Centralia a small, uncontroversial part of the whole. One amendment added almost $9 billion for the International Monetary Fund. The Reagan administration strongly supported the amendment for the IMF, but a significant number of members of Congress did not. Many of the Centralians confused the IMF with the MX missile, an understandable error. To this day, many insist it was funding for the MX missile that almost spoiled their big day.

Speaker of the House Thomas P. O'Neill, aware of Harrison's interest in the supplemental appropriations bill, appointed him to chair the House when the bill came up for debate and vote. The Speaker rarely presides over the House, but it was an honor for Harrison to be chosen nonetheless.

Harrison's staff met the bus from Centralia and immediately began making apologies. It was far from certain the House would even begin debate on the bill that day. The group was taken on a brief tour of the Capitol and then to lunch. While they were eating, word came that debate had abruptly begun. They hurried to the visitor's gallery of the House. Harrison saw them enter and made a quick trip upstairs to brief the Centralians on what would happen. Later he explained:

> I thought that unless they'd been carefully briefed on what was going on, they would think this was very strange. They had come down here to hear a debate on whether they should get some money to relocate. Instead, they heard this violent debate about the debt crisis in Argentina and international bankers. By then, Centralia was a consensus part of the bill. Nobody was going to rip it out. The question was whether the bill passed or failed, and that question really revolved around how bitterly the people were opposed to the IMF."

Sister Murphy remembers the vote on the bill as being a "panicky time." Members of the House voted electronically; a green star next to a name on the tally board meant a yes vote. A red star meant no. The voting was "nip and tuck" for a long time, she recalls.

Mrs. Gasperetti was a bundle of nerves, afraid the bill would not pass and she would be confined to the impact zone forever. She saw green stars light up beside the names of Harrison, McDade, and Murtha. Then she was dismayed to see a red star light up beside the name of Gus Yatron (D–Reading), who represented a neighboring district and was well known to all of them. His vote—apparently against the IMF rather than Centralia—left the Centralians confused and angry. It was a sobering lesson that not everyone considered their plight a top priority. Harrison's groundwork in the House and Specter's in the Senate had made the relocation possible. It was not a gift.

In the end, they won, 226 to 186. Mrs. Gasperetti grabbed herself to suppress a shriek of delight, which was forbidden in the visitor's gallery. Later Thomas Larkin, former president of Concerned Citizens, said, "More than anything, I felt relieved that after several years of pushing for something, that something was finally achieved. By this time, I myself had realized they weren't going to do anything about the fire itself.'' Joan Girolami recalls feeling relieved the money had been approved ''before someone died.'' She considered all that she and the others had done to bring about this day to have been worthwhile. ''It was a shame we had to go through so much, and give up so much,'' she added. Rose Marquardt, who joined CHA after her falling-out with the Unity Task Force over the petition, felt both happy and sad. ''You had a feeling that, thank God it's over, but then you had a feeling that this is the beginning of the end,'' she said.

Ron Ungvarsky escorted the Centralians out of the gallery to a previously planned celebration on the steps of the Capitol. Along the way, he introduced them to whomever they met so they could revel in their temporary celebrity. No citizen group who comes to the Capitol with a large contingent of the press remains anonymous for very long. On the steps, former members of Concerned Citizens—Thomas Larkin, Joan Girolami, Eva and Joe Moran, Eleanor O'Hearn, Mary McGinley, and Theresa Gasperetti—cut a red ribbon to celebrate their approaching freedom from the mine fire.

25
The Lessons of Centralia

A delegation of Centralians celebrated on the steps of the U.S. Capitol in Washington, D.C., on November 18, 1983, after Congress appropriated $42 million for the relocation of Centralia and Byrnesville. From right, in front, are Robert Burge, president of Centralia Homeowners Association, Congressman Harrison, and Sister Honor Murphy, executive director of CHA. U.S. Senator John Heinz (R–Pennsylvania) is at upper left. (Photo: Ron Ungvarsky)

NO one in the Anthracite Region of Pennsylvania, where the potential for new mine fires is as great as ever, will soon forget the tragedy of Centralia and how hard it was for its people to obtain justice. Whenever a new mine fire is discovered, the cry goes up from people who live nearby that they do not want their community to become "another Centralia." It is a phrase that appears to strike fear into the hearts of elected officials and bureaucrats alike. Action against new mine fires, at least those with the potential to harm people, tends to be quick and brutal.

That is the lesson of Centralia for the Anthracite Region, and indeed for any coal region in Pennsylvania or elsewhere. It seems so obvious today, but it took many painful years for citizens and public officials to fully understand that you must try at all costs to prevent a mine fire from igniting, but if one does ignite, you must attack it ruthlessly until it is gone. OSM has emergency funds that it uses to fight dangerous new mine fires. Those deemed less dangerous are supposed to be taken care of by DER.

One example of the impact of Centralia on the people of the Anthracite Region was the fight against the Spruce Creek coal gasification project in Schuylkill County. Spruce Creek Energy Corporation, owned by two Denver firms, Gilman Company and Geosystems Corporation, had proposed generating synthetic fuel gas by setting fire to anthracite coal veins in the Tremont area, which is about twenty-five miles south of Centralia.

Spruce Creek officials insisted there would be no danger of the fire getting out of control and spreading under Tremont, as residents feared. The company said the fire would burn in an artificially created air bubble beneath the mine water level. Gases generated by the fire would be piped to the surface and used by industries that would, theoretically, locate near the project. If anything got out of control, pumping of air would cease and water would rush in to flood the fire.

Tremont residents argued there were too many old mines in the area to make such a scheme safe. They feared the fire would somehow escape into one of the abandoned tunnels. Once the fire was in the mines, their town might become another Centralia. A public outcry arose after the Schuylkill County Commissioners leased 6,500 acres of county coal lands to Spruce Creek and gave the company an option to buy the land at a later date. This led to a countywide referendum in

April 1984 in which 93 percent of county residents voted against the project. Concurrently, two school districts and two townships filed lawsuits to block the company from receiving the coal lands.

State Senator James J. Rhoades of Schuylkill County introduced a bill in the General Assembly that had the effect of banning all underground burning of anthracite in Pennsylvania. The house and senate passed the measure unanimously, and Governor Thornburgh signed it into law on October 12, 1984. Company officials moaned that it was unfair to compare their project to the Centralia mine fire but admitted Centralia was a millstone around the company's neck.

A much more important, though less obvious, lesson of Centralia was that citizens have the power to force government to heed their will, if—and this is important—they have the courage and determination to use that power. Lois Gibbs, who organized her neighbors in the Love Canal area of Niagara Falls, New York, to fight for government relocation of families endangered by toxic waste there in the late 1970s, believed that was the central lesson to be drawn from Centralia, Love Canal, and the toxic waste disaster at Times Beach, Missouri, in the early 1980s. "You can't fight it scientifically and you can't fight it legally," she said.

After her own relocation from Love Canal, Lois Gibbs helped establish the Citizens Clearinghouse for Hazardous Waste. Headquartered in a suburb of Washington, D.C., the group disseminates information about toxic waste and helps citizens around the country organize to fight for government cleanup of toxic waste sites. Mrs. Gibbs, who is president of Citizens Clearinghouse, worked with a citizens group at Times Beach and with Concerned Citizens Against the Centralia Mine Fire and Centralia Homeowners Association. Centralia was not a toxic waste site, but it had many of the same problems as Love Canal and Times Beach.

"You've got to go out and talk to your neighbors, and you've got to fight it with an organized political front," Mrs. Gibbs said. "That's probably the hardest thing for people to accept. Nothing's ever, ever going to move until they go after elected officials with the issue."

It was a lesson the citizens of Centralia learned too late to save their community. Concerned Citizens organized in 1981, but by then the fire had burned for nineteen years and was probably too large and too close to populated areas to bring under control without destroying a major portion of the village. Thomas Larkin, who was president of Concerned Citizens, believed there was still hope in 1981 but agreed that any possibility of saving Centralia vanished shortly thereafter. The best Concerned Citizens could do—and this was no mean feat—was to make the best of a bad situation.

Concerned Citizens worked hard to persuade bureaucrats and elected officials to help Centralia, bombarding them with letters and phone calls. More importantly, Joan Girolami and Larkin stressed in their many interviews with journalists that Centralia needed help, and very likely someone was going to die if that help didn't arrive soon. The constant flow of news stories about Centralia, even after Concerned Citizens fell apart, made it impossible for state and federal officials to ignore the problem, which they probably would have otherwise. Relocation was the eventual result.

Mrs. Gibbs believes Concerned Citizens did not apply enough pressure. She believes the group should have staged news events aimed at embarrassing key public officials, like Governor Thornburgh, over their failure to help Centralia. Indeed, with Thornburgh facing re-election in 1982, Concerned Citizens passed up a key opportunity to perhaps bring a speedier resolution of the problem. "When you affect politicians' public image, then they act," Mrs. Gibbs said during a speech in Centralia in the fall of 1983. "We went out and organized just like you did here. We created political pressure. We picketed city hall. The governor [Hugh Carey] could not stand the pressure. Always remember that politicians are your employees."

With the exception of trips to Washington and Harrisburg in 1981, and the brief standoff in the OSM-DER meeting at the start of 1982, Concerned Citizens did little or none of this. Larkin says such actions were discussed, but only in passing. "We always decided we wouldn't do that," he said. "I don't know why. I think we were a little too conservative. As liberal as we were, we still had a streak of conservatism. The most radical thing we did was march in Centralia with placards [on May 12, 1981]."

How different this story might have been if the citizens of Centralia or Centralia Council had acted to put pressure on their elected representatives in Harrisburg in 1963, when the Scranton administration turned its back on the problem. Instead, council depended on the good will of the Department of Mines and Mineral Industries, an agency far more concerned with the abandoned mine land problems of Luzerne and Lackawanna Counties, where political muscle backed up demands for assistance. Perhaps out of guilt over its own role in the origin of the fire, Centralia Council did little in those early years except claim it was a problem for the Conyngham Township Board of Supervisors to handle.

There was no citizen effort at all until 1969, when Helen Womer and a few of her neighbors, in response to the evacuation of three homes because of dangerous mine fire gas levels, appealed directly to U.S. Representative Daniel Flood. Flood came to Centralia, met with the citizens, and made sure the Bureau of Mines changed, if only partially, the method it planned to use to contain the mine fire. That gave them a taste of what citizen power can accomplish, but they failed to continue pressuring Flood to make sure Centralia was fully protected from the mine fire. Centralia Council was of no help; council president Robert Burge still insisted in 1969 that the mine fire was Conyngham Township's problem.

Robert Lazarski, who served as vice-president of Centralia Council in 1981, believes that some councils "did what they had to do" about the mine fire. His own council was certainly one of them; it is hard to imagine it doing any more, at least in the first eight months of that fateful year. He has drawn some of the same lessons as Lois Gibbs, however, on how a community confronting an environmental disaster like Centralia or Love Canal should act. "Don't let things drag," he said sharply and without hesitation, as if he had thought about it many times. "Get after them right away. Go to the top as soon as you can. You can't start at the lowest level and wait for an answer from them, then go on to the next level. I don't feel you can give each part of that chain [of command] a lot of time. Move up the ladder as quickly as you can."

Mrs. Gibbs's warning that citizens should not rely on medical or scientific evidence to induce government to bring relief to victims of an environmental disaster seems cynical, but events at Centralia bear her out. The Pennsylvania Department of Health consistently downplayed the seriousness of the carbon monoxide problem and devised its own standards for human exposure to the gas, standards that allowed much more exposure than prevailing national standards. Mrs. Gibbs explained:

We find that all across the country there is a standard for some chemicals [and they] are sort of altered and called the state standard. And it's always at least one little degree above what's there. It's just a political game. That's what's hard about this issue.

When I went to Times Beach—I spent a good amount of time with

those folks there—and it was true of the Centralia people I met way before I even came to visit the community. They had such a belief and such
a trust in government and health officials. You know, they grew up there,
their husbands and fathers fought in World War II, and they were the pa-
triots and the American flag people who paid their taxes. To believe that
your government is not protecting you, to think that they are deliberately
fudging data, or ignoring data, or allowing you to suffer is just so hard for
people to take.

In the end, against all expectations, the last Centralia relocation
set a standard for humane treatment of persons who must permanently leave environmental disaster areas. This time, OSM could not
force Columbia County Redevelopment Authority to deduct a penalty
for the mine fire from the money paid for houses of people choosing
relocation. Because of bitter protests from Centralia residents about
the practice, which was the rule during the 1981 relocation, Congress
specifically prohibited such a penalty when it wrote the legislation authorizing $42 million for the relocation.

Homeowners were given almost a year to decide whether to accept the purchase offer made on their homes, not the ten days initially
allowed in 1981. They could even sell the house to the redevelopment
authority, bank the money, and rent the house back until they found
suitable relocation housing. Interest payments were almost enough
to cover the rent. Departing homeowners were permitted to salvage
virtually anything from their house at no cost, and many stripped
their houses of siding, thermo-pane windows, kitchen cupboards, and
the like.

Owners were given the higher of two appraisals made of their
house. Those who were dissatisfied—and there were a few—were en-
titled to a hearing before an administrative law judge appointed by the
state Department of Community Affairs. There was no charge for the
hearing, although if the owner wanted a lawyer to present his case,
the expense was his own. Owners still dissatisfied after the hearing
could make a final appeal to the Secretary of Community Affairs.

The best was still to come, at least for those families who did not
choose (or who were not forced by the gases) to relocate during the
first twelve months of the project. Sister Honor Murphy and Centralia
Homeowners Association began a campaign in the spring of 1984 to
persuade state and federal officials to approve the release of $3.2 mil-
lion placed in the $42-million relocation grant for so-called last resort
housing. This was a bureaucratic term for construction of new housing

if there was not enough "decent, safe and sanitary" existing housing to provide for all the families and individuals displaced by a disaster. CHA wanted to use the money to subsidize development of a completely new community for as many of the relocating Centralians as wished to move there.

It took Sister Murphy months to persuade first state and then federal officials of the need for last resort housing. The problem with the relocation was that a majority of the relocated families chose to stay within an eight-mile radius of Centralia. They preferred to remain close to family, friends, and in some cases jobs, schools, or doctors. New Centralia, as the town they hoped to build came to be called, may have started as a utopian dream, but it quickly became a necessity if scores of families were to avoid being forced to move far away. There were just not that many good houses on the market, and many of the families were leaving homes they had worked for twenty years or more to improve. The prospect of starting over was discouraging and they knew well enough they would not recover more than a fraction of the money they had spent in improvements to their Centralia houses. The appraisal process did not work that way.

To someone who lives in a relatively flat area, the prospect of moving twenty or thirty miles might seem to be no problem at all. In mountainous central Pennsylvania, however, even five miles can take one to a valley where the ethnic mix, predominant religion, and social attitudes are very different from the familiar ones of home.

Centralia Homeowners Association first proposed using the last resort housing money to pay for streets, sewers, and other improvements at whatever site was chosen for New Centralia, costs normally reflected in the price of a building lot. CHA calculated that the subsidy would drop the price of a standard-sized lot by about two-thirds. This, in turn, would bring lower-cost new housing, especially panel or modular housing, within reach of many in Centralia. The subsidized lot, plus what they received for their Centralia home, plus up to $15,000 in additional relocation benefits would, in some cases, make it possible for them to purchase new homes without a mortgage.

After much wrangling between the state and OSM, last resort housing was approved late in the spring of 1985. OSM had initially rejected the idea, suggesting that residents look farther afield for relocation housing, but state officials appealed the decision and won. OSM did not approve the lot subsidy plan but agreed instead to provide each resident who had not already relocated with enough money to build a new house of similar size to his old one at the site of his choice.

The $15,000 cap on relocation benefits was lifted—as the law allows—to make the extra payments possible. Some families who had already moved resented being excluded, but OSM would not make the policy retroactive.

"We won, folks, we won it!" exclaimed DCA Disaster Programs Director Jack Carling at a meeting in Centralia in the summer of 1985. "I've worked all around the country, and I can pretty well assure you that Centralia got itself the best deal any disaster community in the country ever got. It was not just because you are Centralia. The law allows what you got."

One wonders, though, whether the Thornburgh administration pushed for this humane relocation out of altruism or because it wanted to buy the good will of Centralians and possibly forestall lawsuits. OSM might well have considered that, too, when it approved the New Centralia project.

About seventy families had indicated at the time of this writing, August 1985, that they wanted to build houses in New Centralia. Columbia County Redevelopment Authority estimated that fewer than fifty households would remain in Centralia when the relocation ended on December 31, 1986, more than twenty-four years after the fire started. The Womers and Mary Lou Gaughan seem likely to be in this group, although that could change.* Last resort housing induced many of the antirelocation families to leave.

It appeared unlikely in the summer of 1985 that many of the former "stayers," as the antirelocation families came to be known, would end up in New Centralia itself, which was being carved out of a forest south of Kulpmont, seven miles west of Centralia. Led by Father Anthony McGinley and Helen Womer, they had fought both the relocation and New Centralia, and the bitter feelings this caused would not soon fade away. McGinley was particularly despised by some families in the impact zone for his harsh personal criticism of their desire to relocate. When Father McGinley himself moved out of Centralia to a modern house near John Coddington's relocation home in the fall of 1984, claiming there was no place in Centralia to which he could relocate (his landlord had sold his house), the laughter was loud and bitter.

And what of the trench to contain the mine fire? DER had announced no decision by the winter of 1985–86, more than two years after it assured Centralians the trench would definitely be built. State-

---

*Tony Gaughan died on January 3, 1986. Joseph Tighe, who did eventually relocate to Mount Carmel, died on October 31, 1985.

ments about the trench now are carefully worded to avoid any absolute commitment. Mount Carmel officials have expressed their concern about the lack of a plan to stop the fire, particularly since DER now says the fire could reach that community. The GAI report was wrong about that, DER says.

It is ironic that Centralia ended much as it began, with people fleeing turmoil for a new and better life elsewhere. The ancestors of today's Centralians fled the potato famine of Ireland and the wars and repression of Eastern Europe. The people of Centralia fled a mine fire, a modern disaster. Centralians endured much in the years since the fire started, but they have the satisfaction of knowing they set a standard that others will demand to follow. Other communities in America will face environmental disasters of one sort or another, and Centralia can be both a warning and beacon of hope to them all.

Index